My Healing
from
Breast Cancer

My Healing from Breast Cancer

∾

Barbara Joseph, M.D.

FOREWORD BY
Christiane Northrup, M.D.

KEATS PUBLISHING, INC.   NEW CANAAN, CONNECTICUT

My Healing from Breast Cancer is not intended as medical advice. Its intent is solely informational and educational. Please consult a health professional should the need for one be indicated.

MY HEALING FROM BREAST CANCER

Copyright © 1996 by Barbara Joseph

All Rights Reserved

Library of Congress Cataloging-in-Publication Data

Joseph, Barbara.
  My healing from breast cancer / Barbara Joseph.
     p.   cm.
Includes bibliographical references and index.
ISBN 0-87983-711-X
    1. Joseph, Barbara—Health. 2. Breast—Cancer—Patients—
United States—Biography. 3. Women physicians—
Biography.—4. Breast—Cancer—Popular works. I. Title.
RC280.B8J67   1996
362.1 '9 699449 '0 092—dc20
[B]   96-17717
                                                              CIP

Printed in the United States of America

Published by Keats Publishing, Inc.
27 Pine Street (Box 876)
New Canaan, Connecticut 06840-0876

98 97 96   6 5 4 3 2 1

I dedicate this book

- ❧ To my three angels: Zachary, Hannah and Oliver whose presence in my life has assured me of the reality of Grace.
- ❧ To my Dad and Lee for being there through all the tough times.
- ❧ To the memory of my mother Edith.
- ❧ To four creative women who experienced breast cancer as a journey of revelation and transformation: Audre Lorde, Deena Metzger, Virginia Soffa, Treya Killam Wilber.
- ❧ To those who have inspired me to know the depth of our power to heal: Ainslie Meares, Stephen Levine, Tullia Forlani Kidde.
- ❧ To my friend Robin Keuneke for her encouragement to write this book.
- ❧ To my friend Anne who died of breast cancer but lives in my heart.
- ❧ To Jonathan who reminded me that there is life after breast cancer, for shelter in the storm and more.
- ❧ To my doctors who embodied the approach that encourages self-healing—openhearted honesty, enthusiasm, sharing, caring: Dr. Richie Zelkowitz, Dr. Susan Love.
- ❧ And, finally, to all women. May we find the power of the feminine to heal ourselves and the Earth.

Acknowledgments

Thanks to Peggy and Barry for being there and checking in so often in the early days when the wounds were raw.

Heartfelt thanks to John Larson M.D. for his insights and support.

Thanks to Sari Jaffe for helping me through the difficult times as I put my life back together and finished the book.

Thanks to Donny Yance, Udo Erasmus and Joseph B. O'Connell, M.D. for the knowledge they shared with me.

Grateful always to Phyllis Herman, my editor and friend, whose interest, energy, support, and expertise clarified my thoughts, sustained my focus and encouraged me throughout.

Contents

Foreword

Whenever I read a story that embodies the dignity of who we really are as humans, something within me responds deeply and I know that in that moment my health is enhanced. Reading Barbara Joseph's book, *My Healing From Breast Cancer,* was such an experience.

Of all the books about breast cancer I have read, this is the one that best addresses not only how to deal with all aspects of this disease but also what is required for breast healing, both as individuals and as a society. This is the book that I will be recommending to my patients over and over again before they make any definitive decisions about their treatment.

Why? Because Dr. Joseph's experience of healing her life through breast cancer is so eloquently woven through a text that is also medically authoritative. Because she has lived the roles of obstetrician/gynecologist, mother, wife, bereaved daughter and patient, Dr. Joseph knows the anatomy of her own heart very, very well. She also knows how medicine is practiced. It is from these combined viewpoints that she explores our current epidemic of breast cancer: what it means and where we need to go from here, collectively and individually, to create a planet that is safe for our female bodies. She does all this with tremendous compassion both for herself and for others, but without once allowing herself the luxury of the victim role.

Thank you, Barbara, and bless you, for being a beacon of light in an area that has been for far too long enshrouded only in darkness, pain and confusion.

—Christiane Northrup, M.D.,
　　author of *Women's Bodies, Women's Wisdom*
　　Yarmouth, Maine

My Healing
from
Breast Cancer

Introduction

In every crisis there is an opportunity.

My Story

I had just finished breast-feeding. Oliver was eight weeks old and I knew my breasts were empty, yet a huge mass was still there and it was rock-hard. I could no longer pretend I was engorged with milk. I had to face the terrifying truth. As a physician who had felt many similar masses I recognized the likelihood that it was a malignancy. My life was about to drastically change and I was profoundly afraid. Deep inside I knew it was the beginning of a journey into the unexplored parts of my soul.

After the initial shockwaves of my cancer diagnosis subsided, I began to truly live for the first time in my life. In my deepest longing to be with my three children I found they were my greatest teachers in the art of living in the present. My determination to be with my children in the most openhearted way for as long as my future held, led me to the exploration of this crisis in the context of my entire life. My children were grace; in order to be with them I had to be present. It is only in the present that we can heal.

My journey began as I became present to myself and as I opened to my long-buried emotions, the deprivations of my life crashed in. I had never fully processed my mother's death. After her silent battle with ovarian cancer I cracked inside, and cancer grew in that crack. Years of unexpressed anger fueled its growth. My shame in being motherless and the pain of all the precious moments that went unshared found their release and gave my cancer its form.

Each night as my children were sleeping I went into their rooms and breathed the sweet soft air around them; it was an elixir. They nurtured me by night as I nurtured them by day. I began to create a new life—a life of caring about myself for the first time—and in every moment I was glad to be alive, grateful for the opportunity to heal. This is the story of how I breathed through the fear and found my power.

I recovered from Stage III breast cancer using a combination of conventional medical care and complementary modalities. The conventional care included six months of neoadjuvant chemotherapy consisting of the drugs cytoxan, 5-FU and novantrone, before my lumpectomy. Radiation followed the lumpectomy and an additional three months of chemotherapy followed the surgery, until my body finally rebelled and said "no more." The complementary modalities I used included individual counseling, support group therapy, nutritional education (sorely lacking from my medical training), an organic whole foods plant-based nondairy diet, supplements, visualization, affirmations, meditation and prayer, selected readings, workshops, exercise and unconditional self-love.

As I continue my recovery, I see my cancer experience as the catalyst for a powerful redirection in my life, an inspiration which I continue to view with awe. Through years of hard work, I now understand many of the factors that contributed to my illness, as well as how I, with grace, allowed the recovery process. Healing is a process which I actively take part in on a daily basis. I attribute my ability to go through the conventional treatments in good spirits as well as my continued state of health to be a result of the complementary approaches that I made use of then and continue to utilize today. Above all, I feel grateful. Joan Borysenko asked the audience at a healing conference/

workshop I went to in the early days of my illness, "How many of you feel grateful?" At that time I wasn't sure exactly what she meant—grateful for what? Now I understand this question.

This book is based on my personal experiences as a breast cancer patient. I have quoted widely from the sources that have helped me with information and inspiration in my own process. My intent in writing this book is to share the concepts and insights that have helped me in my recovery from breast cancer. It is said that we teach most what we need to learn, and I am very grateful for the opportunity that writing this book has given me. Writing has helped me clarify my thinking and enabled me to begin a new phase of my life—actively sharing my insights, developing my ability to make purposeful choices and strengthening my capacity to pay attention. On a very deep level I believe we all contribute to the world's consciousness and planetary peace by toiling with that small plot of land we have been given—ourselves. It is through our pain and our struggles that our lives ever deepen.

The crisis of breast cancer was the opportunity to turn my life around. Breast cancer was and continues to be a transformational experience. It brought up the issues of my lifetime, the reality of my own mortality, the unexpressed grief of my childhood and the emptiness of our techno-crazed world that denies the power of the feminine. Breast cancer brought into focus the profound chasm between my medical training and my feminine knowing, and the gap between the pharmaceutical bandaids that I utilized as a practicing obstetrician-gynecologist and what my patients and I were really seeking.

Now I understand the nurturance, guidance, reassurance and support women really need when they come in for check-ups. I realize now how profoundly confused women are about the crisis of breast cancer. We need to exercise our right to make informed choices with the help but not the dominance of health care professionals. We need to acknowledge the limitations of conventional medicine without giving up the best it has to offer us. The lack of clear-cut answers in my own treatment decisions and the dismal cure rate gave me the incentive to make my own choices apart from what conventional medicine had to offer.

In the depth of these issues I see breast cancer as my soul's attempt to focus my attention. As I've searched for the truth I've discovered that much of the helpful data I've found is not really new but readily accessible information that has been either downplayed or ignored by the medical profession. Even so, I realize now that the ability to turn one's life around is not the result of an intellectual effort. It cannot simply come out of the information that I and so many others have gathered. As I've uncovered the many pieces of this breast cancer puzzle and realized again and again the simplicity behind the reality, I know that for learning to take place there has to be readiness. For me the pain of a breast cancer diagnosis opened my eyes and set the stage for my own readiness. Pain can sharpen our focus; the healing transformation comes from attention, understanding and will.

Breast cancer has become my guide to a healthier life for myself, my family and the earth. I have become aware that there is no greater way to impact the health of the planet than through our daily food choices. We have all been profoundly affected by our early education: remember The Basic Four Food Groups? It is hard to put aside these outdated beliefs and to find new ones to put in their place. It is difficult to associate the foods that we grew up with, that have soothed us and even replaced love in many instances, with the growing epidemic of breast cancer. Today's convenience foods may ultimately not be very convenient. Our connections with food run deep.

"You are what you eat" is not a new concept, but through the experience of breast cancer it has taken on a very personal meaning. We cannot continue to eat devitalized, contaminated foods and expect to maintain our health and vitality. All vital living processes occur across cell membranes. If our cell membranes are composed of abnormal trans fatty acids that do not fit our biochemical machinery, how are we to stay healthy? Our pantries are filled with cancer-causing partially hydrogenated oils. The power of our food choices is immense.

The animals that provide the standard American diet live in abnormally close quarters and are pumped up with antibiotics to both treat and prevent infections. We ingest these antibiotics as we ingest these animals. The overuse of antibiotics has led to resistant bacterial strains and the development of ever more virulent infections as well as the resurgence of many infectious illnesses thought to have been eradicated by modern medicine. And if that isn't bad enough, hormones are now injected into cattle either to increase milk production or to increase the weight of the soon-to-be-slaughtered animals for no other reason than to add to profits. Research shows that Bovine Growth Hormone (BGH) may very well increase the risk of breast cancer.[1]

Food is political. Pesticides are found in the breast milk of women with breast cancer in higher levels than in women without cancer. Toxic pesticides outlawed in this country are being sold to third-world nations and are then imported back to us sprayed onto foreign produce. Israel's breast cancer rate declined when certain pesticides were outlawed. This is not new information. But we do need to hear it. Why aren't we all eating organic foods? The price, you say. What about the cost of breast cancer?, I say.

Medicine has been run too long by the male scientific model: the model that says, "we can find a cure for breast cancer; let's just look a little deeper into the cells." This mechanistic model is seriously flawed. In this model, breast cancer needs only to be eradicated; however, for true healing to take place the patient must be transformed. In the medical model, breast cancer is seen as one disease; in fact, breast cancer is a different disease in every woman. Medicine ignores the fact that breast cancer is a disease of our society, its attitudes toward women and nature. Medicine forgets that breast cancer mirrors our emotional lives; true healing must address these issues. Medicine needs to see this disease in the context of our lives. Still, researchers continue to look for the answers in our cells, hoping to find a cure for our ills, hoping to isolate a gene to get us out of this mess.

The environmental crisis that we are now faced with has been newsworthy for decades; yet as a society we are still not paying attention. Rachel Carson wrote *Silent Spring* in 1962 during the time she had a radical mastectomy and radiation treatments. Two years after the publication of this landmark book that literally gave birth to the environmental movement, she died of breast cancer. My friend Jane told me, "My mother didn't have to look for a breast cancer support group in Long Island—every one of her close friends had already been diagnosed." Her mother lives in Suffolk County where the alarmingly high cancer rates are clearly related to pesticide contamination of the soil and water, the radioactive emissions from nearby reactor plants, toxic waste dump sites and pollution from the heavy commuter traffic in and out of New York City. Something is amiss. The epidemic of breast cancer is not simple. There are many issues. The challenge is to look deeply.

The mental, emotional and spiritual aspects of breast cancer are no less important than the physical. The majority of women who develop breast cancer have no family history of this disease. There are many women who do not fit the high risk hormonal profile offered by medical science to explain the etiology of this disease. And there are many who already have the healthy eating and lifestyle habits that are supposed to protect against the development of breast cancer. The physical is only one dimension of our complex reality.

As I began to develop a deeper understanding of the nature of health, I learned about these other aspects of myself. We each need to find balance in the mind, heart and spirit as well as in our bodies and to learn what areas need to be looked into, how we are comfortable approaching them and to what degree we need to concentrate our efforts.

The beauty in healing is that wherever one starts is appropriate. A healthy body (not a perfect body) seeks a healthy mind; an emotionally healthy woman will respect and honor her body. Once we initiate our healing work we cannot help but develop in all realms. With the help of my meditations and visualizations, my discussions with my counselor and my support group experience, I never felt healthier than I did in the months after my diagnosis of breast cancer. There was a time during my chemotherapy treatments when I felt lighter than air, as if I were glowing; I arrived at my cancer support group one evening in this altered state. We did a guided visualization; I was asked to visualize the cancer in my body, and I saw a small gray rock disintegrate into sand and scatter into nothingness. I felt I no longer had the disease of breast cancer. I was so alive. I felt such compassion toward myself and the other members of the group. Allowing myself to feel the compassion flow was the healing. As I continue to develop this compassionate self-acceptance, the pain of my childhood and my present life is easier to bear and the anger that hides the pain continues to dissolve. In the ever widening ripples of realization it becomes apparent that we all progress together and that sharing my experience is my imperative. Breast cancer can be the vehicle that transforms pain into compassion.

Breast cancer has been my greatest teacher but not because of fear. I was reborn from a place of health, not disease. We are all in this together. My intention is to share my experiences and the knowledge I've gained for the greater cause, so that other women can make their own proactive choices in the pursuit of their own individual health as well as the health of our planet.

Perhaps my experience can help other women find their own power to prevent breast cancer or, if breast cancer is already present, to transform their illness into a learning experience. We all have the power to lead healthier lives; it is simply a matter of choice. We must all do our own personal work. The emotions that prevent us from making the healthier choices must be processed and healed over time. If we approach the pain in our lives with an open heart, the work of caring for ourselves deeply will lead us to healthier choices and will be reflected in our healing abilities. We need to heal ourselves, our families and the earth with the female principles of nurturance, flexibility, community and respect for nature. With this approach, I am confident that we can begin to heal the breast cancer epidemic.

In the pages that follow, I weave the scientific facts about the causes and the treatment of breast cancer into my own breast cancer story, including strategies for healing, suggestions for vitamin supplementation and guidelines for creating one's own breast cancer healing or prevention program. As a woman, mother, obstetrician-gynecologist and breast cancer survivor I offer my perspective. I've written this book to help women in the crisis of transforming their lives through the breast cancer experience. I hope by sharing my experience I can empower women in the difficult decision-making process that one faces with newly diagnosed breast cancer. My goal is to put the disease into the multifactorial context from which it arises and through which we can approach a healing program. I also hope that this book will inspire those who are cancer-free to make health-supportive changes in their lives. To the extent that we live in each other's hearts, I believe we all face breast cancer together and we must all deal with the issues it poses, both individually and collectively.

∾

In one of my dreams early in the treatment of my breast cancer,

I was riding in a van in the darkness along the edge of a high rocky mountain. It was raining heavily. A bit of lightning flashed here and there giving the only light other than the headlights. It was so dark. There was a van ahead of me that I very much wanted to pass. I kept thinking about accelerating and passing but I knew there were bad road conditions. Should I or shouldn't I? Something stopped me. I decided I wouldn't pass, so I finally just relaxed and continued along. When dawn came, I saw just how high up we were on the mountain and that there really was just one lane hugging the edge of the peak. Had I attempted to pass, I would surely have fallen to my death.

This dream had a profound effect on me. When I woke up I was excited and relieved. I was amazed at how obvious my unconscious had made this message in my dream state. Before my diagnosis I was disconnected from my inner wisdom. The dream graphically illustrated for me the power of my own intuition, or what Christiane Northrup, M.D. calls inner guidance. With excitement I knew it was okay to trust my intuitions regarding all phases of my treatment and in fact my entire breast cancer experience. I sensed that we often can't see the full picture, that we see what we need to see and must trust the rest. What a relief. I didn't have to know everything!

The dreams kept coming, my unconscious was bubbling over. I couldn't write fast enough. With a pen and my notebook at my bedside, images from my past and present life were overflowing. It was abundantly clear that there was a message in all this for me.

Intellectually, we can't always know the reasons. Scientific "proof" is a misnomer. We are all brainwashed to some extent in this culture about the power of scientific studies, all the while knowing that statistics can be manipulated to "prove" just about anything. Throughout the 1980's the Cancer and Steroid Hormones Study (CASH) based in Atlanta published analyses that found no excess risk of breast cancer regardless of the age of exposure to birth control pills.[2] A few years later reanalyses turned around the reassuring CASH studies, supporting a link between oral contraceptives and breast cancer in younger women.[3]

I believe that intuition is far more powerful than intellect. I hope this book enlightens you as a total approach to the issue of breast cancer, but more importantly, I hope you sense for yourself what is intuitively correct in this approach and that it helps you on your healing journey.

PART ONE

~

The Facts You Need To Make Your Decisions

1

Conventional and Complementary Approaches to Healing

Conventional breast cancer treatment by its nature has many limitations. It studies, categorizes, dissects, excises, radiates and medicates the disease by isolating it from its environment, from the woman who has it. The cancer is treated, but not the woman.

BREAST CANCER—INVADER OR MESSENGER?

Conventional medicine treats breast cancer as an invader, the woman-patient as its victim. The medical establishment views the body as a war zone. In a local hospital newsletter bone marrow transplants are heralded as an increasingly effective weapon in fighting cancer. The disease is most often seen as an enemy: we are taught to strike back; the treatments become our armamentarium; our bodies, the battleground.

I see the phenomenon of breast cancer quite differently. I do not believe it descends upon us out of nowhere, striking out randomly. In fact, breast cancer arises from a very specific and individual set of circumstances. Unfortunately, conventional treatments focus on the disease, not the individual in whom it has occurred.

Breast cancer brings with it a clear and very personal message. Something is not working in our lives. Something needs to be changed. Let's not be afraid of this message or attach too many value judgments to it; just allow yourself to take the message in. When I was a guest on a local radio show in honor of Breast Cancer Awareness Month, a call came in from a woman who stated that she was offended by my approach. She said, "Even if you do everything right you can still get breast cancer . . . the body will do what the body will do. . . ." She was angry and felt betrayed. She had tried desperately to be "good" (I did everything right) and didn't want to accept the responsibility of her illness. The energy required to maintain this innocent victim stance and to deny responsibility closes the door on effective healing and effective living. Developing breast cancer is not a failure; recurrence of breast cancer is not a failure nor is dying of breast cancer a failure. The failure is in not paying attention. The failure is in not utilizing our creative potential, not accepting the challenge of the disease, not having the courage to open to the message.

Breast cancer does not manifest randomly. Breast cancer occurs in both a very personal context and a broad social context. Our diagnosis can be a wake-up call, alerting us to alter our diet, our lifestyle, our relationships. Sherry Rogers, M.D. has written, "It's like the car . . . you could just unscrew the oil light when it goes on, or you could smash it with a hammer. Both would make it go away . . . but what for? The light reminds us to put oil in before the engine dies." We need to approach breast cancer on the deepest levels, personally and politically.

∾

I am writing this book to shed light on some of the mechanisms in the development of breast cancer so that women can take active steps both to prevent and heal breast cancer and not get lost in the victim mentality. The victim mentality pervades the topic of breast cancer. Too many experts and spokespeople say, "There are two things we don't know about breast cancer. We don't know the cause and we don't know the cure." This is just not so. We do know quite a lot, it's just not simplistic. Breast cancer is not one disease. We are being misled by the medical approach to illness that worships the magic bullets of surgery, radiation and chemotherapy. Cancer is not a deficiency of the latest generation antineoplastic wonder drug. Cancer is an end-product of a thwarted biological process, a process which is uniquely individual. There are many roads to breast cancer. As long as we persist in looking for the "cure" we are lost and will remain so. Breast cancer is a multifactorial and individual disease occurring in a socio-political context, and the prevention and healing must be addressed in the same way.

℃ *Remember...*

Breast cancer has many causes, and no single cure. By searching for a single cause or a single cure for breast cancer we are misleading ourselves, closing to the real nature of this disease and the possibility of real healing.

THE HEALING PROCESS

We need to strive toward health-supportive lifestyles within health-conscious communities. There is no simple checklist insuring we do everything right. Health is that very process of learning, growing and proactively creating our own path in life. We need to take positive action in our lives and not just give lip service to healthy living. For example, we need to buy and eat organic food whenever possible. This nourishes us, keeps carcinogenic chemicals out of the body and at the same time makes a powerful political and economic statement. Health is not achieved by going for yearly check-ups, getting Pap tests or scheduling mammograms. How we live our lives on a daily basis has everything to do with creating health in our lives.

When we act conscientiously, then all our daily choices reflect wholeness. If we do develop cancer despite our best efforts, there is no shame but room for new approaches. By focusing on the mechanism of the development of breast cancer in a particular individual and trying to understand why the body in all its wisdom has elected the development of cancer as its best adaptation, we can begin to approach healing.

What You Can Do

In order to prevent breast cancer or to effectively heal from a breast cancer experience you can begin by honestly examining every aspect of your life. Ask yourself these questions:

How do you nurture your body? What foods do you eat? Do you exercise regularly? When you look in the mirror, is it with appreciation or criticism?

How do you give voice to your emotions? Do you express emotions openly? Do you put your emotional needs first—or last? Do you honor your own uniqueness?

Do you regularly connect with nature and honor your own creative nature? Do you take the time to watch the sun set, listen to the raindrops, smell the flowers?

Are you aware of your own power to heal?

As we address our personal ecology, a commitment to global ecology emerges. Then we need to reprioritize our lives accordingly.

THE EPIDEMIC OF BREAST CANCER

When a disease occurs with a certain frequency in the population it is termed an epidemic; breast cancer is an epidemic. Breast cancer is the most common cancer among American women. For women in the United States in 1995,

32 percent of the estimated new cancer cases were from breast cancer and breast cancer was responsible for 18 percent of the estimated cancer deaths. There were 183,400 new cases of breast cancer in this country and deaths from breast cancer totaled 46,000. In the U.S., the probability of developing breast cancer in a woman's life is 12.3 percent or 1 in 8.

The breast cancer death rate has not improved from 1930 to the present. Numerous researchers counter the optimistic 95 percent, five-year cure rates for localized breast cancer that we hear about from organizations like the American Cancer Society. The five-year "cure" rate is a misnomer. Researcher J.G. Klijn from the Netherlands reports that half of the country's breast cancer patients will die of the disease.[1] Drs. O. Plotkin and F. Blankenberg note that mortality from breast cancer can be observed up to 40 years from the diagnosis.[2] Other large-scale studies from both Norway and England have concluded that if women with breast cancer are followed for their entire lives, 80 percent will die of the disease.[3]

In the *Townsend Letter for Doctors* the following comment was made. "The manipulation of cancer statistics is not news but when it comes to breast cancer, it is difficult to ascertain the real incidence of mortality. One respected researcher, Dr. C. Barber Mueller, professor emeritus of surgery from McMaster University of Hamilton, Ontario, Canada . . . after following 3,558 breast cancer patients from upstate New York for 19 years, found that 1,660 of those women were dead and 88 percent of them had died of breast cancer. Many researchers feel that the five-year survival without evidence of recurrence is a widely quoted, but inaccurate, definition of cure."[4] We need to realize the seriousness of a diagnosis of breast cancer, its impact on our entire life henceforth and approach the treatment phase as both an acute intervention as well as a long-term modification of lifestyle.

MORE IS NOT BETTER

It's how we live that counts.
What makes life good?
A clear mind.
Free emotions.
Freedom from pain.
To be in harmony with it all.
Precious things.
Cancer destroys them all.
Let's guard them.
But think.
Think deep.
You have seen it yourself.
No turning the blind eye.
The doctor himself may destroy these things,
Destroy what is good in life.
Keep her alive.
At the cost of life.
This is what happens,
Not always,
But more often than you think.

A. MEARES[5]

With breast cancer, more is not necessarily better. Hippocrates, who knew cancer well and coined the term *carcinoma*, urged doctors, "Above all, do no harm." Cancer surgery was not in favor during Hippocrates' time. Paracelsus, a Renaissance physician of note, wrote this about surgery: "It should be forbidden and severely punished to remove cancer by cutting, burning, cautery and other fiendish tortures." He went on, "It is from nature that the disease arises and from nature comes the cure, not from the physicians." And today Deepak Chopra, M.D. echoes this in his highly acclaimed *Quantum Healing*, "Cancer is wild, antisocial behavior, whereby a single cell reproduces itself without check, heeding no signals from anywhere except, apparently, its own demented DNA. Why this occurs, no one knows. It is a good bet that the body itself knows how to reverse the process. . . ."[6]

The modern era of cancer surgery began in the 1900s with the development of anesthesia and asepsis and with the increasing frequency of cancer. With respect to cancer surgery in general, "Often unwilling to acknowledge the limitations of their methods, enamored of technology, and hostile to nonsurgical approaches, many surgeons conceived of progress in terms of greater and greater cutting. In 1948, for example, Dr. Alexander Brunschwig devised an operation he called total exenteration. This involved removal of the rectum, the stomach, the urinary bladder, part of the liver, the ureter, all the internal reproductive organs, the pelvic floor and wall, the pancreas, the spleen, the colon and many of the blood vessels. Patients were hollowed out in the desperate hope that, by doing so, all remaining cancer could be destroyed. Brunschwig himself called his operation 'a brutal and cruel procedure.' "[7]

∾

Hours into the surgery I remember with fascination and horror holding retractors for some of Dr. Goldberg's procedures. I was a gynecology resident and I took shifts with the medical students on this rotation; the surgeries lasted for hours and hours. Goldberg remained focused throughout, he set the tone in the OR. When it was a difficult point in the procedure we all strained, more blood was hung and we went on. At other times music was playing and we gossiped and flirted. Anterior exenterations, radical vulvectomies, radical hysterectomies, staging procedures, this was my gynecologic oncology rotation. Dr. Michael Goldberg was board-certified in this subspecialty. Michael had informed consents on file, yet I suspect the patients had no idea of what the surgery entailed; I could barely fathom it. To this day I am continually awed by the sacredness of the body. We must respect the integrity of our immune systems. As women, we know deeply the power of renewal on a cellu-

*lar level through our monthly menstrual cycles; as doctors,
we need to gently lead our patients back to these essential
principles.*

*Breast cancer rates and mortality continue to climb. Our
"more is better" beliefs are ingrained despite evidence to
the contrary, and it is frightening when we go up against
them. Consider this alarming statistic: 20 years after their
diagnosis, the cause of death in 88 percent of the women
who had died was breast cancer.[8] How then can we make
our individual decisions, knowing both the danger in too
much treatment and the terrifying reality of dying of this
disease? We need to gather information at the same time
that we respect our intuition in each decision we face. Our
intellectual decision making needs to be in harmony with
the deepest and truest parts of ourselves. We can partake of
the wisdom gathered by the women who have gone before
us. Together we will find our way.*

∾

Over time doctors learned that the aggressive surgical approach to breast cancer was not achieving the expected
cure rates. In the mid to late 1800s breast cancer was
thought to spread to contiguous structures, then into the
lymph nodes and finally to the rest of the body. The concept at that time was that breast cancer is at the outset a
localized disease. Based on this thinking, Dr. William Stuart
Halstead developed the radical mastectomy—a surgical procedure removing breast, chest wall muscles, axillary and
supraclavicular lymph nodes. Dr. Sampson Handley advo-
cated removal of part of the breastbone and ribs to facilitate
removal of the internal mammary lymph nodes. The prevailing opinion was to remove all the tissue in the area of the
breast that was possible, advancing ahead of the cancer. As
data was collected and analyzed it was clear that these very
aggressive, debilitating and deforming surgeries were no
better than more conservative surgical approaches both in

terms of survival and recurrence. Many scientific studies in this country and abroad failed to show any benefit to routine radical mastectomy. One of the most widely quoted studies is that of Dr. Bernard Fisher.[9] The results of these studies favored simple mastectomies as opposed to radical mastectomies.

Certainly more conservative surgery results in less disfigurement, less disability in terms of both short- and long-term recovery and no doubt a more positive self-image for the woman undergoing the procedure. Yet even today, the "more is better" myth persists. In an article in the 1994 Connecticut Medical Society Report[10] it is noted that despite the fact that breast-conserving surgery (lumpectomy) is clearly an appropriate option, mastectomy is still being chosen in a larger than appropriate share of cases.

℧ *Remember...*

More treatment (surgery, radiation, chemotherapy, hormones) is not necessarily better treatment. In general, more extensive breast cancer surgery has no better a cure rate than more conservative approaches. Ask your surgeon very case-specific questions. Insist on an answer. Keep an open and inquiring mind. Understand both the short- and long-term consequences of the various treatment options. Inform yourself about the difference between a diagnostic procedure, a staging procedure and a therapeutic procedure (see Appendix); understand why everything is being done. You can say yes to what seems to be a sensible procedure and no to anything that doesn't feel right. It is your right and your responsibility to make your own knowledgeable decisions.

When we want something,
Want it very much,
Want life itself,
There are no limits
To our means of seeking it.
The best, the latest,
The strongest, the most powerful,
And of course the most expensive,
This is what we seek.

A. Meares[11]

The Decision-making Tree

If a procedure is being done for diagnostic or staging purposes, how will the information obtained be of use to you personally in treatment decisions? If an invasive diagnostic procedure is being suggested, be especially sure the results, whether positive or negative, will be of value. It can be helpful to draw a flow chart.

For example, if the results of your lymph node dissection are positive, that might lead to a course of chemotherapy. But it is also essential to think through the results of a negative test. If your lymph node dissection yields negative results, ask your doctor if this frees you from chemotherapy. Perhaps he will tell you that lymph node sampling is not conclusive or perhaps your tumor has aggressive characteristics and therefore he will advise chemotherapy anyway. If, based on the long-term consequences of chemotherapy, you are certain you would not choose this treatment modality in any case, then you must go back up the flow chart and rethink the value of even having a lymph node dissection.

Likewise very aggressive follow-up protocols for breast cancer recurrence, may not only confer additional risk but also decrease one's quality of life. When we feverishly look for subclinical recurrences, treatment dilemmas surface resulting in much anxiety. Respect the integrity of your body and always be gentle with yourself when making these difficult decisions.

THE CONVENTIONAL APPROACH

Medical doctors are educated in a culture that says more is better. We are all part of this culture. So even if cure rates are equal for mastectomy and lumpectomy, a particular doctor may still refer to mastectomy as the "gold standard." Your doctor's education and experience are likely steeped in the myth of "more is better." Be cautious when you hear statements like, "We have more experience with mastectomies." More experience with a particular surgical procedure does not translate into benefit for you. Just because a procedure has been done many times by a surgeon does not give it validity. You are certainly correct to want a surgeon to be experienced in the procedure he/she is to perform but the more important question is, is it the procedure you need?

In his excellent book, *The Cancer Industry,* Ralph Moss cites the reasons for the initial wide acceptance of the Halstead procedure (radical mastectomy) and in so doing sheds light on many aspects of conventional breast cancer treatment. He discusses the allegiance of physicians to this American-born operation, the economic rewards of this challenging and difficult operation, and the essential conservatism of the medical profession. Despite the evidence against this aggressive approach, the Halstead Radical Mastectomy remained the treatment of choice in this country until recently.

So don't cut off your breast just because someone thinks it is the gold standard and doing so promises to be The Cure. *A mastectomy is not the end of breast cancer.* Begin to make informed choices. Perhaps a lumpectomy is enough. And if a simple (as opposed to radical) mastectomy is the reasonable choice, make that choice and honor your self for making it.

Conventional treatment for breast cancer consists of:

1. Surgery.
2. Radiation.
3. Chemotherapy.
4. Synthetic hormones.

Thoughts to Consider Regarding Treatment Dilemmas

Some of the many questions we are faced with today regarding conventional treatment of breast cancer are:

1. Is lumpectomy a reasonable option, and if so, why is it not chosen more often?
2. Should breast reconstruction be done immediately after cancer surgery, delayed or not done at all?
3. Is lymph node dissection a diagnostic or therapeutic procedure? What are the potential and real risks to removing lymph nodes?
4. What are the long-term hazards of radiation therapy?
5. What should the role of chemotherapy be?
6. Is tamoxifen a worthwhile drug and, if so, for whom?

Lumpectomy or Mastectomy?

Surgeons tell us that once the lump is removed and the lymph nodes are negative, the breast cancer is "cured," yet according to published results in the *New England Journal of Medicine*, "We know that 20 to 30 percent of women with negative lymph nodes will still get metastatic disease and sooner or later die of it."[12]

The National Surgical Adjuvant Breast and Bowel Project (NSABP)[13,] along with many other research centers, reported that the chance of survival was the same for the women who were treated with lumpectomy alone, lumpectomy with radiation or mastectomy. A few points are worth noting when comparing lumpectomy alone to lumpectomy with radiation:

- Local recurrences were more common in the group of women that did not have radiation following the lumpectomy but these did not affect survival. Lumpectomy alone is often frowned upon by the medical establishment. However, of those women who choose lumpectomy as their sole treatment, 60 percent do not experience a local recurrence.[14]
- Women with very small tumors (1 cm. or less) had very low local recurrence risks.
- Women over 70 years old had very low local recurrence risks.
- Women in their 30's and 40's had higher rates of local recurrences.
- Women with tumors that were very aggressive histologically (high grade microscopically) and whose initial biopsies showed tumor at the margin were all statistically more likely to have local recurrences.

A few points that are worth considering regarding the role of mastectomy compared to lumpectomy with or without radiation:

- Mastectomy without radiation will afford the same local recurrence rate as lumpectomy plus radiation.
- A local recurrence after a mastectomy will be on the chest wall and is more difficult to treat than a local recurrence after a lumpectomy.
- A local recurrence following lumpectomy and radiation is difficult to treat because of the decreased ability of radiated tissue to heal. In fact, a second course of radiation may damage the tissue beyond repair.
- A mastectomy is a longer and more complicated surgi-

cal procedure with more operative and post-operative morbidity. (In order to avoid the radiation that is almost always advised with a lumpectomy, a woman may choose a simple mastectomy.)
- The change in a woman's body image with the loss of a breast is incalculable.

The type of surgery you choose and whether you opt for a course of radiation therapy will depend in part on whether you fall into a high- or low-risk group with respect to local recurrence. If you fall into a low-risk group for recurrence you may consider lumpectomy alone, forgoing radiation and its attendant risks and deal with a local recurrence when and if it occurs. Even if you do not fall into a low-risk group it is still your option to choose a lumpectomy without radiation. *A lumpectomy plus immune-boosting techniques may offer the best cure rates; the critical studies that would document this just haven't been done.* Radiation does not affect survival therefore it is imperative to inform yourself about the potential side effects and long-term consequences of this therapy before consenting to treatment. The location of the malignancy, the size of your breasts and the pathology all need to be taken into consideration when deciding between lumpectomy and mastectomy; your surgeon can help you with this decision.

Be aware that the surgery a woman gets can be influenced heavily by which hospital she goes to for treatment and where she lives. (See Figure 1 on the next page.) National cancer statistics show strong regional variations in choice of surgery. The reason for this has less to do with science and more to do with a doctor's personal philosophy. Jeanne Petrek, M.D., a breast surgeon at Memorial Sloan-Kettering Cancer Center in New York City, is aware of the strong and often non-verbal ways a doctor may influence a woman's treatment decision. Many women have told Petrek they chose mastectomy because, "It seemed to be what my doctor wanted me to do."[15]

FIGURE 1

THE REGIONAL FACTOR

Where women live often determines what kind of treatment they get, as these percentages show:

	MASTECTOMY	LUMPECTOMY	NO SURGERY	OTHER	UNKNOWN
Northeast	43.4	46.9	6.8	1.5	1.4
Midwest	54.0	35.1	6.8	2.4	1.7
South	63.6	24.8	5.0	2.0	4.6
Southwest	69.2	22.9	5.9	1.9	0.1
West	56.2	39.3	3.6	0.9	0.0

Adapted from the American College of Surgeons, National Cancer Database Annual Review of Patient Care, 1994. *NOTE: These figures represent all breast-cancer cases, including those in which mastectomy is necessary.

ↂ *Remember...*

Since every case is different and there are no statistics that reflect any individual woman's precise situation, take the time you need to educate yourself. Talk with some women who have been through a breast cancer experience and air all questions and concerns with your surgeon. One study noted that a year or more after breast surgery 56 percent of women who had mastectomies regretted their choice.[16] Breast cancer is not an emergency. Do not act out of fear or denial. Trust that after understanding and integrating the facts your intuition will guide you.

Deena Metzger turned the loss of her breast into inspirational creativity. I have a poster she created on the wall of my work area: a photograph of her upper body, naked, arms outstretched, as if to embrace all of life with a tattoo of a branch with leaves across her mastectomy scar. Just looking at it gives me such a powerful and positive message about our possibility to transform this illness—a transformation that goes beyond our personal tragedies and our personal heroism. Somehow that Amazon woman with one breast conveys the essence of Woman, joyfully reclaiming life.

In her book, *The Journey Beyond Breast Cancer,* Virginia Soffa, at her most courageous, relates the difficulties she had in finding a surgeon to perform the more limited surgery she felt comfortable with. After her initial biopsy revealed a small (1 cm.) ductal carcinoma *in situ* with tumor extending to the margins, she writes

> . . . my first choice, a lumpectomy without radiation, was met with great resistance by the medical profession because I had a second area in question, which needle aspiration indicated to be benign . . . Although initially it appeared I had a choice, I was unable to find a surgeon who would perform the surgery I requested. The surgeons felt they would be doing me a 'disservice' to perform such a procedure . . . I was frustrated that my early-detected cancer still required a mastectomy. I felt betrayed because I had heard so much about lumpectomies and the virtues of 'catching it early.'. . . Once I decided that surgery was mandatory, I also found the determination I needed to find the right kind of surgeon who understood and respected my concerns. . . . The important lesson I learned was to recognize the seriousness of breast cancer, the likelihood of a recurrence, and the need to incorporate immune-system-building treatments as an essential part of restoring health.[17]

Interestingly, 10 states now require physicians to discuss alternative treatment options with their breast cancer patients. Higher rates of breast-conserving surgery are found in those states that have enacted breast cancer informed consent laws. The spirit with which this is done, however, can never be mandated. Women need full disclosure of all relevant facts and compassionate help in interpretation of the facts in light of their specific situations.

Lymph Node Dissection: Is It Necessary?

While it has been a long time in coming, there is increasing awareness and acceptance that the more radical surgical procedures offer no better cure rates than the less aggressive options. However, the necessity for lymph node dissection has not been given the attention I believe it warrants and has been included in breast cancer surgery almost as a given.

Recent studies have shown no effect of axillary lymph node dissections on the long-term survival of women with breast cancer. I take issue with a headline in *ObGyn News,* which reported this information: "Without Mortality Benefit, Axillary Dissection Up to *Doctor's* Discretion.[18] The decision of whether or not to have the lymph nodes in the armpit removed is *your* decision. It should be based on:

- Your intuition.
- If and how the result (the presence of malignant cells in the nodes) could influence further treatment.
- Whether those treatment decisions could be made without the operation based on other information (by information gained from physical examination of the axillae, by the microscopic appearance of the tumor and other pathologic criteria).
- The potential for serious complications arising from the procedure (both during surgery, post-operatively and long-term healing issues).

The lymphatic system is a vital part of our immune system, however conventional medicine has placed little emphasis on respect for its function. Sydney Ross Singer, director of the Institute for the Study of Culturogenic Disease writes, "It is unfortunate that the medical profession has typically ignored the role of the lymphatics in the maintenance of health. Apparently the lymphatics are so small that they are easily forgotten. Even the medical textbook,

Gray's Anatomy, admits, 'As these structures [lymphatic vessels] are not readily seen in his dissections, the student is apt to forget the study of lymphatic drainage.' . . . About the only time the lymphatics are mentioned these days is in connection with cancer, especially breast cancer. They are not, however, seen as an important system in the *prevention* of cancer. Rather, lymph nodes are considered pathways for the spread of disease. Surgeons study the nodes' locations so they can remove them when performing mastectomies."[19]

A single lymph node, the size of a kidney bean, is actively involved in both humoral and cellular immunity. Lymph nodes are the sites where both filtering and cleansing of tissue fluids takes place. Thus the lymph nodes have an essential function in resisting the spread of cancer. Michael Baum states that "Lymph nodes themselves may be regarded as actively hostile to the proliferation of tumor cells, owing to [their] inherent anti-tumour activity . . ." In cases where the nodes draining breast cancer are negative, "the removal or irradiation of these uninvolved lymph nodes might be potentially harmful to the patient."

Physician, first do no harm. Lymph nodes which can be felt on physical exam may be exhibiting 'reactive hyperplasia,' part of the immune system's attempt to contain the cancer. On the other hand if lymph nodes are involved with cancer cells, the excision of these nodes according to Dr. Baum, is "unlikely to increase the cure rate"[20] and may not be beneficial unless doing so provides relief of pain or compression symptoms (not a common clinical picture).

Our lymphatic system is intimately related to our venous system; therefore tumor cells that enter lymphatic channels can also enter the bloodstream having access to our entire body. Given this fact, hastily removing lymph nodes is somewhat akin to closing the barn door after the horses have already gotten out. In contrast to the concept of breast cancer spreading in a contiguous manner as conceptualized at the turn of the century, the present understanding is that breast cancer is a *systemic* disease. Dr. Susan Love, my surgeon, explained this to me at our initial meeting.

For the great majority of women with breast cancer the current understanding of the natural history of breast cancer and tumor cell dynamics makes it very likely that tumor cells or micrometastases have already seen other parts of her body. They have not remained strictly in one breast in complete isolation from the rest of the body. If tumor cells have microscopically or macroscopically visited one's lymph nodes, then it is very likely they have also visited one's bloodstream. Tumor cells do not fill the breast, then fill the nodes and then sequentially fill the rest of the body. That model was the old theory of contiguous spread. The very reason that the more radical surgeries are now known to offer no better cure rates is precisely because breast tumors do not spread in this fashion.

So despite the ease of conceptualization and the safety we might feel in believing the old theory, the evidence speaks otherwise. We need to bolster our immune system, not cut pieces out of it. Our bodies are whole; one part is connected to the other parts. The body is dynamic; cutting out a part may seem like the answer but may not serve us well. Don't hand this decision over to your doctor. Think it through, feel it through. Women must begin to make their own choices.

At a recent lecture this topic was addressed by Dr. Love, associate professor, Department of Surgery, and Dr. Dennis Slamon, chief of the division of Hematology-Oncology, Department of Medicine, both of UCLA School of Medicine.[21] Dr. Love said, "As we get better biomarkers, we'll probably abandon lymph node dissection. Certainly, women with microscopic cancers less than five millimeters and women with DCIS (ductal carcinoma in situ) don't need this procedure. At the last couple of meetings I've attended, it was the surgeons who wanted to abandon lymph node dissec-

tion, but the oncologists (chemotherapists) are still clinging
to it." Dr. Slamon added, ". . . In fact, many times the cancer
spreads directly from the breast to distant body sites. We
see women with no evidence of disease in the nodes, yet
their breast cancer has spread to other body sites."

I agree that we need better tumor markers that will alert
us at the time of initial diagnosis whether this is a tumor
that is likely to spread. Yet, in spite of all the evidence that
it may have little impact on the spread of breast cancer to
other parts of the body and is not even a particularly accurate prognosticator, lymph node dissection is still recommended by most surgeons and oncologists.

∾

*I always get a very soft yet powerful feeling when I recall
my decision to decline the lymph node dissection. It was
empowering for me to say no to this procedure. After all the
trauma I had been through it felt so good to protect my
body's integrity. The procedure, although suggested by my
oncologist, made no intuitive sense to me. In my case, because of the size and aggressiveness of the tumor, I had
neoadjuvant chemotherapy first. My initially large axillary
nodes had disappeared during the course of the chemotherapy and I just didn't want anyone exploring the fat and
connective tissue in my armpit in the hopes of finding a
few lymph nodes to look at under the microscope that would
then enable the pathologist to tell me how long I might live.
I was already aware of the poor prognosis associated with
Stage III disease. In terms of treatment value, I had already
had chemo and was at this point planning to get radiation
after the lumpectomy whether the nodes were positive or
negative. The results of a node dissection may have changed
the aggressiveness with which I continued to pursue additional chemotherapy, but overall the operation and its attendant risks did not seem warranted. Just book me for a
lumpectomy please, I'll keep my nodes.*

∾

A woman may decide she does not want a surgical dissection of her lymph nodes. In the majority of cases the decision to proceed with chemotherapy can be made with some degree of accuracy with the information obtained from the combination of physical exam (are your lymph nodes enlarged, i.e., can you feel them? what do they feel like?) and the microscopic examination of the original incisional (removing a sample) or excisional (removing the entire lump) biopsy specimen which grades tumor cells from Grade 1 to Grade 4, Grade 4 being the most aggressive. Other tumor markers are Estrogen Receptor (ER) status, ploidy status and S-phase fraction. The unspoken assumption that the right decision can be made only if we can collect all the necessary data is clearly untrue. There is no single right decision. We are not achieving cure rates to validate our conventional decision-making wisdom, and it is quite clear that breast cancer is an unpredictable disease.

Some of the complications after lymph node dissection are prolonged numbness, restricted mobility, pain and weakness in the involved arm. Up to one-half of the women who undergo lymph node dissections develop lymphedema, swelling in the arm because the lymphatic fluid which bathes the cells can no longer drain properly. In some women this can be extensive and disfiguring. A combination of massage and compressive wrapping can help; it is crucial to treat this complication without delay because if the elasticity of the skin is lost by prolonged swelling the fluid will reaccumulate. Massage, wrapping, as well as specific exercises, can be done after surgery to encourage lymphatic drainage and possibly prevent or lessen the severity of this complication. Meticulous skin care can also help avoid or minimize this complication by reducing skin, subcutaneous and lymph tissue inflammation and infection.

Manual lymph drainage, a form of massage therapy which

has been successful in treating mild lymphedema, can accelerate the rate at which our body processes lymph fluid. This massage technique, by improving lymphatic circulation, helps the body more effectively remove contaminants like estrogenic pesticides and thereby has the added potential of helping to prevent breast cancer. Lymphedema is a problem that you should be aware of and discuss with your surgeon if you are considering lymph node surgery as part of your treatment.

BREAST RECONSTRUCTION— IMMEDIATE, DELAYED OR NOT AT ALL

Breast reconstruction can make a big difference to a woman who feels physically unbalanced with one breast, particularly if her breasts are large. Emotionally, reconstruction can be beneficial as well. In our breast-worshipping culture many women need to feel cosmetically acceptable. The fashion needs of one-breasted women are certainly not being met. Not long ago, pregnant women were also supposed to hide their physical reality.

A reconstruction can help some women release the past and move on. In 1994, 25,933 women with breast cancer chose to have total breast reconstructions after their mastectomies.[22] For some a too hasty decision to do an immediate reconstruction can inhibit the process of grieving the loss that is part of the mastectomy experience. Approximately 49 percent of women who have had breast reconstruction with implants had the procedure immediately. Some women are choosing to forego both reconstruction and prostheses and to become comfortable with their new physical realities. The poet Audre Lorde had said, "If we are to translate the silence surrounding breast cancer into language and action against this scourge, then the first step is that women with mastectomies must become visible to each other. For silence and invisibility go hand in hand with powerlessness."[23]

PROSTHESIS

The mirror captures
for an instant
your little-girl body yearning
for breasts
  —like mine.
I watch
as you hold the soft
contoured form to your chest
and imagine
what it will be like.
I am tempted to seize the image
etched on my consciousness.
You ask: "May I have it?"
And I say softly: "No daughter, never
—No, never."

—SUSAN B. MARKISZ[24]

One-Breasted Women: The Question of Prosthesis, Implants and Breast Reconstruction. Every now and then there would be a patient who sat on my examining table and, after we chatted and I had checked her pulse and blood pressure, heart, lungs and thyroid gland, she would lift her cotton gown and her bravery would hit me right in the middle of my chest, dead center. There was a mastectomy scar emblazoned across her chest. I always felt it so deeply. It wasn't pity, although the emotion I felt had an element of sorrow and it wasn't "better you than me." At that time I doubted that such misfortune could befall me (I thought being a doctor conferred protection). It was more an admiration for her battle scar, an overwhelming sense that this woman had given up her breast for her life and that she was a living testament to the power of women to make such choices in their lives. Sacrificing one's breast is not an easy thing to do in this culture; women are so profoundly indoctrinated to associate their value with their youth and beauty. Yet over and over women chose life and therein lay my admiration. It was such a powerful bond I felt for these women, and I always tried to examine their scars in a tender way, with the respect they deserved.

Not all women with breast cancer will have a mastectomy and of those that do, not all women choose to live with their mastectomy scars. Some women recover from their mastectomies and at a later time have breast reconstruction; others have the reconstruction at the time of their original cancer operation. Personally, I think we all need to process what we go through and, knowing that emotional issues need emotional time, I worry about women who choose to have immediate reconstructive surgery.

Perhaps there is something to be gained by being a one-breasted woman, an Amazon woman. Perhaps the power of that sacrifice and the ability to transcend it can teach and empower some of us. For others, the pain of having one breast is too much to bear. There is also a lesson in exploring the need to look normal, in not letting the world in on this secret. I've seen reconstructed breasts, not only after mastectomies, but after cosmetic breast surgery, and the feeling for me was different. As I did those breast exams there was no feeling of life in those breasts only the sense of a tightly filled water balloon buried just under the skin of their chests. If the plastic procedure was done for cosmetic reasons alone I noticed that often women did not mention it when I questioned them about previous surgery. The procedure had been done with such expertise and the healing was so excellent that I sometimes had no idea that I was about to feel an implant until my hand was upon it. I much preferred the feeling of flesh, the sometimes thick mastectomy scars abutting the ribs. There was so much possibility in that raw pain, so much more to learn, while the implants had a formless kind of feel, looking one way, feeling completely otherwise, an entirely different offering.

If *I* have to lose my breast, let me be an Amazon, a warrior. Deena Metzger lost her breast and wrote:

I am no longer afraid of mirrors when I see the sign of the Amazon, the one who shoots arrows. There is a fine red line across my chest where the knife entered, but now a branch winds about the scar and travels from arm to heart. Green leaves cover the branch, grapes hang there and a bird appears. What grows in me now is vital and does not cause me harm. I think the bird is singing. When he finished his work, the tatooist drank a glass of wine with me. I have relinquished some of the scars. I have designed my chest with the care given to an illuminated manuscript. I am no longer ashamed to make love. In the night a hand caressed my chest and once again I came to life. Love is a battle I can win. I have the body of a warrior who does not kill or wound. On the book of my body, I have permanently inscribed a tree. . . . I am no longer ashamed of what I know, nor of the scars I suffered to gain that knowledge. I am not afraid of the power which is in us. I am not afraid of the dawn, of being alone, of making love, of announcing myself as a part of the revolution."[25]

I certainly believe that all women should have the opportunity to feel physically beautiful but I hope that this in no way interferes with their ability to fully process and deeply learn from the experiences that their lives present. In her moving reflections on the experience of breast cancer Audre Lorde remembers a post-op visit to her by a Reach to Recovery volunteer,

. . . a kindly woman from Reach to Recovery came in to see me, with a very upbeat message and a little prepared packet containing a soft-sleep-bra and a wad of lambswool pressed into a pale pink breast-shaped pad . . . what she said was, '*You'll* never know the difference,' and she lost me right there, because I knew sure as hell *I'd* know the difference . . . I looked away thinking, 'I wonder if there are any black lesbian feminists in Reach for Recovery?' . . . it was the wrong color, and looked grotesquely pale through the cloth of my bra. Somewhere, up to that moment, I had thought, well perhaps they know something that I don't and maybe they're

right, if I put it on maybe I'll feel entirely different. I
didn't. . . . For not even the most skilled prosthesis in the
world could undo [the] reality, or feel the way my breast had
felt, and either I would love my body one-breasted now, or
remain forever alien to myself."[26]

Prostheses are made in different sizes and shapes and
can be a cosmetic solution for some women. They are sold
in surgical supply houses, lingerie stores and in shops dedi-
cated to the special needs of women with breast cancer.
The breast cancer epidemic has actually inspired the creation of a new line of specialized lingerie. Prostheses are
made of different materials and can even be customized.
However they are not everyone's solution, marketing efforts
notwithstanding. Virginia Soffa talks about her comfort in
abandoning her prosthesis:

Eventually I decided to make my own [prothesis], which I
now understand is *not* uncommon. . . . After the initial adjustment I soon switched to cotton T-shirts and abandoned my
homemade prosthesis.[27]

Betty Rollins' description of her first evening out after her
mastectomy, in *First, You Cry,* stuffing her bra, coura-
geously attempting to reintegrate her life, and her hilarious
and poignant attempts to find the perfect nipple are very
grounding. She too fashioned her own prosthetic device:

I felt that I could not go one more day without a nipple.
Whereupon it occurred to me that perhaps I could make one
myself—attach something small and pointed to the nylon
cover of the Dacron wad. I headed for my sewing box, rum-
maged through spools of thread, buttons, pincushions, and
cards of needles and pins, and there, in one corner of the
box, under a green button, was a black nipple. Actually it
was a black cloth cuff link. But I knew right away it would
work . . .[28]

**Zero-breasted, one-breasted or two-breasted women—
We all need support.** It is important to remember that all
women recovering from breast cancer need to be supported. Having breast-conserving surgery does not in any
way imply that a woman need not make psychological adjustments to the crisis and aftermath of breast cancer in her
life. In Sandra Levy's study "Mastectomy Versus Excisional
Biopsy: Mental Health Effects on Long-Term Follow-up,"
129 women with Stage I and II breast cancer were followed
for 15 months after surgery. Patients who received breast-
sparing surgery were rated as more functional by observers;
these same patients felt they received less emotional support over the entire recovery period. Because of the accumulating scientific evidence substantiating the value of
emotional support in healing, this finding is troublesome. It
is important to attend to the mental health needs of *all*
women being treated for breast cancer. We cannot assume
that women who have had breast-conserving surgery need
less emotional support.

> Dr. Levy concludes, Breast-sparing surgery is likely not a
> psychosocial panacea, and patients spared their breasts have
> psychological symptoms that appear acutely worse in the
> short run, and in the end similar to those who experience
> more extensive surgery. Women who are diagnosed and
> treated for breast cancer, particularly younger ones, have
> significant mental health needs requiring support and poten-
> tial interventions. The patterns differ as a function of surgery,
> but based on these data we cannot conclude that those re-
> ceiving a lumpectomy are psychosocially better off for elect-
> ing that treatment option.[29]

No one has said it better than Audre Lorde: the experience of breast cancer must be made visible no matter what
our chests look like. We must honor each other for the
experience whether our treatment leaves us with no breasts,
one breast or two is not really the issue.

When Moishe Dayan, the Prime Minister of Israel, stands up in front of parliament or on TV with an eyepatch over his empty eyesocket, nobody tells him to go get a glass eye, or that he is bad for the morale of the office. The world sees him as a warrior with an honorable wound, and a loss of a piece of himself which he has marked, and mourned, and moved beyond. And if you have trouble dealing with Moishe Dayan's empty eye socket, everyone recognizes that it is your problem to solve, not his.[30]

Implants vs. flaps

Silicone implants. Between 1962, when silicone breast implants first became available, and January 1992, when the FDA called for a moratorium on these implants, approximately two million women underwent breast procedures involving these implants.

Silicone is a dangerous manmade substance whose chemical name is *polydimethylsiloxane*. This substance has been used in breast implants and in the semi-permeable membrane covering both the silicone and saline breast implants as well as in a number of other devices used in human bodies. Silicone molecules may leach out of these devices, exerting damage by initiating inflammatory reactions and by releasing free radical oxidants.[31]

Severe chest wall, shoulder and breast pain are examples of direct organ damage. Although the medical establishment is not convinced, ("Unexplained Pain from Implants Still Reported" was the title of an article in the December 1994 issue of *Ob.Gyn. News*[32]), the problems continue to be reported, and the evidence and cases are accumulating. The reason these problems are unexplained is because they go beyond the expertise of conventionally trained physicians. Localized hardening, discomfort and pain from the occasional breakage and spillage of the gel filling are breast-related complications. Distant effects from the small amounts that can migrate out of an intact implant and from larger leaks include autoimmune diseases such as rheumatoid arthritis, systemic lupus erythematosus and scleroderma/systemic sclerosis, pancreatic exocrine dysfunction, fatigue, flu-like illness, nuerocognitive problems such as tremors, burning pain in the extremities and short-term memory loss. The FDA has also received inquiries about a study reported by the *Journal of the American Medical Association*[33] suggesting that the children of women with silicone breast implants may be at risk for developing abnormal esophageal motility and as yet has not drawn any conclusions.

In February 1994, facing a class-action lawsuit, the manufacturers agreed to pay $4.75 billion to compensate women allegedly harmed by the implants. Women with saline implants are also eligible to participate in the settlement. Interestingly, the manufacturers continue to claim the implants are safe while at the same time agreeing to pay $5 billion dollars in damages! In 1992, a few months after calling for a moratorium on silicone implants, the FDA's advisory panel recommended that their use be limited to controlled research studies for women who have had mastectomies for cancer. So the women who are already compromised with respect to immune function are those who can, according to the FDA, be experimented upon.

Our shortsightedness in thinking about implant technology needs to be addressed; we cannot expect to insert synthetic materials into a living system with no adverse consequences. Some xenobiotics found in nature can be processed by the body, just as the body can deal with some background radiation. However, there is no detoxification pathway for polydimethylsiloxane.

Saline implants. Saline implants, which are silicone shells filled with saline, may be subject to some of the same complications as silicone implants. The FDA is still uncertain about how to regulate these implants, which have been in use for over 30 years. The investigations have not proceeded as rapidly as originally planned. There are currently three ongoing national studies evaluating the safety of saline implants with silicone shells, the results of which will be available in 1998. Additionally, reports have surfaced regarding bacterial and fungal infections initiated by leaking saline implants.[34]

๛   Remember...

Take the time to discuss all the options of breast reconstruction with your surgeon and a plastic surgeon before any procedures are done; have all options clearly defined beforehand. Decisions about reconstruction should be made in the same way as decisions regarding breast cancer treatment, yielding well-thought-out and emotionally suitable choices. Do not rush the process.

Any of the procedures can be done immediately at the time of a mastectomy or at a later time. The advantage of having it done immediately and not facing another operation at a later time must be weighed against the longer time in the operating room, the additional recovery issues both short- and long-term and the difficulties of making another major decision at a time when you are facing the crisis of breast cancer. If we can step back and give ourselves time to adjust to the diagnosis and aftermath of breast cancer, then I believe the decision about reconstruction will come easier.

Flaps. Several procedures have been developed using one's own tissue to form a breast. In a myocutaneous flap, a flap of skin, muscle and fat is taken, generally from the abdomen (tranverse rectus abdominus muscle—TRAM flap) or back and introduced in a tunneling procedure into the mastectomy site. The blood supply remains intact and, because the tissue is real, the breast reconstructed in this way may be more acceptable esthetically. Depending upon the area from which the flap is taken, there may be a corresponding weakness at that site; however, the myriad of problems associated with synthetic materials are avoided. The breast, as in the case of artificial implants, will have little sensation.

Is Radiation Hazardous?

> How is cancer treated?
> Radiation will kill the cancer cells,
> Shrivel them up.
> That's what they say.
> And of course it does.
> And shrivels up other cells too,
> There in the skin where you see it,
> And deep in your body as well.
>
> —A. Meares[35]

Radiation does not alter your chance of survival with breast cancer. Radiation is used as an adjuvant or additional treatment with lumpectomy, to reduce the local recurrence rate; it is also used for palliation, to relieve suffering, in locally advanced cases. If survival is not improved by this modality, then we must be very sure that we understand the risks involved with its use.

Radiation itself is a risk factor for developing breast cancer. Perhaps incongruously, it is also a breast cancer treatment modality. The medical literature is replete with documentation linking radiation to breast cancer.

Thirty-five years after the bombings of Hiroshima and Nagasaki the data on breast cancer incidence is still being collected as the girls and women exposed to the atomic bomb approach mid-life. The results of studies by the Radiation Effects Research Foundation show that the exposure of female breast tissue to ionizing radiation at any age prior to menopause can cause breast cancer later in life.[36] The risk of developing breast cancer in atomic bomb survivors depends on where they were at the time of the bomb, i.e., the level of exposure and the age at which they were exposed. For example, women exposed at age 10 through 19 to the highest levels of radiation showed a relative risk of seven times that of women without known risk factors.

The radiation of the thymus gland in infants[37] and multiple series of diagnostic x-rays on adolescents for scoliosis[38] have resulted in a statistically higher incidence of breast cancer when these females reach adulthood. One study in the *Journal of the National Cancer Institute* evaluated women with scoliosis who had frequent low-dose diagnostic exposures. The women were treated at an average age of 12, getting an average of 41 films and were followed on average for 26 years. Follow-up of these women revealed an almost twofold risk.

Like the studies of the atomic bomb survivors showed, the carcinogenic effects of radiation are more pronounced at certain times in a woman's life (when breast cells are more vulnerable). Radiation effects are modulated by a woman's hormonal milieu and potentiated under certain conditions. This study and others impel us to question the potential harm of frequent diagnostic procedures and to be aware that there is a cumulative effect of low-dose radiation exposures.

In the past women have been treated with radiation to alleviate the pain of postpartum mastitis[39] and have developed breast cancer at higher than expected rates. Thirty and forty years after being treated with flouroscopy for tuberculosis, women develop breast cancer.[40] We also see women with breast cancer after radiation treatment for Hodgkin's disease. Certainly radiation is not a benign procedure. It must be well-considered before automatically incorporating it into every woman's treatment plan. Hodgkin's disease happens to be one of the few diseases for which radiotherapy is curative and for which a calculated risk may well be worth taking. However if radiation does not improve survival for breast cancer we must be aware of the potential dangers before agreeing to its use.

Dr. John Laszlo of the American Cancer Society acknowledges "it is impossible to . . . give radiation treatments without injuring normal cells . . . Depending on the site treated, large doses of radiation can cause nausea and vomiting, loss of appetite and reduction in bone marrow function.[41] Radiation has these effects because it creates burns causing cell and tissue death. The body's natural attempt to heal from radiation may result in scarring, including fibrosis of internal organs.

After my own six-week course of radiation, follow-up chest x-rays revealed scarring in the apex of my left lung. Functionally, my lungs have also been impaired; I have had two protracted bouts of pneumonia and one prolonged episode of bronchitis in the four years since my treatment has been completed.

It is also unlikely that a breast that has been radiated can lactate, which may be a concern for some women. Deep scarring can cause hardening of the breasts, making future examinations by both physical exam and mammography less accurate as well as significantly increasing the difficulty of any future surgery should it become necessary to treat a recurrence or do a reconstruction. Texas surgeon Richard Evans, who does not support routine radiation after a lumpectomy, uses the term "local persistence" to describe many local relapses and notes that second tumors of this sort can be detected and removed.

In terms of self-image and sensuality, there may be changes in sensation; a lack of sensitivity and/or discoloration of the breast may result as well as a change in the size and consistency of the radiated breast. Radiation also can impair the natural healing ability in that same tissue. The process of radiation burning and healing by fibrosis damages the blood vessels and lymphatics that are so important in the health maintenance of breasts. Because of these damaging effects, once radiation is used to treat cancer, its future use in that organ is all but precluded. Radiation can occasionally cause hairline fractures of ribs. The extent of damage to the normal cells depends on the direction of the beam and the dosage. Damaged chromosomes can not only have a negative impact on future generations, but the destruction of bone marrow and the immune function that resides within it can lead to cancer in other sites.

The younger you are at the time of radiation the more likely it is that radiation itself will cause another cancer. A study at Columbia University concluded that "women who received radiation treatments for breast cancer are twice as likely to develop lung cancer as breast cancer patients who didn't receive radiation treatments."[42] Author Cathy Hitchcock asserts that for her, "Agreeing to a procedure that was in itself potentially carcinogenic seemed ludicrous."[43] Commenting on adjuvant radiation, one researcher noted that "certain recent studies have thrown the medical community into confusion by showing that metastases may be more frequent in cases that have received radiation . . ."[44] And the *British Medical Journal* published a study on women who had post-op radiation wherein there was "no significant effect on survival up to ten years, but beyond ten years the mortality in the irradiated patients was significantly increased."[45] In a systematic overview of 17,273 women in 36 trials, the Early Breast Cancer Trialist's Collaborative Group confirmed that radiotherapy did not affect 10-year survival but did confirm an excess of non-breast cancer-related deaths in the decade following radiotherapy.[46] Dr. John C. Bailar III, commenting on this metaanalysis, pointed out the need to ascertain the long-term effects of radiotherapy on both survival and quality of life.[47]

Smoking and breast radiation is a lethal combination. Women with breast cancer who smoke at the time they receive radiation treatments have a high risk of developing lung cancer on the irradiated side.[48] Women who smoke and are already at high risk need to take this into account when planning treatment.

Breast cancer patients treated with radiation and chemo-therapy are at a much higher risk of treatment-induced leu-kemia than those who receive chemotherapy alone. Dr. Eleni Diamandidou of the M.D. Anderson Cancer Center in Houston reported a cumulative 10-year leukemia rate of 2.5 percent in patients who received both therapies as com-pared to 0.6 percent in those who got chemotherapy alone. These facts were revealed during a retrospective review of 1,474 patients presented at the annual San Antonio breast cancer symposium.[49]

The possibility of side effects and after effects from radia-tion were minimized in my discussions with radiation oncol-ogists and in the patient literature I was given. I was informed only that my skin might redden and that I might be somewhat tired toward the end of the six weeks of treatments.

ର

I knew where the changing room was. I slipped out of my layers—cotton bra and undershirt, long-sleeved T-shirt and bulky sweater and I put on a paper gown. I had gotten so thin on my strict diet, I was always chilly. They showed me into the room with the red X on the door, CAUTION— RADIATION HAZARD. They led me in, I laid down on the steel table and was left there alone. The beam was aimed at my breast and the surrounding tissues.

ର *Remember...*

Radiation is far from innocuous. Lumpectomy without radiation is a reasonable choice for some women. Care-ful selection, meticulous surgery and wide margins of resection could reduce local recurrence rates. Lumpectomy and radiation are presented as a package deal: buy one get the other one free. This may not be the deal you want, so each treatment should be considered separately. Gather all the information you need and then make your decision with your heart as well as your intellect. Trust in your inner wisdom; then give yourself total support.

If you choose radiation, be sure to be especially gentle with yourself and your breasts: refrain from wearing bras or any constrictive clothing, wear only cotton undershirts, do not expose your breasts to the sun, use only natural products to moisturize and be sure to use visualization to protect your breasts from side effects during the treatments. Certain foods including miso and sea vegetables may be especially beneficial during radiation treatments. At Hiroshima University's Atomic Bomb Radiation Research Center, people who ate miso regularly were up to five times more resistant to radiation than those not eating miso.[50] Following research by scientists at the Gastro-Intestinal Research Laboratory at McGill University in Montreal, Canada, alginates, derived from sea vegetables, were used to decrease the ill effects of radiation. Through their biological activities, various marine algae function as natural decontaminators.

Besides miso and seaweeds, other good food sources to counter the ill effects of radiation are dark leafy greens, broccoli, cabbage, cooked carrots, winter squash, burdock root and lentil beans. Antioxidants, specifically the carotenes and selenium, are valuable immune boosters and are DNA-protective during radiation therapy. Do not minimize the effect of radiation on your body; rest during radiation treatments is essential.

∾

At the time of my treatment I did my wholehearted best; I never really questioned the wisdom of radiating my body. I bought the package. Recurrences. NO. I don't want that. I'll take some rads, why not? It doesn't hurt, just lie back and get zapped. In fact, it was the combination of the immune-depressing effects of radiation and chemotherapy, administered simultaneously in my case, that landed me in Norwalk Hospital in December of 1991 when my white count plummeted to dangerously low levels. Still not quite getting it, I was worried that the hospitalization had interrupted my final days of radiation. Did I need to finish the course? Had I accumulated enough rads? More to the point: Perhaps my body in all its wisdom had landed me in the hospital precisely to get away from all the treatments; my body had had all it could tolerate.

Because I had chemotherapy and radiation simultaneously it was hard to know how much of my fatigue during the radiation treatments was from radiation, but boy, did I feel depleted. It was something like the feeling of exhaustion after being up all night with several patients in labor. Each time I went back to the doctor's on-call room that exhaustion gave way to immediate sleep. Well, I felt as if I'd done an all-nighter every afternoon around two o'clock. I simply had to lie down; I just couldn't make it any further. My whole body started to vibrate, my body craved sleep and sleep was my restorative. I had no choice but to listen to my body; it wouldn't take no for an answer. Listen, do you hear your body's whispers? If you do, listen. If you don't, listen harder. If we don't listen, the messages get louder and louder until the body screams at us.

I experienced none of the immediate local radiation side effects; the skin on my breast was fine. I made every radiation session a holy experience. I was finally alone with myself. As a mother of three children under age four, I finally had some longed-for time for myself. Too bad it was flat on my back on a steel table! I tried hard to bring a meditative awareness to this experience. My thoughts turned to the energy source and imaged the rays going to any cancer cells, not touching or harming my healthy body. After a two-week gap in the treatments because of my hospitalization for viremia, finally, on New Year's Eve, 1991, the radiation treat-

ment was completed. Five years later, I still feel the site of the radiation along the left side of my irradiated breast and into the armpit; a throb, a constriction, a tightness, is always with me even when my mind is elsewhere. I'm not in a great deal of pain, but there is a physical awareness— a constant sensation—that the treatment imprinted as the radiation penetrated my body, forever changing the course of my life.

Author Sharon Batt's reflections echo my own thoughts, "In retrospect, I don't feel I made an informed choice about this aspect of my treatment. I was not aware of radiotherapy's limited function or possible harmful effects. I didn't realize how little firm evidence exists, either to support routine radiation ro to permit anyone to assess the risk of long-term damage."[51]

CHEMOTHERAPY, YES OR NO?

How is cancer treated?
Drugs to kill the cancer cells.
That's what they say.
And they kill other cells too.
And it does not feel too good.

—A. MEARES[52]

The "more is not better" idea applies equally well to chemotherapy. The new technologies of autologous bone marrow transplants allowing for the infusion of ever greater dosages of toxic chemotherapies may or may not be in your best interest, especially as a first approach. My friend Anne Fredericks died wondering if she might have done better had she not chosen the most aggressive chemotherapeutic treatment initially.

ॐ

Up to Boston to Dana-Farber for a fourth opinion. I was scheduled to see an entire team. The surgeon, Dr. Linda Harrigan, actually was a friend of a medical school classmate of mine; it made me feel better having spoken to her ahead of time. Dr. Helena Friss* was the radiation oncologist, and Dr. Richard Stein,* the medical oncologist. Because of the complexity of my case all the doctors would be in one place, I was told, and we would review my case together; in this way I could get a full picture of their recommendations. That was the plan.

Dr. Linda Harrigan* was tall, beautiful and Boston-businesslike. I thought she should have shown more concern. But then I rebuked myself: do you expect people to fall apart just because you, a perfect stranger, has breast cancer? No, but perhaps a little more sympatico, some acknowledgment of my personal disaster. She looked at me and she asked me the same unsympathetic questions I'd been answering for the past two weeks. No one asked, so how are you feeling? And then I got on the paper-lined examining table. What incredible loneliness—was it really me sitting on the table? To this day, I can still remember that incredible sense of helplessness. I felt like a child. Her hands and the many other hands palpating my breast over and over. I could hardly believe it. How could this mass the size of a tennis ball appear so suddenly? Could I, the obstetrician-gynecologist, somehow have missed this? She finished her exam and she left.

She returned in a short while after looking at my studies: mammos, CXRs, CAT scans of chest and abdomen, bone scan. I simply waited. I just wanted a little bit of hope held out. Something positive, a little goodie to keep me going. But what she did say was, "Well, the way we read it here, your bone scan is questionable." I looked at her in utter

---

* not their real names

disbelief. You mean I came 300 miles to hear you tell me that what was read in Norwalk as completely normal is now, in your opinion, abnormal? Did I just go from Stage III to Stage IV in the blink of her eye? Was she serious or was she just covering her ass? (a common practice in medicine whereby the doctor does every possible test or tells you every possible poor outcome so that you, the patient, don't come back at some later point claiming something was missed.) What in the world was going on here?

The next docs in were the radiation oncologists, Dr. Friss and her assigned medical student or resident. Two women. They both stood up the entire time they were in the room with me while I sat up on the crinkly paper-lined examining table. They asked fewer questions, looking much more sympathetic than Dr. Harrigan had, and then they examined me. Another four hands all over my breasts. My breasts (and I) were in a state of shock, still engorged and desperate to feed Oliver. They felt so especially painful and private in the context of having so abruptly stopped nursing that it made all the examinations so difficult. It was as if my intimate bond with Oliver was being publicly demolished. My breasts ached with the fear of not having enough time to know Oliver. The radiation oncologists left saying they would report to Dr. Stein and wished me well. I sensed their fear.

I lay on the examining table trying to get some rest. I was beginning to realize how precious every moment was. I was trying so hard not to be totally overwhelmed. After what seemed a long time, Dr. Stein came in. He repeated the process, more questions, another exam. Finally, three hours later, I got dressed and went down the hall. We were led to a lounge and we sat down with Dr. Stein. You can have cytoxan, adriamycin and 5-FU in this dosage with or without CSF or in higher dosages with a bone marrow transplant. He delineated numerous and varied protocols. "Which one would I prefer?" "Well, what do you think?" I asked, trying my best to sound rational about this. "Which was best? What would you suggest if I was your wife?" Dr. Stein was honest: there was no best. They didn't know. He couldn't say and I knew it and my husband knew it and we all kind of sat there together with this realization.

The protocols I was offered were the drug company's and university medical center's answer to research in breast cancer. Is drug combination CAF given for two weeks with a one week break better than CAF at a higher dose given for three weeks with CSF and a one week break, or is C & A given at super high dosages in a bone marrow protocol for Stage IIIA the best?

Well, I asked, knowing full well that bone marrow protocols could themselves be lethal, "What percentage of people die from the treatment with bone marrow?" "Oh, about five percent," he said, rather nonchalantly. Goddammit! I refuse to die from the treatment. My heart spoke loud and clear; I knew more was not better. I would take the standard chemotherapy and forego the five percent mortality from the bone marrow protocols. And vitally important to my decision, I would not participate in a higher-dose protocol at Dana-Farber, but take the standard triple chemotherapy in Norwalk where I could be near my children and where I could take my elixir of love every night, never toxic, always healing from Oliver, Hannah and Zachary.

∽

Understanding the natural history of breast cancer helps us in our approach to treatment and healing; Dr. Love writes:

The problem is that most [breast] cancers have been there a long time by the time we find them. The average cancer has a doubling time of 100 days; it takes 100 days for one cell to double and become two. You need 100 billion cancer cells to have one centimeter of cancer. If you do the math, you'll see that most cancers have been present for eight to ten years by the time you can feel the smallest of lumps. A long time. The tumor gets a blood supply, however, at around year three. This means that cancer cells can be shed into the bloodstream very early on, way before we have the ability to detect the tumor. Some of these cells will be killed by the immune system, but others may find their way into other organs, slowly growing and eventually surfacing in a way that is indeed life-threatening.[53]

FIGURE 2

BREAST CANCER EXISTS PRECLINICALLY FOR MANY YEARS
PRIOR TO DIAGNOSIS

Size of tumor in relation to cell doublings

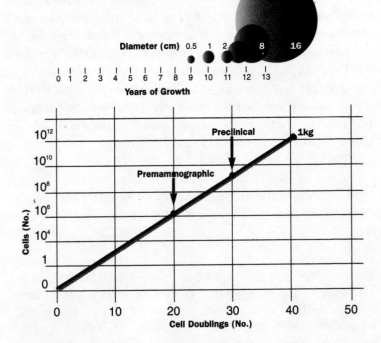

Although it sounds like a grim tale of dread, what this really means is that there is no urgency in the decision-making process in the treatment of breast cancer. If a disease process has been going on for 10 years, let's not fool ourselves into thinking that we must get our treatment going in the next 48 hours. Read, think, feel, consult, process, then decide. The most important part of your treatment will be the systemic approach—the whole person approach—and that goes beyond what is offered by conventional medicine.

Because breast cancer, from early in its course, is a systemic disease, it does not mean all women need chemotherapy. It simply means that it is likely that breast cancer cells have already been through your system, that they have left the breast through the circulatory and lymphatic channels; not that they have necessarily established themselves elsewhere but that the cells have not been strictly confined. In *Dr. Susan Love's Breast Book,* the author explains, ". . . the question we have to ask is not whether the cancer cells have gotten out, but how well we think the patient's body has taken care of whatever cells might have gotten out."[54] If these malignant cells have not established themselves in other sites it is because the immune system is functioning.

Enhancing this immune function is vital. The cancer cells that have left the original tumor are called "micrometastases." The function of systemic therapy in women who have no demonstrable metastases is to eradicate these micromets. Systemic means treating the entire system; chemotherapy is a systemic treatment. It is not the only such treatment but it is the conventional approach to systemic therapy. A well-researched nutrition program and daily meditation are also systemic approaches.

∾

My initial reaction to getting chemo was, "I'm dead; if I need chemo, I'm dead." Our collective belief about cancer is that it is a death sentence and that chemo is a demonic torturer. Don't underestimate the power of our negative beliefs.

My having gone through medical school did nothing to lessen my fears; in fact, if anything, my experience in Gynecologic Oncology heightened my anticipation of the horror. I had seen the protocols, I had written the orders, I had followed the temp curves of in-patients getting chemo, watching for sepsis in those whose immune systems were being attacked by the same toxic regimens that were bombarding the cancers; I had monitored the urine output in women receiving nephrotoxic drugs; I saw women come back after chemotherapy failed—for more surgery, for more rads, for more chemo. And I saw tumors spread in unusual ways even after all this therapy.

I had to acknowledge all that and then, having done so, befriend my would-be assailant. Chemotherapy was the best option I had for my initial treatment, this I knew. I felt good. I had decided on the approach and I was going to cooperate with my body in accepting the treatment in the best way I could. I brought my meditation tapes with me to the treatments. As the chemotherapy was infusing, the lights were out in the small examining room, and I visualized the drugs going directly to the cancer in my breast and axillae, avoiding all my healthy tissue. I pictured healing in process, healing light streaming in from the top of my head, I relaxed with my breathing. As the infusion began I felt heat, then a wave of revulsion (a total body nausea) and a toxic metallic taste. I allowed these sensations to pass through without fighting them. I let nothing distract me from my purpose. Month after month the tumor began to melt away in the light of my healing visualizations. Imperceptible at first, but by the third round of chemo the tumor was obviously smaller; it had shrunk from about six to four cm. My spirts soared, I was learning how to take care of myself. Throughout the first six months of my triple chemotherapy (which consisted of cytoxan, novantrone and 5-FU) I was immersed in my healing. I learned how to prepare nourishing food; I rested; I began to visualize, to meditate and to journal. My dreams were incredibly vivid, almost every night powerful images guided me to the areas of my life that needed clarity.

As for the side effects of the chemo, I was spaced out from the premedication on the day of the treatment. For two days afterwards I felt extremely tired and my appetite was poor. I got a few painless ulcerations in my mouth and my hair thinned a bit. However, I let nothing distract me from my purpose.

∾

Chemotherapy, like every other area in the treatment of breast cancer is controversial. Here are some basic points of information:

- Premenopausal women with positive nodes are helped most by chemotherapy. In the Early Breast Cancer Trialists' Collaborative Group,[55] one out of eleven women taking chemo was spared a recurrence, after 10 years. One woman in 15 remained alive more than 10 years because of the chemo.
- Chemotherapy is not as effective in postmenopausal women. In the study just noted, one life was saved for every 50 postmenopausal women (in their 50s) taking chemo, and for women in their 60s a life was saved for every 34 women taking the chemo.
- Ovarian ablation, (removal of the ovaries) may be as effective as chemo for premenopausal women. In fact some, if not most, of the effect of chemotherapy is due to its suppression of ovarian function in premenopausal women.
- 70 to 80 percent of node-negative women will not have a recurrence, but 20 to 30 percent will die of metastatic breast cancer. In 1988, the National Cancer Institute took the stand that all women with breast cancer should have chemo. Remember that several drug com-

pany officials serve on NCI advisory committees. In the 1992 Collaborative Study, for every 25 node-negative women treated with chemo, one life was saved after 10 years.

You may be tempted to say, well if there is any improvement in disease-free survival or survival at all then perhaps I should take the treatment. Here again, though, we have to be careful. Author Sharon Batt quotes Texas physician William McGuire:

If all 70,000 women diagnosed annually in the U.S. with node-negative breast cancer were to have one of these courses of chemotherapy, the direct financial cost would be $338,174,200 per year and 50 to 100 women would die from the treatments. These figures did not include the cost of treating toxic effects or indirect costs, such as days lost from work. About 5,040 women would gain some disease-free time. "I would argue," Dr. McGuire has written, "that the considerable cost outweighs the benefits of treating all node-negative patients, especially in the absence of a proved survival benefit."[56]

❧

12/18/91. I was very scared when I broke out with Zoster. It was almost as if I had had a recurrence of cancer. I'm not sure why I was relying on my body to hold up, as if it would take anything and keep going . . . I felt awful for two days, 105 fever and shaking chills. After going back and forth with my doctor for a few days, he insisted I see Dr. Chang,* an infectious disease specialist. Dr. Chang promptly assured me that I could certainly die of viremia if I did not agree to be admitted to the hospital and get IV acyclovir. I looked at my husband; he looked worried. I didn't know what else to do so I acquiesced . . . I was in the hospital overnight for the first time in all this, hospital wrist band

* not his real name.

and all; only a few months ago I was making GYN rounds here—what a homecoming!

I had been having a great deal of difficulty ending my treatments; Dr. Love informed me that there was no data supporting continuing the treatments beyond those I'd completed, my body agreed; Dr. Zelkowitz thought there was some value in continuing the chemotherapy for an additional three to six months, my mind agreed. My soul had to cast the final vote.

1/16/92 . . . I continued treatments despite my deep-seated doubts. Finally, after nine months of chemo, I was able to say no more. What had been so difficult to end was over. Nine months: an appropriate amount of time for an obstetrician, the time for a gestation to mature. I was ready to be born anew!

∾

Breast cancer is a systemic disease *prior* to its detection. What protects us from diffuse metastatic disease is the ability of our immune system—our greatest ally—to contain the cancer. Immune support is a fundamental principle in both the treatment and prevention of breast cancer. A treatment that damages our immune system must be viewed with caution.

In my case, chemotherapy was used to debulk a very large and aggressive Stage III tumor. Although chemotherapy can be a life-saving treatment modality in advanced disease, I am certain that chemotherapy is not the best approach to preventing recurrence in early stage breast cancer. I strongly advise restraint regarding the use of these very toxic drugs. When I tell my story I never forget to mention the ways I supported my immune function during and after my chemotherapy treatments. I will never know which part of my program had the most impact on my recovery. I sense that the complementary therapies I utilized—from my macrobiotic diet to my visualizations—were as crucial to my recovery as they were to diminishing side effects from chemo.

Side Effects

One evening in group
Lori took off her headscarf
She was naked in front of us
Her baldness was startling
Her boldness more so
We were a privileged few
Allowed to share her grief
As she pulled off the covering
And revealed what lay beneath
She embraced her own bald vulnerability
In our presence

—B.J.

Side Effects—Short- and Long-term

The short-term side effects of chemo can be ameliorated by attending to nourishment on all levels. Short-term side effects include nausea, vomiting, loss of appetite, hair loss, menopausal symptoms like hot flashes (in premenopausal women), mouth sores, conjunctivitis, bowel problems (both diarrhea and constipation). The drop in white blood cell count is not only an expected side effect but the crude way your doctor will monitor your treatment. If your white blood count is normal, that means you're tough—you can take more. And your dosage will be increased. When your bone marrow is suppressed enough and can't maintain a normal white count you've reached an "effective" dose. If your count is dangerously low, the next round of treatment will be delayed and in the meantime, you will become susceptible to infections and bleeding complications until your body is able to rebound.

Long-term side effects are even more worrisome. Chemotherapy clearly works as a systemic poison; one of the effects of this poison is the increased incidence of second malignancies. The incidence of leukemia in breast cancer patients who have received chemotherapy was reported as .5 percent by the National Surgical Adjuvant Breast and Bowel Project.[57] This may not be an impressive statistic, but for the woman who develops leukemia it is, especially if she was one of the 24 of 25 node-negative women for whom chemotherapy did nothing in terms of breast cancer recovery. In general, when radiation and chemotherapy are given together, the incidence of second malignancies increases to 25 times the expected rate. Somewhere between five and ten percent of surviving cancer patients (from all cancers) die of leukemia in the first ten years after treatment with chemotherapy.[58]

How to Protect Yourself

If you choose to undergo chemotherapy, it is essential to protect yourself. Women who are taking toxic pharmaceuticals must do everything possible to nourish body and mind simultaneously, thereby enhancing immune function. Your detoxification system also needs to be functioning optimally so that the body can excrete these pharmaceutical chemicals and metabolic debris from tumor breakdown. Complementary systemic treatments such as the use of whole foods, supplements, rest and mindbody techniques are essential in this regard.

- **Food.** There is no substitute for wholesome food. The anti-cancer substances in foods are only beginning to be isolated. A balanced diet should be high in plant foods, unprocessed, low in animal fat, hydrogenated fats and sugar. Organic foods are key. We know that 40 percent or more of cancer patients die of malnutrition and that chemotherapy and radiation can exacerbate this condition.[59] See Chapter 3

- **Supplements.** Nutritional supplements can boost the immune system. When therapeutic levels of nutrients are achieved, the immune system responds with more activity. There is good evidence that antioxidant supplements can prevent or ameliorate many of the side effects associated with chemotherapy. Tumor cells do not absorb antioxidants as well as normal cells, therefore therapeutic levels of these substances make chemotherapy more selective in targeting cancer cells.

One study found that taking 1600 IU of vitamin E daily for one week prior to treatment allowed 69 percent of chemo patients to keep their hair.[60] Adriamycin, used frequently in triple agent chemotherapy for more aggressive or advanced breast cancers, is known to be cardiotoxic. In fact, chemotherapy can damage the heart so much that heart failure, not cancer, may be the cause of death. Antioxidants like vitamins A, C, and E can prevent this but unfortunately are not included in chemotherapy protocols.[61]

In her book, *Wellness Against All Odds,* Dr. Sherry Rogers writes, "It is criminal not to prescribe nutrients for patients on chemotherapy in this age with all that is known about antioxidant chemistry and the universal cell damage created by chemotherapy . . ."[62] Dr. Charles B. Simone, in *Breast Health,* writes, "All cellular studies using vitamins (C, A, K, E, D, beta-carotene, B6, B12), minerals (selenium) and cysteine concomitantly with chemotherapy and radiation show the same effect: increased tumor killing and increased protection of normal tissues.[63]

I recommend a minimum of 400 IU a day of vitamin E for women on chemo. To help prevent adriamycin toxicity, I suggest 100-300 mg daily of coenzyme Q10.

- **Mind-body techniques.** There is a strong connection between emotions and health—a fact that is finding more and more acceptance in the medical establishment. In the late 70s, David Spiegel, M.D. analyzed the outcomes of 86 women with advanced breast cancer who had been randomly assigned to either routine cancer care (the control group) or a support group. The women in the experimental support group had improvements in mood, were demonstrably less anxious and depressed and in half as much pain as the control group.

A few years later Dr. Spiegel set out to prove that although the psychological intervention was helpful to these women with breast cancer in terms of quality of life, it would have no impact on the eventual progression of their disease or their survival. Interestingly, by following the outcomes of these same women 10 years later, he proved himself wrong. Indeed the psychotherapeutic intervention affected not only the quality of life for these women but extended their lives as well. Referring to his book *Living Beyond Limits,* Spiegel shares, "What we think and feel is relevant to the course of disease, but it does not provide us with straightforward control over it either. In this book I describe what I have learned from cancer patients about how one can live fully in the face of illness, how mind and body work together, how facing dying can intensify living."[64] Join a support group; talk to a counselor; pay attention to your dreams and learn from them, give credence to the impact of your emotional life on your disease process.

I certainly attribute my ability to go through the conventional treatments with a minimum of difficulties to the immune-enhancing effects of my overall health program.

Knowledge is Power. Our Information Is Limited.

Treya Wilbur wrote:

How many women have heard this word CANCER pounding like an endless drumbeat inside their heads, relentless, unforgiving. . . . I sit here, on this couch, wrapped in my blanket, these papers and pamphlets piled in my lap. I turn to them, obsessed with wanting to learn more . . . The reading soothes me. This night information is my lifeline out of useless fear and worry. This night information is the best kind of therapy. I was to find this was always true for me in the future. The more I knew, the more secure I felt, even if the news was bad. Ignorance frightens me; knowledge soothes me. The worst part is not knowing . . . definitely the worst part is not knowing . . .[65]

Since 1975 the number of breast cancer patients receiving chemotherapy has increased 300 percent. Yet, the mortality statistics do not reflect a benefit from these treatments that is proportionate. Perhaps chemo is overutilized. Certainly the recent advice from the National Cancer Institute (NCI) recommending the use of chemotherapy for *all* breast cancer patients must be viewed with skepticism. For years the NCI, the American Cancer Society, Memorial-Sloan-Kettering Cancer Center and the major pharmaceutical companies have directed our country's priorities in cancer research, have set the stage for acceptable treatment protocols and have dominated the media and the minds of the public with self-serving choices.

The National Breast Cancer Coalition, a grassroots advocacy effort, is calling for new voices in decision-making, taking it out of the hands of the few who often have conflicts of interest and into the hands and hearts of those who are affected and whose lives are at stake. Statistics can be manipulated to show just about anything. On paper even a small but statistically significant benefit seems worthwhile, but nowhere in that small but present benefit statistic is the suffering calculated, the side effects measured or the quality of life addressed. A treatment needs to make sense to you intellectually, to feel right emotionally and to potentially benefit you in a life-affirming way.

∿ *Remember. . .*

Chemotherapy is a systemic poison that can be part of a well-planned treatment strategy. The primitive, more rapidly dividing cancer cells are killed more easily than normal cells; however, the destruction wrought by chemotherapy is relatively non-specific.

In order to derive the maximum benefit during chemotherapy treatment a woman must support her normal cells nutritionally so that they can resist and recover from this toxic treatment. Do not fall prey to the "more is better" philosophy. With chemotherapy, less may be life-saving. Resist the use of chemotherapy for prevention; with breast cancer this aggressive treatment is more suited to advanced disease. If you do choose to utilize chemotherapy, protect your immune system with wholesome food, supplements and mind-body techniques.

WHAT ABOUT BONE MARROW TRANSPLANT?

A metaanalysis done under the auspices of the World Health Organization showed that high-dose chemotherapy and autologous stem cell rescue (HDC/ASCR) with autologous bone marrow transplantation or peripheral blood stem cell rescue was no more effective than conventional chemotherapy for metastatic breast cancer. The concept behind the bone marrow transplant and stem cell rescue procedure is simple. The immune/blood cells are removed from a woman's body so that she can be given very high chemotherapy doses which would otherwise kill her. Her blood cells are later replaced. This high-dose chemotherapy is sometimes referred to as dose-intensification. To me, this makes no intuitive sense. If cancer cells are not sensitive to the usual therapeutic doses, why would they be responsive to such massive doses? Again the "more is better" philosophy is flawed. Dose intensification is to medical oncology

what the radical mastectomy was to surgery in years past.
When bone marrow therapy was offered to me, I refused
it. There wasn't even a split second in which I thought that
this Draconian procedure could possibly be the right thing
to do.

The Bone Marrow Transplant

I had a friend
I wanted to know her better
we really laughed together, belly laughs
women in their thirties
everything before them
She stopped by and we sat at the kitchen table
Emily and Oliver played while we talked
Who needed to meet over breast cancer?
We wished we had met at the PTA
but alas
Anne had a bone marrow transplant
she thought it would help
she saw no other way
I couldn't tell her—I didn't know for sure
I cooked her some cereal and miso soup
And I brought her a book
for inspiration
What else could I do?
And then she died
It was too much for her
women in their thirties
beautiful women
one died

—B.J.

"Based on the published literature, we found no evidence
of benefit from HDC/ASCR compared with conventional
chemotherapy under any circumstances," Dr. Jeffrey Lerner
stated in an interview. Conversely, he said, "There is evidence of harm . . ."[66] The National Cancer Institute is cur-

rently attempting to increase the enrollment of women with metastatic breast cancer in three clinical trials involving high-dose chemotherapy and autologous bone marrow transplant or peripheral stem cell support. The results from these studies will not be available until the end of the decade. The December 1995 issue of *News From the National Cancer Institute* reported, referring to treatment with high dose chemo, "patients are opting for the risky and expensive treatment outside of trials, despite the lack of conclusive evidence that it is any more effective than standard therapy."

WHAT ABOUT TAMOXIFEN?

Currently, tamoxifen is being offered to just about every woman with breast cancer after her dues are paid in the surgery, radiation, and chemotherapy departments. Moreover, for women at "high risk," tamoxifen is now being offered as "preventive medicine." Half a year after it was halted amid a scandal of faked data, the largest study of breast cancer prevention (that is, *chemoprevention*) ever undertaken is getting back in gear. I can feel the collective fear in my chest as Dr. Ronald Herberman, principal investigator of the Breast Cancer Prevention Trial and director of the Pittsburgh Cancer Institute said, "During the study hiatus, we received countless inquiries from women across the country asking to be evaluated for entry."

How Tamoxifen Works

Tamoxifen is a drug that has a number of mechanisms of action, the most well-known is its ability to block estrogen receptors on breast cancer cells. Women with higher concentrations of estrogen receptors have the most potential benefit from tamoxifen. Tamoxifen also works by inactivating circulating estrogen, increasing its bound portion and thereby decreasing its availability to receptor sites.[67] In addition, tamoxifen has a number of estrogen-independent effects: decreasing insulin-like growth factor[68] and TGF-alpha,[69] which both stimulate breast cancer cells and increasing a potent breast cancer cell growth inhibitor.[70] Paradoxically, tamoxifen increases levels of estrogen, perhaps in reaction to its blocking function, and indeed has some pro-estrogenic effects in other parts of the body. Tamoxifen causes a cascade of reactions throughout the body, some recognized, some unknown.

Who Does Tamoxifen Help?

The Early Breast Cancer Trialists' Collaborative Group published a large review in 1992 after following 30,000 breast cancer patients for an average of five to six years. The reviews showed that 74.4 percent (744 out of a thousand women) of the patients taking tamoxifen survived vs. a 70.9 percent (709 out of a thousand women) survival rate for those not taking this drug. These numbers indicate that an additional 35 women will live for every 1,000 women taking tamoxifen compared to those with similar disease and treatment without tamoxifen. That is, 3.5 percent of women overall were helped by this drug within the time frame of the study. In the same study, when the statisticians evaluated survival without evidence of recurrent disease, 66.4 percent of women taking tamoxifen vs. 59.9 percent of women in the no-tamoxifen group were apparently disease-free after a five-year follow-up. So here 65 additional women out of a thousand taking this drug were recurrence-free at the five-year mark, due to the ingestion of tamoxifen. Statistics can be tricky, misunderstood and/or misinterpreted. How one interprets the benefit of tamoxifen depends on who you are. If you were one of the 35 women who presumably lived because of this drug it may be heralded as a great therapy. Yet 709 women out of the 1000 who didn't take tamoxifen also lived, as well as a matching 709 women who lived taking tamoxifen but who by statistical analysis would also have lived without taking it. So 744 women taking tamoxifen believe that they are alive because of it when in reality that is clearly untrue.

When various groups of women are analyzed for the purposes of investigating who may derive the most potential benefit from tamoxifen, certain characteristics clearly emerge. Estrogen-receptor status makes a difference. Women whose tumors are ER-positive clearly get better results with tamoxifen. Some researchers have found no effect at all for women with ER-negative tumors.[71]

In general, postmenopausal women do better than premenopausal women on tamoxifen. According to the statistics available in this large study, tamoxifen saved one life for every 20 postmenopausal women taking the drug. This contrasts with the one woman whose life was saved for every 100 women taking tamoxifen in the premenopausal group. In this same study the postmenopausal ER-positive group showed promising survival advantage. That is, for every four women who died without tamoxifen therapy, one woman was alive in the tamoxifen group. The large Collaborative Group study found no benefit at all for premenopausal women who were ER-negative. Women who have positive lymph nodes (cancer in their axillary biopsies) have a better overall response to tamoxifen. This same study found that 50.4 percent of women with cancer in their lymph nodes who were taking tamoxifen were alive after 10 years compared to 42.4 percent of node-positive women not taking the drug. Some researchers have found no survival advantage to women with negative lymph nodes, even if they have an ER-positive status.[72]

The greatest advantage in terms of survival benefit for patients taking tamoxifen is to postmenopausal women with positive nodes and high ER levels. Doctors who have nothing else to offer in terms of treatment now have this "harmless" therapy to prescribe to all takers. According to the pharmaceutical house that manufactures tamoxifen, it is nothing less than a miracle and, in fact, some would have healthy women take this drug as a primary prevention.

Side Effects Include Second Malignancies

Tamoxifen's anti-estrogenic action results in menopausal side effects including hot flashes, vaginal dryness, discharge and menstrual dysfunction. The pro-estrogenic effects result in a tamoxifen-linked uterine cancer.[73] The NSABP (National Surgical Adjuvant Breast and Bowel Project) reported a two-fold increase in the relative risk that women taking tamoxifen assume regarding the development of a uterine malignancy.[74] The American College of Obstetricians and Gynecologists Committee on Gynecologic Practice writes, "The increased risk of endometrial cancer in women treated with tamoxifen seems to be dose and time dependent, with higher cumulative doses and exposures resulting in greater relative risk."[75]

And if a second malignancy is not serious enough, recent reports indicate that the endometrial cancers that do develop in women taking tamoxifen are more aggressive, so much so that even the NCI (which has historically aligned with the pharmaceutical industry) warned investigators that women on tamoxifen treatment trials must be informed that they have an increased risk for developing uterine cancers and that these cancers may be fatal. A retrospective study done at Yale[76] revealed that 10 out of 15 women on tamoxifen for the treatment of breast cancer and who then developed uterine malignancies had either poorly differentiated endometrioid or other aggressive uterine tumor types. Dr. Peter Schwartz followed up on these 10 cases: 5 of the 10 women died of their uterine malignancies and 4 of the remaining 5 had recurrent endometrial cancer.[77] In addition to uterine malignancies, women receiving tamoxifen have also developed contralateral breast cancer as well as second malignancies of the lung and gastrointestinal tract.

Other gynecologic problems associated with tamoxifen use include bleeding from any of the following conditions: atrophic endometrium, endocervical and endometrial polyps and adenomatous hyperplasia. Benign uterine fibroids have grown in women receiving tamoxifen, and malignant uterine sarcomas have been reported as well as ovarian cysts. Tamoxifen can induce menopause in some women.

Other non-gynecologic but serious side effects from tamoxifen include: blood clotting disorders in about one percent of patients and damage to the eyes, which is reported in six percent of patients.[78] Although liver cancer has been induced experimentally with this drug, it has rarely been reported in women taking tamoxifen. Since liver cancer is considered to be invariably fatal, even a rare occurrence is worthy of note. Importantly, most women in tamoxifen trials have not been followed long enough to determine whether liver carcinogenesis is a problem. In breast cancer patients, liver cancer is invariably assumed to be metastatic, so there certainly may be an element of underreporting if indeed women are developing primary carcinomas in the liver.

Other side effects include nausea, usually in the initial few months, loss of appetite, headache and depression. That's a rather impressive list of side effects for what is considered a relatively innocuous drug!

How Long?

The optimum duration of therapy with tamoxifen has not been established. The National Cancer Institute recently issued a clinical alert urging a five-year limit on tamoxifen therapy. This occurred after the National Surgical Adjuvant Breast and Bowel Project prematurely halted a clinical trial when interim results demonstrated no additional benefits from tamoxifen therapy beyond five years when used as adjuvant therapy in node-negative, estrogen-receptor positive breast cancer. Dr. I. Craig Henderson, former director of cancer programs at the University of San Francisco School of Medicine said, "Lots of physicians have been overexuberant in their use of tamoxifen. We've had a tendency in this country to assume more is better and put patients on tamoxifen for life. I'm more concerned about overtreatment than I am about undertreatment with this agent. I don't believe in going beyond the data—and there are no data showing more than five years of tamoxifen to be beneficial."[79] Numerous trials comparing two years to five years are in progress, and another randomized trial of tamoxifen comparing five years of therapy to longer duration is planned. Definitive answers will not be available until the year 2000.

The Rationale for Using Tamoxifen as a Chemopreventive Agent

Women with diagnosis of breast cancer are at a higher risk of developing cancer in their opposite (contralateral) breast as compared to the general population. A number of studies have shown that this risk is reduced for women who have taken tamoxifen as adjunctive hormonal therapy. This observation has been the basis for the development of the now ongoing trials using tamoxifen as a preventive agent in perfectly healthy women. Even if the trial is successful in preventing breast cancer in these healthy women, statistical analysis reveals that 99 percent of the women who take this agent will reap no benefit and indeed will be exposed to all the side effects mentioned above as well as any yet undiscovered complications. I think this is a very dangerous situation. Instead of reducing our exposure to synthetic estrogens and looking to ways we can naturally, effectively and safely reduce our risk of breast cancer we are instead attempting to expose more women to additional estrogens. This, I fear, will surely compound our problems.

A Cautionary Note About Statistics

It bears repeating that statistics can be misleading. We hear about five-year survival and ten-year survival rates. We have studies that show the benefits of various surgeries, chemotherapeutic agents and hormonal therapies at the five-, seven- and ten-year marks. Yet breast cancer is a chronic disease whose biology shows an extraordinarily wide range of behavior. The results of a classic study by Drs. Brinkley and Haybittle,[80] which followed over 700 cases of breast cancer over a 25-year period, estimated that the excess risk of dying as a result of breast cancer did not disappear until after 20 years had passed. Understanding the natural history of breast cancer, recognizing that this disease can be a very slowly progressing disease resulting in death 20 or more years after treatment, throws into question the preliminary results of various medical and surgical interventions.

ᑿ *Remember...*

There are many unanswered questions regarding tamoxifen as an adjuvant treatment for breast cancer and even more questions regarding its place, *if any,* as an agent of primary prevention. Survival is not affected by tamoxifen for the great majority of patients.

How does the idea of taking a hormonal therapy feel to you? Consider which group you are in and the likelihood of a significant advantage. Consider the potential for minor and life-threatening side effects. Feel, think, discuss, decide.

Soyfoods—A Natural Alternative to Tamoxifen

Soybeans, a dietary staple in Asia, contain a number of beneficial compounds that are active against breast cancer. Soy is rich in isoflavones which are converted in the body to phytoestrogens (plant estrogens). Phytoestrogens are similar in structure but less potent than the estrogens we produce. By competing for receptor sites, these plant hormones protect us against the damaging effects of too much estrogen that we are exposed to as a result of poor diet, high stress and environmental contamination.

Genistein is an isoflavone unique to soy which has been shown to have particular benefit in breast cancer. Mark Messina, Ph.D., who worked for many years at the National Cancer Institute, says: "Women under treatment for breast cancer often receive 20 mg. of tamoxifen per day. For comparison purposes, one half cup of tofu or one cup soymilk contains approximately 40 mg. of isoflavones. Clearly, soy foods are rich enough in these anticarcinogens to have potential preventive and therapeutic use."[81] Soy foods offer their value as therapeutic agents without any damaging side effects (see Chapter 3).

Making The Appropriate Choice— Only You Can Do It

Keep with you at all times the knowledge and the power of your inherent wisdom. In each treatment decision there will be choices, but in one of the choices there will be a greater level of comfort. If you are uncomfortable, don't deny the feeling. A supportive counselor can help you clarify the issues and sort through the turmoil. You have the wisdom to connect with the right choice. Develop the power of inner listening. Your intuition may speak to you in a meditation, in a dream or through your gut sensation. Just give yourself the time you need to listen.

THE INTEGRATED APPROACH—HOW TO MAXIMIZE YOUR HEALING POTENTIAL

The Inextricably Interwoven Factors

Since there is no one cause of breast cancer, there can be no one cure. There are multiple factors; each woman has a different pattern with her own unique interconnections. Every breast cancer patient has:

1. A particular genetic endowment.
2. A dynamic internal environment, which includes
   - An individual pattern of estrogen metabolism.
   - A possibly deficient nutritional status.
   - A metabolic status reflecting present and past level of physical conditioning.
   - A particular mental-emotional milieu which is reflective of learned behavioral responses and one's ability to express various emotional needs.
3. An external environment including
   - Outdoor air and water pollutants.
   - An incredible array of toxic indoor pollutants emanating from synthetic materials and exacerbated by tight insulation.
   - A socio-political arena that professes a war on breast cancer but has not made health care for women a national priority.

○ᴡ᾽ *Remember. . .*

All of the areas of concern for women with breast cancer, including genetics, diet, hormone status, physical fitness, emotional health, stress levels and exposure to toxins, interact. No area is fixed. You can intervene in any and all areas. Begin wherever you find the most comfort.

COMBINING APPROACHES FOR REAL HEALING

Complementary approaches aim at helping the body optimize all systems, particularly immune function, thereby enabling us to select a better adaptation than cancer for survival. Understanding on a physical, mental and deep emotional level some of the reasons why breast cancer has occurred opens up vast possibilities for healing. In the spirit of deep respect for individuality, my recommendations are broad. Every woman, with guidance from her chosen team of health, fitness and counseling professionals, needs to tailor a program to her own specific circumstances.

In doing my own work of healing I began to tune into an everyday spirituality that I had been unaware of prior to my illness when I lived the fast-paced lifestyle of a 20th century woman, mother and obstetrician-gynecologist. Now the living that had gotten lost in the rush became mine. The daily events that I never really noticed became heaven: Oliver's dimples, cleaning and cutting my fresh organic vegetables, Hannah's laughter, the beauty of Long Island Sound on a clear summer day, the gleam in Zachary's eyes, running my hands over my boys' crewcuts, the hugs, one more goodnight kiss. I knew I was blessed. The powerful healing effects I had tapped into overflowed into my appreciation of every aspect of my life. The painful awareness of the finitude of my life was adding splendor to every moment.

∾

Complementary breast cancer treatment and preventive approaches include:

For the body
- Diet and supplements.
- Exercise.
- Environmental detoxification.
- Touch, massage.

For the mind/body
- Readings, ongoing education and re-education.

For the emotional body
- Emotional processing.
    Individual psychological counseling.
    Group support.
- Lifestyle approaches.
    Stress management.
    Engaging our creativity.

For the soul
- Visualization, affirmation, meditation, dream work, prayer, love.

As we engage ourselves in the work of looking inward, our sense of connection with other women will grow, and each of us according to our own timetable will reach out in our own way. After personal needs have been met, you may be ready for:

Spirit in action
- Social action, networking with other breast cancer patients.
- Political action, grassroots advocacy.
  Environmental issues (pesticides in our food supply).
  Breast cancer organizations.

I will explore these approaches with you in later chapters.
Both conventional and complementary treatment approaches have a unique role to play in your healing program. The appropriate conventional treatment addresses the immediate relief of the burden of cancer, providing that it is not too toxic, while the complementary approach allows the body/mind to reestablish balance, making the healthy choices that enhance the immune system, thereby promoting healing and preventing recurrence.

There is an intrinsic wisdom within us, given certain raw materials such as essential nutrients and emotional nurturance, that enables our bodies to create energy, reestablish order and heal cancer just as our surgical wounds know how to mend without any instructions.

The Healing Process—There Are No Failures

The work of Ainslie Meares, M.D., which I quote throughout has been inspirational to me. Dr. Meares' work with the power of healing rang so true for me; for months I carried his book with me, sharing it with people at the various workshops and conferences I attended in the early days of my illness. The book made poetry of my cancer. He refers to the issue of success and failure, an issue that comes up again and again especially for woman diagnosed with breast cancer.

> Of those who have come to me,
> Some have made it,
> And some have failed.
> Why did they fail?
> With most the darkness of the shadow
> Was almost black.
> Then blackness came
> Too soon.
> And failure it was.
> But those who were dear to them,
> In strange procession,
> One after the other,
> Have come to me,
> And denied the failure.
> They've said,
> When the dark
> Becomes black
> With such calmness,
> No failure in that.
>
> —A. Meares[82]

Dr. Meares was way ahead of his time, working with terminal cancer patients who attempted through deep meditation to access the healing powers of the body. Death is not a failure when we make our own decisions. There is an exquisite balance between the effort to overcome the disease of breast cancer and the surrender necessary for all healing to take place: the acceptance of what is. No one has expressed this better than Reinhold Niebuhr, the author of the Serenity Prayer:

O God, give us
>   serenity to accept what cannot be changed
>   courage to change what should be changed
>   and wisdom to distinguish the one from the other.

Some of the time we need to back off and stop trying so hard. We need to *accept.* Sometimes we need to quietly gather strength in very personal ways so that we can take on the challenges; we need *courage.* If we are pushing against our own comfort, we need to stop fighting our own *wisdom.* There are amazing lessons within the experience of cancer; it is an *opportunity.* Let us open our eyes and be willing to move on. *Insight.* When the time is right we need to let go of the disease. *Faith.* And then we will see. The differences between our medical cures and deep healing begin to reveal themselves if we pay attention. *Patience.* What about *success?* When I reflect on all the personal work I have done and the grace of my experience, I realize that success comes in as many forms as there are snowflakes.

∾

Success

I'd been waiting for the call.

After six months of neoadjuvant chemotherapy, the mass had shrunk just as we'd all hoped it would. I went in for surgery clutching my tape recorder; I was anxiously waiting for someone to try and take it away once we went into the OR. After all I'd read about "pain-in-the-ass" patients doing better and living longer, I had brought in my soothing music, à la Bernie Siegel, and was ready to do my part to defend this right. Nobody made any attempt to take my tape recorder away, so I relaxed.

My husband and I had gone away the weekend before surgery. We'd been through a lot, three babies and now breast cancer, and we'd only been married four years. So

*with two shifts of babysitters, we drove up to Bridgeport to
ferry across Long Island Sound for a weekend together. We
got off at Port Jefferson and drove across Long Island to
Montauk. We stopped along the way and got some fresh-
baked bread and peach preserves. We'd brought along some
food; I was being so careful about my diet. I was as thin
as I'd ever been but I felt that it was good for my condition
at that time. My hair was cut into a crew, in anticipation
of going bald, and was thinned out a bit from the chemo.
We were alone together overnight for the first time since
Zachary was born. We walked the beach. We kissed and
hugged sensing how tenuous it all was. One of the very few
joyful times in our tumultuous marriage. The October wind
blew through us on the Montauk beach, pale blue the ocean
blended into the sky, gray misty, waves crashing.
I went into surgery with this beauty fresh in my mind
and here I was waiting for the pathology report. It was late
Friday evening, I'd already reconciled myself to not knowing for another few days. I had been hoping to find out
before the weekend. I grabbed the phone each time it rang,
my heart in my mouth. I flashed back to that first consultation in Dr. Love's office. Sitting across her desk, Susan explained the phenomenon of breast cancer. It could've been
me on the other, more comfortable side of the desk. I had
explained so many times to young women about their abnormal PAPs, the results of cervical biopsies, endometrial
biopsies, always trying to make it simple. Now Dr. Love was
simplifying breast cancer for me. Somewhere in the expla-
nation, Stage III Breast Cancer was OK. No one else explained it this way. Somehow in her presence I deeply felt
it was OK. OK, OK, OK, it wasn't a death sentence. I had
some options, and as we discussed further, we came to the
point that if I did choose neoadjuvant chemotherapy (that
is, chemotherapy prior to surgery), which I did, and if I
had a good response (meaning the tumor shrank rather
than growing or remaining the size of a tennis ball), which
it did, I would then find myself, after about six months,*

*ready for surgery, which I did. And at that time I would
choose the type of surgery, which I did. I had only a lumpectomy. I declined any other procedures. Dr. Love had said
there were various possible outcomes: the chemo could possibly shrink the tumor, and the pathology could reveal some
residual tumor of the type I started with or there might be
an overwhelming response and there might be no residual
tumor. There were quite a few treatment options and various outcomes leading to further crossroads in decision making. One road lead here, one there, but this one, AH . . .
No tumor. I liked that possibility. Did that happen often, was
it possible? Susan Love opened the door to that possibility for
me. I knew then that it was possible. I am eternally grateful
to Dr. Love for leaving that door open.*

*The hour was late, the phone rang, and I picked it up,
my heart was racing, I pulled the phone into the bathroom
pushing the door closed on the wire; this was personal, very
personal. I had never worked with such easy intensity. This
was my report:*

≈

LEFT BREAST MASS

1) Previous biopsy and up-front chemotherapy.
2) Focal foreign body giant cell reaction consistent with previous biopsy site.
3) Focal nodular benign fat-laden histiocytic infiltration (possibly the result of tumor regression).
4) Lobular atrophy and focal reactive atypia and focal squamous metaplasia of duct epithelium attributed to chemotherapy effect.
5) **No residual tumor identified.**

I DID IT!

*10/19/91
Done—cured.
No cancer.*

I feel freer than I have.
A weight is lifted.
The mind is difficult.
What ifs are still there,
but their power is stripped.
Let me rejoice
and thank God
for my power and courage.

—B.J.

I remembered Richard Bach's words:

There is no such thing as a problem without a gift for you in its hand. You seek problems because you need their gifts . . . Every person, all the events of your life are there because you have drawn them there. What you choose to do with them is up to you.[83]

I continue to integrate into my life the various complementary approaches that I learned as part of my breast cancer healing program. My diet has changed, yet it is no longer something I do out of fearful necessity but out of wholesome love for myself, my family and the planet. I continue my relationship with my counselor, Tullia, who has helped me to process the experience of a life-threatening illness and transform it into the challenge and redirection that it has become in my life. Tullia continues to support me in the emotional struggles of my life. Yes, there is life and even problems after breast cancer. I continue to approach my lifestyle with as much gentleness as three young children will allow. My career in medicine begins anew. Daily I reach into my heart to find the love that was always there for me when I was so in need. My children provide me with daily practice in patience meditation. I cultivate a deep respect for the healing power of nature. I read, read, read and try to integrate knowledge into a more wholesome understanding of life. I love my life and pray for the strength and courage to share and expand what I have learned.

PART TWO

❧

Who We Are from the Inside Out

The great majority of us are required to live a life of constant, systematic duplicity. Your health is bound to be affected if, day after day, you say the opposite of what you feel, if you grovel before what you dislike and rejoice at what brings you nothing but misfortune. Our nervous system isn't just a fiction, it's part of our physical body, and our soul exists in space and is inside us, like teeth in our mouth. It can't be forever violated with impunity.

BORIS PASTERNAK

2

Genes and Hormones

WE ARE NOT DOOMED BY OUR GENES

THE GREAT DEBATE

Always center stage in the debate about what causes breast cancer is the genetics vs. environment issue—the inside forces vs. the outside forces. I believe that we have as much influence over our internal environment as our external environment has on us. We are not passive victims of our genetic machinery but cocreators of our internal milieu. Our personal choices profoundly affect both the microcosm (our body) and the macrocosm (our earth).

In an interview in *Psychology Today*, Deepak Chopra was asked about the genetic component of illness, the component that we are apt to think has nothing to do with personal responsibility, "What if, for example, we inherit a bad gene?" Dr. Chopra's response:

> We have the ability to change the morbidity of future generations—because what is genetic information other than the sum total of the metabolism of the experience of our ancestors? Every stress that I inherit is genetically there because it is an end-product of how my ancestors metabolized their own experience. And if we gain self-knowledge and change our behavior now we can affect future generations. If we don't then we share the responsibility for it.[1]

My hope is that we can make use of this understanding to inspire us to take more responsibility for the way we live our lives and not allow guilt, blame and victimization to interfere with authentic empowerment. Our genes don't write our script but dynamically reflect our metabolic experience.

HEREDITY DOES NOT STAND ALONE

No woman is risk-free with respect to breast cancer. We hear the frequently quoted and ever-escalating cancer statistics: one in three Americans will develop cancer and one in eight or nine women will develop breast cancer. We need to put this into a meaningful context.

While much research is being directed at isolating the genes responsible for breast cancer, it is important to maintain a balanced perspective on the genetic vs. the environmental component in the cancer equation. It is generally accepted that 75 to 80 percent of all cancers are caused by dominant environmental factors in contrast to a dominant hereditary component.

Dr. A.G. Knudson[2] has proposed a theory that unifies our understanding of hereditary breast cancer. He says that two sequential mutations are needed to get breast cancer. The woman who has an inherited genetic mutation already has the first mutation and therefore needs only the second to get the disease, thus she is more susceptible to breast cancer. The critical second mutation could be caused by dietary factors, toxins in the environment, hormones or any combination thereof. A woman without the hereditary component would need two mutations, so statistically she would be at a lower risk for the disease. Dr. Knudson's theory in effect describes the interplay between the hereditary component and the environment in the etiology of breast cancer. In point of fact, we don't know how many mutations are critical or the sequence of the events necessary for a particular individual to manifest breast cancer nor can we be sure of an individual's vulnerability to particular risk factors. We can, however, alter the likelihood of sustaining genetic mutations by attending to our lifestyle choices.

No matter how we conceptualize the process, the environment surely modifies any inherited tendency to breast cancer. The genetic mechanisms which control cell growth are not absolute but dynamic processes.

GENES ARE DYNAMIC

There is new and mounting scientific evidence that genes are not static. As a culture we do not recognize the tremendous impact of major risk factors for cancer—diet, environmental exposures and the emotional context of our lives. Undue emphasis has been put on the simplistic association between genetics and breast cancer without a fuller understanding regarding its interplay with these other factors. In fact, our diet, the environment and our emotional milieu interact with and strongly influence our genetic and hormonal expressions. Deepak Chopra has written:

> Your genes are damaged every day by radioactivity, ultraviolet light, chemical toxins and pollution, random mutations, X-rays, and even the process of life itself. Highly reactive oxygen molecules are released when food is metabolized in the cells, and among the many chemicals they bond to and damage is DNA . . . Long thought to be an inert chemical that sits unchanged in the cell's nucleus, DNA is now known to have a remarkable capacity for self-repair . . . Under the assault of free radicals and other damaging influences, at least seven different kinds of mistakes can appear in a strand of DNA . . . It can sense exactly what kind of damage has occurred, and via special enzymes the appropriate missing links are spliced back into place . . . [an] astonishing display of intelligence . . . [3]

The expression of genetic material depends on the environment bathing the DNA. The intracellular environment in turn depends on the extracellular environment—the two are in dynamic equilibrium. And both the intracellular and extracellular environment of the cell in turn depend on how the individual interacts with the external world in a variety of ways, including but not limited to diet. Breast surgeon Dr. Robert Kradjian writes, "Each time we eat a foodstuff, within minutes, molecules from that food enter or surround each of the trillions of cells in our body. By age 65, many humans have ingested over 100,000 pounds of food, making food our most profound, intimate and decisive involvement with our environment."[4]

Gene expression is nutrient dependent and toxin sensitive. The choices we make in our daily life impact our biochemical milieu and therefore the expression of our very essence. A mutation in one generation may be genetic in the next. Genetic susceptibility, environmental exposure and nutritional adequacy are all related to the manifestation of cancer.

We Are Not Doomed by Our Genes

Understanding the role of genetics is important. Women who have a family history of breast cancer often feel unnecessarily alarmed, and those who don't may feel a false sense of security regarding the possibility of developing this disease. Family history is the risk factor most overestimated by women. Having a first-degree relative—a mother, sister or daughter—with breast cancer or a second-degree relative—an aunt, grandmother or cousin—with breast cancer increases one's risk; however, the degree of risk depends on the type of relationship, how many relatives have been affected, what age the disease occurred and whether or not the disease was bilateral.

On a molecular level breast cancer is a genetic disease, but it is not necessarily an inherited one. This means that something happens to the genes that regulate cell growth, be it hormones, radiation, chemicals or something in the diet; it does not necessarily mean that we inherit our disease from previous generations. Blaming only our genes may be an expedient method of blaming the victim for her disease and a rationale for funneling excess research money into gene-hunting.

The fact is, the great majority of women with breast cancer, 80 percent by most estimates, have no family history of the disease and develop what is known as sporadic breast cancer. If 80 percent of breast cancer patients have a negative family history then a purely genetic basis for this disease is unlikely.

There is a very small group of women who have an especially strong genetic component in the development of breast cancer. Dr. Susan Love calls this group "the pure hereditary group." This type of inheritance, which involves dominant cancer genes, contributes to approximately 5 to 10 percent of breast cancer cases. In these cases a dominant gene is passed from mother or father to offspring. It is currently believed that $BRCA_1$, sequenced in 1994, is responsible for about 45 percent of breast cancer due to a single dominant gene disorder and $BRCA_2$, mapped late last year, accounts for a roughly equal percentage. Other dominant genes are also involved in breast cancer, including the p53 gene.

Both male and female carriers of $BRCA_1$ are at increased risk for developing colon cancer. Families who have a mutation of the $BRCA_1$ gene also have a higher incidence of ovarian cancer. While male $BRCA_1$ carriers do not generally develop breast cancer, male carriers of the $BRCA_2$ face a lifetime breast cancer risk as high as six percent (the relative risk is increased one hundredfold). Male carriers of $BRCA_1$ are also reportedly at increased risk for developing prostate cancer.

In terms of breast cancer, the positive identification of this gene for women is said to be tantamount to living with the certainty of this disease. Yet even for those women who test positive for the $BRCA_1$ gene, 10 to 15 percent will not develop breast cancer. While scientists know that only a small percentage of our genetic material is actually expressed, the mechanisms responsible for this expression are not known. It remains unclear exactly what factor or group of factors turn the expression of a gene on at any given point in a particular woman's life. The majority of cases of "pure hereditary" breast cancer are in younger women, which is a feature of most hereditary forms of cancer. There have been conflicting studies regarding the type of breast cancer that occurs when a dominant gene is involved, whether it occurs exclusively premenopausal or is predominantly bilateral.

It turns out that there are more than 20 different mutations of $BRCA_1$ and this gene may confer different risks in different families. The National Cancer Institute has recently begun a study to explore a particular alteration on the $BRCA_1$ gene that is thought to occur three times more frequently in Jewish women of Eastern European descent. The results expected by the fall of 1996 will be helpful in determining the significance of a particular two-base deletion for Ashkenazi women without a family history of breast cancer. Until now alterations in the $BRAC_1$ gene have been linked to increased risk only in women with a very strong family history of the disease.

The largest group of women with an identifiable genetic component are those with polygenic breast cancer. Most family history cases of breast cancer fall into this category. Polygenic breast cancer means rather than inheriting breast cancer as a dominant cancer gene that passes through each generation, one inherits a particular susceptibility on a genetic basis which gives rise to a less pronounced family history. It is thought that perhaps 13 percent of breast cancer is on a polygenic basis.

An example of polygenic inheritance is the ataxia-telangiectasia mutant gene.[5] The ATM gene, responsible for the rare life-threatening neurological disease ataxia telangiectaisa, is carried by an estimated one percent of American women. People who inherit two copies of this gene suffer a life-threatening disorder; those with one copy of the gene do not become ill but are extremely sensitive to radiation. According to researchers at Tel Aviv University, women with the ATM gene are five times more likely to develop breast cancer. Dr. Barbara Weber, the director of the Breast Cancer Program at the University of Pennsylvania Cancer Center, noted that the ATM gene may play a role in as many as 8 percent of all breast cancer cases in this country. At the University of North Carolina, 19 women with the ATM gene who had developed breast cancer were studied; 53 percent of them had histories of extensive diagnostic X-ray use. Of the 57 female carriers of the gene who did not develop breast cancer, only 19 percent had comparable x-ray studies.[6] Dr. Michael Swift, now director of the Institute for the Genetic Analysis of Common Diseases at New York Medical College, estimates that between 9 and 18 percent of women with breast cancer in the U.S. may have the ATM gene. So far there is no general test available to identify carriers of the ATM gene. If carriers of this gene have a heightened sensitivity to radiation, then mammography may pose significant risks to these unidentified women.

Just like radiation, and on a very individual basis, one or more components of our environment may be significantly deleterious in terms of polygenic susceptibility, so that the balance is tipped to the development of breast cancer. A woman may, for example, inherit a vulnerability to a high-fat diet; thus, in this case, breast cancer may not be expressed except in conjunction with this type of diet. Another woman may not manifest breast cancer unless a certain hormonal milieu is achieved, perhaps that associated with early and prolonged exposure to oral contraceptives.

Looking at the expression of breast cancer in identical twins provides an opportunity to compare the strength of genetic influence on the development of this disease. If an identical twin develops breast cancer, fewer than six percent of the remaining twins go on to develop this disease. This certainly points toward additional factors at work in the expression of our genetic inheritance.

GENETIC ENDOWMENT VS. GENETIC EXPRESSION

Genetic endowment (inherited genetic material) is a given; genetic expression is not a given. The genetic component that is ultimately expressed is affected by a host of variables, one of which is diet; another is environmental carcinogens. We inherit our genetic material from our parents; what happens to our DNA after conception depends on the surrounding environment. An inherited disease seems to imply that we are powerless, but this is not the case. The inheritance aspect means that on a genetic level there is a potential for the expression of breast cancer. So if breast cancer is in your family, fear not; an individual's genetic *expression* is the key.

All cancer on a molecular level is a genetic disease whether inherited or otherwise acquired through our interaction with the world around us. Dr. John Lee offers another theory about the etiology of cancer which holds that certain toxic environments within a cell stimulate the latent ability of otherwise undamaged chromosomes to switch to a more primitive mode of expression. This implies that we can prevent cancer by maintaining a healthy intracellular environment. Philosophically it can also lead us to pursue nontoxic treatments that address cancer from the inside. Dr. Lee's theory differs from a more traditional genetic theory that maintains that DNA accumulates damage over time from a variety of sources (radiation, viruses, toxins) and is unalterably damaged. Perhaps the middle ground is that the intracellular environment can act as a promotor, affecting the expression or nonexpression of cancer and is amenable to dietary and other lifestyle changes.

Dr. Lee's theory is consistent with recent research on the $BRCA_1$ gene. The latest studies from the University of Texas at San Antonio suggest that in cases of familial breast cancer, the mutated $BRCA_1$ gene codes for a faulty protein which does not function properly as a tumor suppressor. However, in most other breast cancer patients, the normal

$BRCA_1$ gene codes for a protein that appears structurally normal but is not functioning properly. These studies suggest that something within the intracellular environment may be responsible for this structurally normal but functionally abnormal protein, coded for by a structurally intact DNA. Therefore the intracellular environment may be the most important mediator in the process of genetic expression and functional impairment that can lead to the uncontrolled cell growth we know as cancer.

∽   *Remember...*

We cannot change our family history, but we can help create our future by the way we live today. Genetics, diet, environment, hormones and breast cancer are inextricably linked. Genes themselves are not static. Genetic expression is a reflection of who we are and how we live.

We can use the awareness of our genetic predispositions as a wake-up call, alerting us to make positive changes in our lifestyles. We can use what we perceive as our vulnerability to open our eyes and fearlessly build strength by taking a preventive approach.

WE PARTICIPATE IN THE CREATION OF OUR HORMONES

Hormones are an integral part of us, a most intimate expression. We in turn are very sensitive to the hormones in our system, both those hormones that we naturally secrete and the synthetic hormones we knowingly and unknowingly ingest. "After 15 years of medical practice," Dr. Christiane Northrup writes, "I continue to be amazed by how clearly menstrual cycles and bleeding are connected to the context of our lives ... there is no way any condition can be 'just medical.' "[7]

In my gynecologic practice, women have come with a variety of complaints. Their symptoms can be addressed on many levels. On the most superficial level, testing and medication can be specifically directed at irregular bleeding, alleviating a vaginal itch or eradicating a cervical dysplasia. However, by exploring the context of the life in which that bleeding, itching or abnormal cellular maturation is taking place, we can do much more than just relieve the symptoms. The exploration of one's current and past emotional life—one's deepest issues—can reassure a woman that her symptoms are body talk and that her body is her friend. Women often do not understand that we create our own hormones; they are not separate, distinct or apart from who we are.

When a single woman in her 40s who had had amenorrhea for four years began to menstruate again it was crucial to understand that she had recently met a new partner and had embarked on the most sensual relationship of her life. Her hormones expressed her new sense of self.

Estrogen—Friend or Foe?

The secretion of estrogen:

- Is measurable in the first trimester of fetal development.
- Is part of an incredible feedback system that reacts to the decline of maternal estrogens at birth.
- Is responsible for resetting the hypothalamopituitary system until puberty. Very low levels of estradiol in childhood serve to repress the brain's central mechanisms that later help to establish our female cyclicity.
- At puberty is involved in the development of the complex feedback loops that eventuate in ovulation.
- Begins the orchestration of an adolescent girl's growth

spurt, breast development, menarche as well as the development of ovulatory cycles.

Could this key hormone be intrinsically bad? Does such dualistic good/bad thinking make sense in light of the evidence for estrogen's key role in our normal development? Does balanced cyclic ovarian activity put us at risk? I think not. I believe the problem lies in an unbalanced hormonal state of relative estrogen excess and progesterone deficiency, the result of our poor diets, stressful lifestyles, the continuous exposure to a hormone-impregnated food supply and industrial xenoestrogenic pollutants. Therein lies the key to the link between hormones and breast cancer.

Among the three major natural estrogens, estradiol (E2), estrone (E1) and estriol (E3), estriol is by far the least stimulating and the least apt to cause problems. There is strong evidence that unopposed estrone and/or estradiol are carcinogenic for breasts, while estriol may well be protective against breast cancer. Some researchers have identified a 50 to 100 percent increase in breast cancer risk for women in the upper two-thirds of overall estrogen level compared to the lowest third[8][9].

Women with vegetarian-style dietary practices, including lacto-ovo vegetarians, macrobiotic and traditional Asian women, all have lower total serum estrogen and lower breast cancer rates compared to women who eat the standard American diet. The breast tissue of vegetarian eaters is exposed to lower levels of hormones. A woman on the typical American diet absorbs more estrogen from her gastrointestinal tract, which is then filtered by the kidneys and excreted in larger quantities in her urine. Animal fats in the diet stimulate colonic bacteria both to synthesize estrogen from dietary cholesterol and to promote the breakdown and reabsorption of estrogen complexes contributing to the total estrogen load. Vegetarian diets, high in fiber, promote the excretion of excess estrogen from the body—and thus more estrogen is found in the feces of vegetarian women.

The causative role of estrogen in breast cancer was first demonstrated in 1932 when a French scientist, A. Lacassagne, injected estrone into mice who then developed breast cancer. It is probable that sufficient estriol impedes this carcinogenic effect. H.M. Lemon, M.D.[10] demonstrated in 1966 that women with breast cancer have a reduced urinary excretion of estriol. He later went on to show that women without breast cancer have naturally higher estriol levels, compared to estrone and estradiol, than women with breast cancer. In Dr. Lemon's study, breast cancer patients receiving endocrine therapy who went into remission were those women whose estriol quotient rose. The quotient is simply the ratio of cancer-inhibiting estriol to the sum of the other major estrogens, estradiol plus estrone.

Estriol levels are high in pregnancy, when estriol is produced by the fetal placenta. Estriol has been shown to inhibit breast cancer in animal studies. A. H. Follingstad, M.D. reported[11] that when small doses of estriol were given to a group of postmenopausal women with metastatic breast cancer, 37 percent experienced a remission or arrest of the metastasized lesions. Estriol's effects are thought to be due to the hormone's weaker estrogenic characteristics, blocking the stimulatory effect of more potent estrogens on the breast. High levels of estriol are found in vegetarians and Asian women who have lower rates of breast cancer. The types of estrogen used in conventional Hormone Replacement Therapy (HRT) are estradiol and estrone. Estriol is used in other countries for HRT much more extensively and is thought to be a safer alternative. See Chapter 6.

Estradiol is metabolized through two different routes. Pathway 1 leads to 2-hydroxyestrone (2-OHE-1), Pathway 2 results in 16 alpha-hydroxyestrone. Some scientists believe that breast cancer risk is linked to these pathways and that dietary factors such as indole-3 -carbinol[12] and environmental chemicals affect these pathways in salutary or detrimental ways.

Estrogen metabolism is also thought to be the final common pathway linking alcohol intake to breast cancer. Women who drink alcohol have higher estrogen levels than nondrinkers, reflecting changes in liver function induced by alcohol. An analysis of more than 50 studies revealed that two drinks per day increases the risk of breast cancer by 25 percent. The more one drinks the higher the risk.[13]

ESTROGEN/PROGESTERONE IMBALANCE

Observations suggest that excess estrogen, especially when unopposed by progesterone, is related to the development of breast cancer. Puberty and perimenopause are known to be periods of unopposed estrogen stimulation and therefore, by definition, times of progesterone deficiency.

The role of progesterone deficiency in the etiology of breast cancer has been overlooked. When measured prospectively, women with progesterone deficiency were found to have 5.4 times the risk of developing premenopausal breast cancer and a tenfold increase in deaths from all malignant neoplasms compared to women with normal progesterone levels.[14] Breast cancer is more likely to occur in premenopausal women with normal or high estrogen levels and low progesterone levels. Dr. John Lee has done a great deal of work in the area of progesterone and women's health and has written extensively about his observations.

There have been some interesting, albeit inconclusive, studies relating to progesterone, the timing of breast cancer surgery and clinical outcome. Some studies show that in premenopausal women with breast cancer treated by mastectomy, those who underwent mastectomy during the latter two weeks of their menstrual cycle (when progesterone was the dominant gonadal hormone) developed significantly fewer late recurrences or metastases than those women whose surgery occurred during the first two weeks of their menstrual cycle (when only estrogen is being produced by the ovaries). This finding was published in an article in the respected medical journal, *The Lancet,* authored by Dr. Ian Fentiman,[15] the deputy director of the Imperial Cancer Research Fund's Breast Unit at Guy's Hospital in London. The article came out in the May 25th issue in 1991, exactly one month after my diagnosis. My sister clipped a newspaper article[16] reporting on this study and sent it to me. In response to the reports, Dr. Jay Harris, Clinical Director of Harvard University's Joint Center for Radiation and Therapy, noted that many women prefer to have surgery immediately and that trying to time operations to a patient's menstrual cycle would create scheduling problems for busy medical centers. "For people in the field, we have viewed this skeptically, because it's not obvious why this might be true."

Although there have been a number of conflicting reports with regard to optimal timing of surgery, the report and the response above underline several points.

- Breast cancer is incompletely understood by those in charge of treatment protocols.
- New ideas, unlike new drugs, are not easily accepted by the medical establishment, which is very often conservative and territorial; I assure you, if a drug produced the survival benefit of 84 percent vs. 54 percent at 10 years, which the timing of surgery did in the quoted study, it would be headline news, the pharmaceutical companies would be marketing it and doctors would be utilizing it.
- Convenience and scheduling should not be health care priorities.
- Women need to be given choices within the limits of available knowledge in order to make responsible decisions about their own healthcare. The physician's role is to compassionately assist in this process.

THE LINK BETWEEN HORMONES AND BREAST CANCER NOT UNDERSTOOD

"The good news is that we know breast cancer is related to ovarian/hormonal activity. The bad news is that we have known this since 1896—almost one hundred years."[17]
—Dr. R. Hoover, National Cancer Institute

There is a powerful but incompletely understood connection between reproductive hormones and breast cancer. We need to put the information together in a meaningful way to prevent this disease, to assist us in its treatment and to help us live fully in its aftermath.

We secrete estrogens and progesterone (and a host of other hormones) in response to a genetic program which is profoundly influenced by what we inhale, ingest, absorb, think and feel. The balance of these hormones is key. Dr. Susan Love expresses medicine's incomplete understanding of the hormone–breast cancer link: "It seems that the more periods a woman has over her lifetime, the more prone she is to breast cancer ... if she menstruates for more than 40 years, she seems to have a particularly high risk ... The key time seems to be the amount of time between the first period and the first pregnancy ... As you see ... we still don't know why or how internal hormones affect breast cancer."[18] The epidemiologic conclusion—that cyclic ovarian activity is a risk factor for breast cancer and the more years duration, the higher the risk—is incomplete and therefore misleading.

EPIDEMIOLOGY POINTS THE WAY

Although many epidemiologic studies[19] give support to the role of hormones in the onset of breast cancer, it is far from clear whether it is estrogen, progesterone, absolute levels or relative levels of these hormones or the timing of the exposures which is most important in affecting the risk of breast cancer. The following statements are well-accepted epidemiologic observations regarding the risk of breast cancer:

- Pregnancy exerts a protective effect.
- Breast-feeding is protective.
- Increased risk with early menarche.
- Increased risk with late menopause.

Let's take a close look at each statement.

Pregnancy Exerts a Protective Effect

Harvard epidemiologist Brian MacMahon was an early investigator who published results regarding reproductive factors and breast cancer risks from seven different countries.[20] Women having their first full-term pregnancy before age 20 have approximately one-third the risk of women bearing children after age 35. Women without children are at higher risk than those having borne children. Having borne several children is independently protective, and recent evidence suggests that shorter spacing between children decreases the risk of breast cancer.

Why is pregnancy protective? The major hormones of pregnancy, estriol and progesterone, appear to be protective against breast cancer. During pregnancy, the dominant estrogen is estriol, a weak-acting estrogen produced by the placenta. Estriol causes much less breast stimulation than estrone or estradiol, the ovarian hormones that dominate during the first two weeks of the menstrual cycle. During pregnancy there is also a naturally high and protective level of progesterone present. The hormonal milieu associated with a full-term pregnancy completes the developmental cycle of the breast. Permanent changes occur that reduce the pre-existing susceptibility of the developing breast to carcinogenic influences.

Breast Feeding Is Protective

Breast-feeding protects women from breast cancer. Studies in our culture show mixed results for a number of reasons including the relatively short time most women in our society choose to nurse and the fact that many women breast-feed on a part-time basis, supplementing with bottle feedings. Over half the women in China breast-feed and do so for at least three years; Chinese women have low breast cancer rates. All agree that where there is evidence of protection, the longer you nurse, the less your risk of breast cancer. Whereas some of the early studies suggested that the protective effect was contingent on years of nursing, a recent Canadian study shows that women who nurse for only two months gain some protection from premenopausal breast cancer.[21] This was corroborated by research conducted by the United Kingdom National Case-Control Study Group.[22] Another large-scale investigation conducted in 1993 demonstrated that four to six months of nursing offers protection against the disease.[23] Most studies on breast-feeding demonstrate the protective effect for premenopausal breast cancer.

Clearly the diminished value of breast-feeding in our culture is implicated in the breast cancer epidemic. The Tanka boat women of Hong Kong breast-feed only on the left side and have higher rates of right-sided breast cancer. Women who consistently use one breast for suckling likewise have a higher risk of developing breast cancer in the unsuckled breast.[24] Apparently breast-feeding acts on a hormonal as well as local anatomic level.

By proactively choosing to breast-feed we can consciously reduce our own breast cancer risk and possibly the risk for our daughters. Not only does breast-feeding have health benefits for mothers, but it also has beneficial effects on our infants' immune systems. Immunologically, colostrum which is secreted during the first few days after birth, is very protective to the newborn. Who can say how this exposure may enhance future immune function and even by extension impact on our infants' future breast cancer rates.

It has also been shown that the antepartum hormonal milieu may effect an infant's breast cancer rates in adult life.[25] Exposure to maternal estrogens during the pregnancy may have implications for future breast cancer risk in female offspring (and unknown effects on hormone mediated functions in males). *Lancet* published a study which analyzed the pregnancy records of 1,655 women from Sweden.[26] The results suggested that female babies who weighed more than eight pounds at birth had a 30 percent increased risk of developing breast cancer. Female babies whose mothers were diagnosed with preeclampsia/eclampsia had a 75 percent decrease in risk of breast cancer. It is indeed possible that a mother impacts on her daughter's risk for breast cancer both through a direct effect of hormone levels in pregnancy and postpartum as well as via a more general effect on the development of immune function.

Increased Risk With Early Menarche

Hormone imbalance, estrogen excess/progesterone deficiency, predictably occurs at the time of puberty when menstrual cycles are beginning to be established. During the time between menarche and the completion of the first pregnancy, the cells of the breast are vulnerable to an array of carcinogenic influences. Completion of pregnancy has a maturing or stabilizing influence. Delaying menarche may significantly reduce a woman's risk of breast cancer, perhaps by reducing this vulnerable window of time. A 1993 study found that a two-year delay may decrease a woman's risk by 10 percent or more[27]. Early menarche (younger than 12 years old) may set estrogen levels higher throughout a woman's reproductive life.[28]

Over the last century the age of menarche has consistently fallen. In countries with low breast cancer rates such as China, girls start their periods at around age 17 while the average age in the U.S. is now 12.8. Adolescence sets the stage for breast cancer. We know the developing adolescent breast is acutely sensitive to hormones, and what takes place at this critical time likely has far-reaching implications. By ingesting the standard American high-protein, high-fat diet, ovarian hormone production is altered and puberty is induced earlier than it would have otherwise begun.

Just consider this typical week's school lunch menu:

- *Monday:* footlong hot dog, oven fries, choice of fruit, milk.
- *Tuesday:* crispy chicken nuggets, fluffy whipped potato with gravy, baked vegetable, milk.
- *Wednesday:* Italian pasta with meat sauce, garlic bread, tossed salad, fresh fruit, milk.
- *Thursday:* double burger with lettuce and tomato on a bun, crispy fries, fresh apple, milk.
- *Friday:* Domino's pizza, milk.

There is not a single whole grain on the entire week's menu. All the main dishes are either meat or dairy and every meal includes milk. The lack of vegetables is glaring. The fruit is not organic and therefore has multiple pesticide residues. The diet of adolescent girls is a crucial area of concern in the breast cancer epidemic. Susan Love has written:

> . . . Breast tissue seems to be more sensitive to carcinogens during adolescence than it is after the first pregnancy. It may well be possible that the time to study a low-fat diet is at puberty rather than in post-menopausal women.[29]

Japanese women have one quarter the breast cancer rates of American women[30] yet Japanese-American women living in both Hawaii and California now have breast cancer incidence rates approaching those of the Caucasian American women.[31] This tells us something about the strength of environmental influences over heredity. Optimistically, if the risk can double in a decade it should also be possible to reduce it proportionately. When Japanese families immigrated to the United States, the second-generation women were more affected by the high-protein, high-fat diet than first generation women attesting to the sensitivity of the developing breast and the importance of diet in childhood-adolescence.[32]

The growing reliance on fast foods is a cultural phenomenon that appears to be accelerating and is very worrisome. I fear we will see severely increased cancer rates among adults who grew up on diets of junk food in their sensitive developmental years. Not only are these foods high in fat and protein, but they are low in fiber and nutrients.

An early onset of puberty and the late onset of menopause are not genetically predetermined events. The declining age of puberty since the industrial revolution early in this century corresponds to our increasingly high-protein, high-fat and processed diet since that time. Diet affects menstrual patterns. The link is clear: diet affects hormones and hormones affect breast cancer.

Menstrual patterns reflect what is happening on a deeper level: that is, how we are actively creating our internal hormonal environment. Diet affects menses both directly and indirectly: directly by its effect on ovarian function and indirectly by affecting genetic expression via alterations in the intracellular environment.

4. Increased Risk with Late Menopause

Estrogen/progesterone imbalance again occurs with increasing frequency in the perimenopause (the years leading up to the complete cessation of cycling). There are many studies that show a protective effect of early menopause on breast cancer risk. According to a study published in the journal *Cancer* of over 63,000 Norwegian women the risk goes up by around 3.6 percent per year increase in age at natural menopause. There are also several studies indicating that early menarche is a risk factor; this particular Norwegian study showed a corresponding increase in risk by around four percent for every year earlier than 17 that the first menstruation begins.[33] If a woman menstruates for more than 40 years she has a higher risk of breast cancer.

WE ARE NOT SEPARATE FROM OUR HORMONES

Our hormonal environment is not a given; we can consciously have an impact on our own hormones and perhaps our daughters' hormones:

- Although we cannot retrospectively change the age we began to menstruate, we can certainly influence our daughter's first menses through the foods we put on the table during her childhood and adolescence.
- We can influence the age and the pace we go through menopause through our diet and lifestyle choices.
- In many cases we can choose at what age we will bear children and whether or not we will breast-feed.

In theory we have control over our fertility; exercising this control in the current cultural climate is another issue. Our culture pushes women in conflicting directions. Delayed childbirth is often seen as desirable and fits in with the goal of completing one's education before raising a family and satisfying the demands of our so-called "equal opportunity" job market. Perhaps we need to rethink the current trend of postponing families well into our 30s and beyond. The trend in delayed childbearing has been taken by some to an absurd extreme. There are even cases of artificially induced menstrual cycles for the purposes of conception in postmenopausal women! Perhaps we need to cultivate a bit more respect for the natural rhythms of our life cycle.

I believe we need to prioritize our health concerns and create social and health policies in the areas of childbearing and childcare that respect women's dual role in society. The expression of these concerns might take the form of bearing children earlier, supporting women who make this choice, increasing financial support for the education and career development of women and expanding our workplace attitudes to allow women and men more diverse parenting options.

THE WEB WE WEAVE

We are each an incredibly complex web of many important influences and choices: genes (our ancestral influences), prenatal exposure (our postconceptual and intrapartum experiences), infancy (breast-feeding and other primary nurturant experiences) our childhood and adolescence (diet and early sexual experiences) and finally our adulthood (choices regarding childbearing, breast-feeding, hormonal contraception, diet, hormone replacement therapy, emotional expression). The further along we progress, the more conscious the influences can be and the more empowered our choices can become.

We have an important role to play in spinning this intricate web of genetic susceptibility, hormones and cultural factors. The changes we make can also impact on both the recurrence and survival rates of breast cancer patients in a positive way. Take time to view these interventions as powerful opportunities to change the course of your life.

- A whole-foods diet will lead to lower fat stores and decreased circulating estrogen levels throughout a woman's life. This diet will not only contribute to preventing breast cancer but also to preventing a host of afflictions with which our culture is plagued—from heart disease to infertility.
- We can, with awareness, make an informed choice re-

garding childbearing and become comfortable with breastfeeding.

- We can choose not to take certain exogenous or synthetic hormones and explore more natural and ecologic alternatives for birth control and the menopause transition.
- We can become more knowledgeable about xenoestrogens in our food supply and household products and avoid them.
- We can seek physicians and other health professionals who are familiar with products like estriol and progesterone—products which research shows to be cancer-preventive rather than cancer-promoting—cooperating with our body's inclination toward balance and healing rather than adding to the total load from which it must detoxify.

ᘯ *Remember...*

Only with our vision can our risk of breast cancer—and our daughters'—be reduced. By changing our diet and the diets of our daughters, by releasing our emotional blocks, by providing an atmosphere where our daughters can freely express themselves and make informed choices and by cleaning up our environment, we can make meaningful changes in our hormone balance and genetic expression, and thus the risk of breast cancer itself.

3

Nourishing Body and Soul: Food, Supplements, Herbs

WE ARE WHAT WE EAT

As I began to investigate how to nourish my body, I embarked on the path to nourishing my soul.

Making Choices

It was the summer of '91, still early in my treatment. I was driving up to Litchfield, Connecticut to see Bill Spear, a well-respected macrobiotic counselor. I was very serious about healing.

Perhaps a month before that I had followed my therapist's suggestion and had a consultation with Dr. Robert Silverstein, an M.D. knowledgeable about nutrition. He had intense penetrating eyes, a short beard, wire-rimmed glasses and a noticeably trim body. I was relieved about that. It told me he practised what he preached.

There was a treadmill in his waiting room and a low table with samples of natural foods for patients to examine. After a physical exam, he gave me some handouts which included his version of a basic whole foods diet along with his world view. He philosophized, "Freedom means eternal vigilance." I agreed; the greatest freedom is that of responsibility. I wanted so much to be responsible to my illness; sharing what I have learned is part of that responsibility. "Aim for 90 percent," Dr. Silverstein said. I liked that— trying to be practical about radical changes in my diet.

Let's be gentle with ourselves; I couldn't agree more. He suggested that I see a macrobiotic counselor.

I knew I was committed enough to my healing to undertake a radical dietary shift. I had already read some basic macrobiotic literature. In fact, I hired Josie, a macrobiotic cook that Dr. Silverstein had suggested, for a couple of cooking lessons I took with a few friends. One of them was Marion, Zachary and Hannah's teacher at Tot Shabbat, our temple's toddler class. "How are you?" she asked me one beautiful Spring morning. "Not that great—I just found out I have breast cancer." Her jaw dropped; my heart sank. When I told Marion I wanted to get a few women together for a macrobiotic cooking class she quickly helped put a group together. There was something so warm and supportive about her helping me do this. Marion was one of the women in my life who was able to accept my illness and be there for me; she had a generosity of spirit that helped sustain me through a very isolating time. But while I was listening to Josie with all my heart and soul, the other women in the group were dabbling in just another cooking style—you know, French, Italian, Mexican, macrobiotic! So I felt very much alone, but the classes got me started, anyway.

So off I went to meet with macrobiotic counselor Bill Spear, firm in my conviction that I could make a major dietary shift (after all, it was my life hanging in the balance). I was really excited about the possibility of macrobiotics as a complementary treatment. Bill reviewed a questionnaire I had filled out as we sat there. He turned to me from across the room looking oddly familiar—a ponytailed hippie from the 60s. Bill asked me how he could help me. I said, "I want your best advice." He answered that I had to start making choices in my life.

∾

Bill was right on target. Breast cancer is about making choices—healthy choices—regarding our diet, our treat-

*ment, our doctors, our consultants, our personal environ-
ment, our lifestyle. Before breast cancer I felt I was just
being dragged along with the current. So much of the time
I felt powerless and even passive. I didn't make things happen. They happened to me. My first marriage came about
through a combination of friendship and misconstrued ob-
ligation; the second happened in the wave of relief that
followed. Even going to med school was somewhat of a hap-
penstance; always a straight A student, I wanted a challenge . . . science majors applied to med school . . . I rode
the current.*

*So interestingly, instead of coming home with strict di-
etary guidelines, batches of recipes and formulas for medicinal drinks—which is what I had expected—I was given
advice: an Rx for emotional work. I was to work on "bioen-
ergetics," whatever that was! Bill suggested I read some of
Elizabeth Kübler-Ross's work and go to her next workshop
on Life, Death and Transition. He really blew me away;
instead of telling me my cancer was caused by diet, he told
me 80 percent of my illness was emotional in nature! In
essence, Bill thought my breast cancer was largely caused
by my emotional blocks. Stop "swallowing the anger and
the love," he said.*

*After my mother died I remember silently witnessing my
sister Peggy and Dad fighting incessantly. "Drop dead," she
said to him. I listened. "Quiet," she begged. Peggy always
wanted absolute silence as she did her homework. She was
so nervous. My father told her if she wanted quiet to get it
in the cemetery. I listened. And I silently watched. I was the
good girl. No anger. Not like Peggy. Poor Peggy was always
fighting with Dad. I, the good girl, locked it all up inside to
explode 25 years later into breast cancer. As Woody Allen said
in one of his films, I don't get angry, I grow tumors instead.*

ɔɤ

*While Bill Spear did give me an overview of the macrobiotic
diet and guidelines for food choices, he was very general*

about the diet. Obviously, no junk food, no soft drinks, candy or salty, high-fat commercial corn chips, crackers, potato chips (that's okay, I didn't eat much junk food anyway). No sugar (white or brown), molasses, corn syrup, artificial sweeteners, chocolate or caffeine. No processed foods; no partially hydrogenated oils. I would have to read labels carefully. Eliminate red meat and chicken. Eliminate all dairy products (butter, cheese, cream, ice cream, milk, yogurt). Greatly reduce tropical produce (bananas, coconuts, dates, oranges, cashews) and the nightshade family of vegetables (tomatoes, potatoes, peppers, eggplant, tobacco). Even with this daunting list of no-nos, I wasn't worried, there was still plenty to eat! I was damn serious about getting well, and whatever that entailed, well, that was fine with me.

✑

After seeing Bill I got started right away. The Elizabeth Kübler-Ross workshop he suggested was in a couple of days. It took hours on the phone making the arrangements. The workshop was on a campus outside of Albuquerque, in the middle of nowhere, so I would have to get local transportation when I disembarked from the plane.

Wait—watch it—why was I doing this? Did Bill tell me to go to this workshop or did I choose it myself? Was I just obeying again, being dragged by a new current? I was scared, let's face it. I was at a point in my life when I was searching in all directions. At this same time I was beginning to make connections inside that would enable me to make more comfortable decisions later on.

I talked to Tullia, my counselor. She said she thought the workshop would be too intense. She did not think it was appropriate for me right then. From what I understand, the Life, Death and Transition workshops are geared to people who are facing death imminently. Although cancer had pushed me to a place where I was acutely aware of my mortality, death was not in my immediate future, as far as

I could tell. Nevertheless, I was set on going, come what may. The adventurer in me wanted to go—the challenge, the hope. I desperately wanted to open to new possibilities.

Lucia, my babysitter, took Zachary, Hannah and Oliver with me to the Connecticut Limousine terminal to wave goodbye, and I was on my way. So there I was reading, writing and listening to tapes on the way to the airport, excited and scared about the journey ahead. It was an unusually gray day. When we arrived at the airport I ran into the terminal to check in. The sky darkened. Lightening cracked the sky. The rain poured down. Divine Intervention. The airport was closed for the night. There was no way I could get to Albuquerque or anywhere else this night. I waited for a few hours at the airport gate, looking out the huge windows at the crackling sky and the gray runways. Finally it was clear that no matter what other connections I could possibly make, there was no way I could get to the workshop. I was told that if I arrived late on the other end there would be no transportation to get me to the site, which was a three hour car ride from the airport.

Some things are decided for us. I took the Connecticut Limo home and arrived to find lights flashing outside my house. A number of Con Ed trucks and employees were working there. A large tree had been struck by lightning. The electricity was out.

∽

As I began to search for ways to nourish my body I also began to look for ways to nourish my soul. Not so surprisingly, my respect for my own body's nourishment led me to a more ecological and spiritual approach to all life. The wisdom of the body encourages us to find the path of our soul. The deepest honoring of our bodies ushers in soulful respect for our true nature, the reality beyond the physical. As we become clearer on our paths to health we find that circumstances will guide us, that there are no coincidences!

THE POWER OF OUR PLATES

Of more than 100 human studies on diet and cancer, 93 percent show that those who regularly eat lots of fruit and vegetables have a lower likelihood of developing cancer than similar people who don't.[1] The basic principles of healthy eating have been quite clearly established. We must strive to educate ourselves, use our innate common sense, remain open to new ideas, maintain our flexibility and never underestimate the power of our plates.

In order to heal cancer, we must more than meet our requirements for all the essential macro and micro nutrients. We must eat the best quality foods we can obtain, keeping in heart and mind the principle that what is good for the planet's health is ultimately good for our own personal health. Eating organic, locally grown foods is an excellent way to stay close to nature and in harmony with the seasons. Having a small vegetable garden, even if you grow only a very small quantity of food, is a wonderful symbolic gesture of appreciation for the cycles of Mother Nature and her immense transformational and restorative powers.

CANCER CAN BE HELPED BY A NUTRIENT-DENSE DIET

Cancer clearly has a latent period. Based on the time it takes a single cancer cell to double, calculations show that most cases of breast cancer have been present for eight to ten years prior to detection by mammography or the discovery of a lump. The initial detectable focus of disease does not just instantaneously appear; it has a long history behind it. The history behind the initiation and promotion of breast cancer is disturbed biochemistry, a poorly functioning detoxification pathway and overloaded carcinogenic influences. These factors can in great measure be corrected or overridden by a nutrient-dense diet.

It is vital to understand that the way we live our lives,

especially what we and our daughters eat now, will make a difference in our future. Food choice is clearly not the sole factor in the development of cancer but it is certainly a very important one. We each have unique nutritional requirements as well as unique and dynamic abilities to deal with environmental stressors. The concept of "total load," used in the field of environmental medicine, is a useful one. We are all exposed to a variety of harmful substances, some more inherently dangerous than others; some are toxic only in certain amounts while others are potentiated by specific substances or conditions. Some of these toxins are external (DDT, lead, gasoline vapors); others are produced internally when normal operations go awry. All these exposures add up to what is known as total load.

The greater the environmental stressors, the more important is nutritional replenishment so that our detoxification pathways can function. The more depleted our diet the more likely that less dramatic environmental stressors will tip the scales into the full-blown manifestation of disease. Each individual's body has unique inborn nutritional requirements which can be obtained from food and supplements. Nutrient requirements vary from person to person, and optimal functioning can best be achieved by individualized programs. Blood tests and established population norms notwithstanding, no one but you can be the final arbiter of how you feel.

ᴄᴡ   *Remember...*

Nutrients can help neutralize environmental toxins that initiate and promote breast cancer. Assure a nutrient-dense diet of foods as close to their natural state as possible and use supplements judiciously for prevention and treatment of breast cancer.

A Single Mineral Deficiency ...

A single mineral deficiency can cause a myriad of symptoms including back and neck pain, muscle cramps and twitches, constipation, menstrual cramps, insomnia, anxiety, panic disorder, premenstrual irritability and breast tenderness, numbness, tingling, palpitations, arrhythmia, hypertension, mitral valve prolapse and fatigue.[2] Documented relief from all of these symptoms has been achieved with the ingestion of a single mineral—magnesium. If a single mineral deficiency can have such far-reaching effects in a variety of target areas, just imagine the health problems in store for those who consume the overly refined, processed, extremely depleted standard American diet.

Food Runs the Biochemical Machinery

We need to eat a wide variety of nutrient-dense foods to run the machinery of the body, which does its job of digestion (making nutrients available to the body from the food we eat), absorption and delivery (getting nutrients from the gut, across membranes, into cells), metabolism (utilization of the nutrients in a variety of cellular activities) and elimination (moving cellular waste products across membranes and out of the body). All these nutritional functions depend on enzymes which require very specific vitamins and minerals to do their jobs. Likewise, the body has enzymes that are essential to processing carcinogens (many of which have been introduced into our environment by 20th century technology). Detoxification, the processing of chemical carcinogens, requires nutrient-dense food so that the necessary enzyme-mediated, mineral dependent biochemical reactions can take place.

If your body has too many chemicals to process and does not have the energy, enzymes or cofactors required to do so, these chemicals will remain in your body doing damage, sometimes permanently impairing the very mechanisms which are meant to detoxify them. Cancer may be the final pathway if we do not provide our bodies with the nutrients necessary to take us down the path to health. Cancer is not just a stroke of bad luck. So, whether breast cancer has been promoted by a poor-quality, high-fat diet, initiated or promoted by carcinogenic chemical exposures or fed by constant stress, anger or fear, a clean and nutrient-dense diet cannot fail to help.

The Secrets of Nature Are Found in Food

Every day science is discovering that nature has more secrets. Our scientific methods are valuable, but limited. We can never, outside the laboratory, control all the variables in the situation we are studying. In the name of scientific study, we isolate one nutrient and measure its effects in the lab and then in randomized clinical studies. Yet in nature one nutrient can never work alone. Nutrients are synergistic and work cooperatively in the ecosystem of our bodies.

We know that the whole is inexplicably greater than the sum of its parts, but we often discredit and devalue what cannot be accurately measured and reduced to its component parts. If we wait for the elusive definitive evidence it may be too late to arrive at workable solutions to the breast cancer epidemic. Nature has provided us with a multitude of anticarcinogens in our foods, but they are often not taken seriously until a pharmaceutical company extracts them and synthesizes them as over-the-counter or prescription medications.

Perfectly designed well-controlled double-blinded scientific studies regarding the influence of diet on breast cancer pose difficulties for many reasons. Foods themselves are greater than the sum of their nutritional parts and as such cannot be broken down, measured and compared like Drug A vs. Drug B. There are aspects of nutrition that do not lend themselves to the methods of large-scale studies which evaluate food intake only:

- The manner of food preparation can greatly enhance or markedly diminish a food's nutrient value: raw foods contain beneficial enzymes; overcooking destroys vitamins and enzymes; frying destroys essential fatty acids and creates toxic by-products.
- How a food is grown (organic vs. non-organic), as well as the degree of mineralization of the soil in which it has grown affects the inherent value of a food.
- Chewing, digestive capacity, enzyme levels and the assimilation of nutrients are crucial factors that depend very much on biochemical individuality.

There is a wholeness inherent in natural foods, especially when they are prepared with love and eaten with the intent of healing, that cannot be measured by scientific analysis. This is not to say we cannot scientifically study diet and analyze food; we have, and the results are continuing to show the relationship between breast cancer and refined, depleted, high-fat, high-protein diets. However, people are intricate, uniquely complex beings, each with so many interacting factors. No matter what the multifactorial picture of causes for any individual's breast cancer, good nutritional practice can aid in the healing.

INCORPORATE HEALING FOODS INTO YOUR DIET NOW

Every woman with breast cancer is unique, both in her set of causes and in her responses to treatment. Of two women with Stage 1 disease, one will be cured while another dies of metastatic disease; still another woman with Stage IV metastatic disease will have a spontaneous remission. No doctor will argue with this. Individuals defy statistics precisely because that is the nature of individuality. This concept can empower you no matter what your disease status or medical prognosis. One of the keys to understanding breast cancer is the appreciation of the concept of biochemical individuality, that each woman needs an individualized approach and, more importantly, that each woman needs to approach her own disease as an individual.

With this in mind, it is unarguable that the standard American diet is not health-supportive. The studies we do have are clear in linking breast cancer to a high-fat, high-protein, overly processed diet. We cannot afford to wait for all the studies that would be necessary to show us exactly what to put on our plates at every meal. I'm not even sure that would be optimal. Freedom, choice and variety are part of the beauty of food and life. What we need to do is use guiding principles and take on the responsibility for our own personal health and the health of the planet.

The best diet for healing from and preventing breast cancer is a whole foods diet consisting largely of unprocessed, unrefined whole grains and a wide variety of organic vegetables. This diet is mineral- and vitamin-rich, naturally low-fat, low-protein, high-fiber and non-dairy. This is the diet I recovered on and continue to stay healthy on.

By eating plant foods (grains and vegetables) rather than animal foods (meat, poultry, dairy), we are lowering fat and protein consumption, and by choosing organic foods lower on the food chain we are decreasing our consumption of toxic residues.

After eating in a more wholesome way I became aware of the interconnectedness of all living things. Our personal dietary habits not only affect our individual health but have far-reaching global consequences. As the boundaries between personal healing and global healing merge we will move forward as a compassionate culture.

∾

I continued to eat the low-fat, lower-protein non-dairy diet that I had begun shortly after my diagnosis. At the end of October 1991 I travelled up to Brookline, Massachusetts to consult with the leader of the macrobiotic community on the East coast, Michio Kushi. He made various recommendations, suggesting that I go on a strict healing phase mac-

robiotic diet for four months and then widen the diet to the more standard macro diet. I followed his strict and quite elaborate suggestions.

I found myself up in the early hours of the morning shredding carrots and daikon for my morning tonic. Other days I was chopping cabbage, carrots, squash and onions for a sweet vegetable drink. And every third day I was boiling black soybeans and drinking the thick black water that they produced. At night I was up late cutting vegetables for my morning miso soup and reviewing recipes for the following day. And throughout the day I was washing, soaking, cutting and otherwise preparing all sorts of strange looking and even stranger tasting concoctions. I took this on completely. I felt sure this was the right dietary approach for me, and I knew my life was in the balance.

If there was magic at work here it was that from deep within I knew unequivocably how essential it was to care for my body in this way and wholeheartedly embrace this new way of life. Macrobiotics is a philosophy of which dietary principles are only a part. It seemed intuitively right for me; I chose to pursue macrobiotics without any hesitation.

> Until one is committed,
> there is hesitancy,
> the chance to draw back,
> always ineffectiveness.
> I have learned a deep respect
> for one of Goethe's couplets:
>
> Whatever you can do,
> or dream you can, begin it.
> Boldness has genius,
> power and magic in it.
>
> —W.H. Murray
> *The Scottish Himalaya Expedition*

Looking back, I give myself credit. At the time I didn't have a moment to pat myself on the back. I was too busy

*figuring out if I should be cooking dried daikon with
kombu, kinpira (burdock and carrot), nishime, steamed
greens, sauteed vegetables, pressed salad, or what? It was
kind of like, if it's Wednesday I must be cooking arame!
After many weeks of this very strict regimen I continued to
follow a macrobiotic-style diet. After a few months my diet
became somewhat less strict. In my current life I still incorporate the basic principles. It is only years later that I understand from a scientific perspective why, in fact, the
macrobiotic diet was so healing.*

∾

The Evolution of the Standard American Diet

Incredible changes in food consumption have occurred
since 1900. At the same time, the incidence of breast cancer
has increased as natural foods have been eliminated from
our collective diet and artificial foods have replaced them.
Grain consumption has decreased by 51 percent since 1900
and vegetables by 23 percent. Consumption of frozen foods
has gone up a dramatic 2,764 percent. Instead of consuming
fresh fruits and vegetables we are substituting nutrient-
depleted frozen and canned produce, and not much of that
either. The consumption of artificial foods continues to es-
calate; for example, soft drinks are up 2,678 percent since
the turn of the century (see Figure 3). Many diseases of
modern civilization have appeared following the introduction of white flour, white rice, sugar, canned items and
other processed foods. Jane Brody's research[3] indicates that
for the last million-and-a-half years people have been eating
three times as much plant food as animal food. This is the
exact reverse of what the average meat-eating American
consumes today.

The dietary goals for the United States which were set by
the Senate Select Committee on Nutrition and Human Needs
in 1977 and which linked the modern diet with cancer,

FIGURE 3

FOOD CHANGES 1910–1976
Per capita annual consumption in pounds unless noted otherwise

CATEGORY	1910	1976	CHANGE
Grains	294.0	144.0	−51%
Fresh Vegetables	188.0	144.5	−23%
Canned Vegetables	12.6 (1920)	53.0	+320%
Frozen Vegetables	0.57 (1940)	9.9	+1,650%
Fresh Fruit	123.0	82.0	−33%
Processed Fruit	20.5	134.6	+556%
Frozen Citrus	1.0 (1948)	117.0	+11,600%
Frozen Foods	3.1 (1940)	88.8	+2,764%
Meat	136.2	165.2	+21%
Beef	55.5	95.4	+72%
Poultry	18.0	52.9	+194%
Eggs	305 whole	276 whole	−10%
Fish	11.4	13.7	+20%
Dairy	320.2	354.3	+11%
Cheese	4.9	20.7	+322%
Frozen Dairy	3.4	50.2	+1,376%
Sweetners	89.0	134.6	+51%
Corn Syrup	3.8	32.7	+761%
Soft Drinks	1.1 gal.	30.8 gal.	+2,638%

Source: U.S. Department of Agriculture

stated that the goal should be to increase carbohydrate consumption to approximately 60 percent of calories, to reduce overall fat consumption, to reduce saturated fat consumption, to reduce cholesterol consumption, to reduce sugar consumption by 40 percent and to reduce salt consumption. This message has not been effectively communicated to the women in this country, who in large measure control the food choices. What these goals translate to in terms of food selection are an increased consumption of whole grains, vegetables and fruit and vast reduction in the consumption of foods high in fat—including meat, poultry, eggs, milk, butter and other dairy foods—a decreased consumption of sugar and a decreased use of table salt and canned and processed foods.

After two years of public hearings, the doctors and nutritionists consulted by the Senate Select Committee stated:

> During this century, the composition of the average diet in the United States has changed radically. Complex carbohydrates, fruits, vegetables and whole grains—which were the mainstay of the diet—now play a minority role. At the same time, fat and sugar consumption have risen to the point where these two dietary elements alone now comprise 60 percent of total calorie intake . . . In the view of this committee, this has amounted to a wave of malnutrition, both over and under-consumption, that may be as profoundly damaging to the nations' health as the widespread contagious diseases in the early part of the century.

Malnutrition in this context means we are starving for vitamins and minerals. We, as a culture, have lost our connection to real food. As our agricultural society became industrialized we began to purchase convenience foods at supermarkets geared to our fast-paced lifestyles. Chemicals and preservatives abound. The committee went on, "The overconsumption of fat . . . as well as cholesterol, sugar, salt and alcohol have surely been related to cancer, as well as numerous other diseases."[4] This report was a turning point; until this time the government and most of the scientific and medical communities had given uncritical support to the high-fat, high-protein standard American diet. Within a few years following this report many national and international scientific and medical organizations reached similar conclusions and published similar guidelines.

The U.S. Surgeon General issued a report in 1979 entitled *Healthy People: The Surgeon General's Report on Health Promotion and Disease Prevention,* in which the recommendations of the Select Committee were reiterated as well as highlighting the dangers of food processing.[5] Following this, The National Academy of Sciences issued *Diet, Nutrition, and Cancer*[6] in 1982. In this study the modern diet—high in fat, animal protein, sugar and chemical additives—was associated with the majority of cancers, including breast cancer. The panel reviewed hundreds of current medical studies associating long-term eating patterns with the development of 60 percent of the cancers in women, which naturally includes breast cancer.

There is a general consensus in the scientific communities both here and abroad that animal fat should be reduced and that nutrient and fiber-rich plant foods should be increased to prevent disease. It is unfortunate for the American public that dietary recommendations are so highly charged with politics. The basic conclusions and the food choices that naturally follow were not and still are not given the undiluted publicity they deserve. In fact the Food Guide Pyramid released in 1992 by the U.S. Department of Agriculture is an outgrowth of this consensus. Even with its moderate guidelines, the publication of the Pyramid was unduly delayed by the meat and dairy industries who have much to lose if the American public cuts back on meat and dairy products. In the last few years various modifications of the U.S.D.A. Pyramid have been published by nutritional educators including a Mediterranean Pyramid, an Asian Pyramid and a dairy-free Vegetarian Pyramid. Designed to enhance breast health, my Organic Food Pyramid (Figure 4) will help you create your own health-supportive diet. Your entire family can benefit from these guidelines.

A Word about Organic Foods

Organic foods are essential choices in healing from breast cancer as well as for a breast cancer prevention diet. Organic foods not only are free of toxic residues, including xenoestrogens (estrogen-like chemicals which are foreign to our body, see Chapter 6) but are richest in the minerals

FIGURE 4
Dr. Joseph's Organic Food Pyramid*

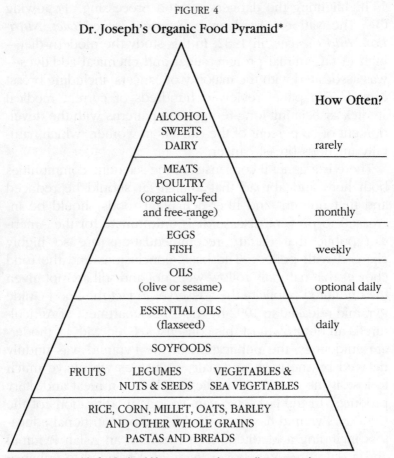

	How Often?
ALCOHOL SWEETS DAIRY	rarely
MEATS POULTRY (organically-fed and free-range)	monthly
EGGS FISH	weekly
OILS (olive or sesame)	optional daily
ESSENTIAL OILS (flaxseed)	daily
SOYFOODS	
FRUITS LEGUMES VEGETABLES & NUTS & SEEDS SEA VEGETABLES	
RICE, CORN, MILLET, OATS, BARLEY AND OTHER WHOLE GRAINS PASTAS AND BREADS	

*Whenever possible foods should be organic and minimally processed.

which cancer patients vitally need. The mineral content of organic produce is dramatically higher than non-organic. The choice, when possible, should always be organic.

When pesticides are ingested they need to be detoxified and excreted rather than incorporated into our cells. Some substances bioaccumulate and will never be excreted because the human body cannot process certain chemicals. Detoxification requires proper nutrient levels including healthy levels of essential vitamins and minerals. The liver, digestive system, kidneys, lymphatics and the circulatory system are important components in detoxification and removal of toxic waste. But constant detoxification takes a toll on the body; it consumes energy that could otherwise be used for healing.

Proper mineral balance is necessary for healthful functioning of the body in general and is vital for the functioning of the various enzymatic pathways necessary for clearing cancer. Every biochemical reaction in the body depends on enzymes and their mineral cofactors. Attention to mineral levels is especially important for women undergoing the conventional breast cancer treatments—surgery, radiation and chemotherapy—and for those women trying to rebuild their health. All repair mechanisms depend on these minerals.

FOODS TO EMPHASIZE

Whole Grains

Whole grains, unrefined and unprocessed, offer maximum nutrient density. Grains are the seeds of plants and have an outer fibrous coat which contains water-soluble vitamins, proteins and minerals. The bulk of the grain is endosperm, carbohydrate starch which holds the calories for the grain's germination. Within the germ of the grain are fat-soluble vitamins and unsaturated fatty acids. Modern processing has virtually destroyed our grains. The germ and the outer bran coating are discarded or removed and sold back to us as a health food. We are sold only the starchy endosperm as bread or white flour, cereal and pasta. Whole grains should form the backbone of our meals. Some of the grains to be included in your diet:

short- medium- and long-grain brown rice	millet
	pearl barley
sweet brown rice	quinoa
amaranth	rye
buckwheat	whole oats
corn	wild rice

The Importance of Fiber

Whole grains are high in fiber. According to the American Health Foundation[7] and a plethora of scientific studies there is convincing evidence that whole grain cereals, and other foods high in fiber specifically protect against breast cancer. Dietary fiber increases the fecal excretion of estrogen and thereby decreases plasma concentration of estrogen.[8]

Fiber helps the bowels function properly, binding carcinogens from diet or environment. It increases the weight and amount of stool which dilutes the effect of the carcinogens by helping to move food and breakdown products so carcinogens are excreted more rapidly with less time to contact the gut wall. Fiber also helps keep our intestinal flora healthy. Well-balanced intestinal flora is important for digestive function as well as general immune function.

∾ *Remember...*

Fiber is protective for breast cancer. Whole grains are rich in fiber, vitamins and minerals and also provide a good energy source. Eat whole grain foods daily in the healing phase and incorporate whole grains as much as possible in a health-supportive proactive prevention diet.

Other Whole Grain Foods

Other grain foods include various pastas, breads and dry cereals. Eat much less of these on a healing diet; however, these are fine foods for a prevention diet and for the family.

PASTAS

corn noodles
Jerusalem artichoke pasta
quinoa noodles
ramen noodles (instant)
rice noodles (Chinese)
sesame noodles

soba noodles (part buckwheat)
somen noodles (whole wheat)
spelt pasta
udon noodles (whole wheat)

BREADS

corn bread
corn rolls
rice bread
Rudolph's unyeasted rye breads
sourdough bread

spelt bread
sprouted wheat or spelt bread
whole wheat or rye bread (yeasted)
whole wheat pita bread

CEREALS (Serve with rice or soy milk)

corn grits
dry cereals like Erewhon's Crispy Brown Rice or Glenny's Maple Corns
rolled oats

steel cut oats
whole grain puffed dry cereals (rice, millet, corn, wheat, Kashi)

OTHER GRAIN FOODS

bulgur wheat
cornmeal
mochi
popcorn
rice cakes

seitan
whole grain wheat, rye or rice crackers
whole wheat couscous

Vegetables

A large part of a healing and health-supportive diet will consist of fresh organic produce, especially vitamin-and mineral-rich land and sea vegetables. Make friends with these vegetables, learn their names and their tastes. A good way to try a new vegetable is to steam it or add it to a soup, then experiment from there with different ways to cut, cook and flavor these vegetables. I never tasted kale and most certainly never heard of eating dandelion greens before getting sick!

alfalfa sprouts	mustard greens
beets	onions
broccoli	parsley
bok choy	peas
brussel sprouts	pumpkins
cabbage, red or green	radishes
carrots	romaine
cauliflower	rutabagas
celery	scallions
collard greens	string beans
corn	summer squash
cucumbers	turnips and turnip greens
dandelion greens	winter squashes (butter-
daikon	nut, buttercup, delicata,
kale	hubbard)
leeks	yams

Letha Hadadi, an herbalist who lectures frequently at the Open Center in New York City on breast cancer and has traveled extensively in the Far East, remarked that the low rates of breast cancer in China in part reflect the regular use by Chinese women of produce for prevention. She learned that dandelion greens aid in the prevention of breast cancer by improving circulation of blood and lymph in the breast.

Sea Vegetables

Research shows that the majority of Americans have mineral deficiencies, both clinical and subclinical. ". . . if you look at the composite deficiencies in one person, they are generally multiple. And, of course, if they have any illness or symptoms (and always if they have cancer) or are on any chronic medications, it is almost guaranteed that there will be deficiencies according to Sherry Rogers, M.D."[9] This means that even if you have no specific complaints your body may not be functioning optimally. Mineral deficiencies are common because of the abundance of processed foods that are found in the majority of American pantries.

When brown rice is converted to white rice by grinding and bleaching 80 percent of trace minerals—including magnesium, manganese, copper and zinc—are lost. When whole wheat berries are turned into white bread, it is similarly depleted. Thus it is not surprising that the average American consumes less than 40 percent of the RDA (recommended daily allowance) of magnesium.[10] Over 300 enzymes depend on magnesium, underscoring the importance of adequate levels of this mineral and the potential vast array of bodily functions that might be disturbed by its deficiency. Since the majority of the population is magnesium deficient, the incorporation of sea vegetables can be a very effective way of correcting this and other mineral deficiencies.

Sea vegetables are a great source of minerals, especially calcium. There is a great misconception about our ability to get enough calcium from our diet if we eliminate dairy foods. The following list[11] underscores this point:

FOOD SOURCES OF CALCIUM*

almonds	234	kukicha tea	72
broccoli	103	sesame seeds	1,160
kale	179	parsley	203
mustard greens	183	hijiki	1,400
salmon	213	agar agar	400
low-fat yogurt	183	nori	260
collard greens	156	wakame	1,300
skim milk	123	dulce	567

mg of calcium per 3.5 ounces

When I first became ill and discovered sea vegetables through macrobiotics, I'll never forget my children's faces as they looked at and then, believe it or not, sampled many of my initial attempts at cooking with sea vegetables. What a display of courage! I will admit that some of the sea vegetables are difficult to develop a taste for, but many are delicious.

Start with nori—norimake rolls of brown rice and veggie slivers wrapped in sheets of nori are fun for the whole family; nori can be crumpled up and used as a garnish on salads or grain dishes. Add two to three inches of kombu to stocks or soups; use it instead of salt when cooking rice or other grains. Wakame is an essential ingredient in miso soup; miso is the nutritious soybean paste that flavors the soup and is an essential addition to your healing menu. There are many different types of miso paste that can be chosen for both taste and seasonal variety; lighter ones are more appropriate for the summer and darker ones in winter. Similarly, the vegetables in miso soup can be varied according to what's on hand or, even better, what's in season. Dulce is a sea vegetable that can be prepared as a crispy filling for a sandwich. Vegetarian jello made from agar-agar and various combinations of fruit juices and slices is another rich source of minerals. For those who have developed a taste for sea vegetables, arame and hijiki can be prepared as side dishes. See Resources for recommended cookbooks.

Garlic

Garlic contains large amounts of sulfur, which is part of the protein content of every cell. Muscles, tendons, cartilage, hair, nails, eyes, brain all have sulfur-containing proteins. Our digestion, absorption and the assimilation of our food are all dependent on enzymatic processes. All our metabolic pathways are enzyme-mediated. And all enzymes have sulfur-containing proteins as their basic unit. The liver, our detoxification clearinghouse, has over 1,000 sulfur containing enzymes.

Sulfur compounds inhibit carcinogens. Specifically, garlic, onions, leeks and chives contain allyl sulfides which increase glutathione-S-transferase activity which enhances the excretion of carcinogens. John Milner, Ph.D. of Pennsylvania State University found that high garlic diets slowed breast tumor growth and reduced the number of tumors in laboratory animals.[12] Sulfur compounds inhibit enzymes that facilitate cancer spread. The National Cancer Institute is studying garlic as an immune enhancer and cancer preventive agent.

LET VEGETABLES BE YOUR MEDICINE

The substances listed below are what Charles Simone, M.D. refers to in *Cancer and Nutrition*[13] and his more recent book, *Breast Health*,[14] as natural food protectors. These substances and many others are the rationale behind why we can trust certain foods to be our medicine. As we continue to isolate more and more of the natural food protectors and gain new respect for their healing potential I believe that our personal and planetary healing will follow. Once we get in touch with the sanctity of food on a daily basis, we will all heal in unexpected ways.

Carotene

Many studies have shown that people who consume foods with high amounts of carotenes have a lower risk of developing cancer.[15] The carotenes are a group of potent immune enhancers that can reverse precancerous conditions. The carotenes are powerful antioxidants. Antioxidants are a group of diverse substances which neutralize free radicals which are chemical by-products of the environment as well as our own metabolism. If free radicals are not properly eliminated they can do harm: damaging membranes, alter-

ing DNA and eventuating in cancer. Adequate levels of antioxidants enhance immune function. Carotenes are found in
yellow and orange fruits and vegetables and dark leafy
green vegetables such as: carrots, sweet potatoes, yams,
pumpkins, squash, cantaloupe, kale, broccoli and bok choy.

Indoles

A compound called indole-3-carbinol (I-3-C) obtained from
cruciferous vegetables—which include cabbage, Brussels
sprouts, broccoli, bok choy and cauliflower—can destroy
or otherwise inactivate estrogen, thus reducing breast cancer risk.[16] In animal studies, I-3-C reduces mammary cancer.

Isothiocyanates

The group of compounds known as isothiocyanates are also
found in cruciferous vegetables. Sulforaphane, which is part
of this group, increases the enzyme activity associated with
the detoxification of cancer-causing substances. Broccoli is
a good source of sulforaphane.

Fruit

Fruit contains natural sugars and its refreshing quality makes
it a wonderful choice for snacks and desserts. Fruits contain
valuable vitamins, minerals, enzymes and fiber. The importance of eating organic fruit cannot be overemphasized.
Sprays and chemical fertilizers work their way through the
entire plant, influencing its growth and quality; washing will
not effectively remove residues nor will peeling, usually.

In late 1995, the Environmental Working Group, a research and advocacy group in Washington, D.C. published
the following list of fruits[17] that have the highest levels of
pesticides residues: strawberries, cherries, peaches, Mexican
canteloupe, apples, apricots and Chilean grapes. To be on

the safe side, if you can't afford or locate organic varieties of these fruits, simply avoid them.

Always choose fruits that are in season. Tree- or vine-ripened fruits, are more nutritious and local produce is always preferable, from both a seasonal and ecologic perspective.

LEGUMES

Beans or legumes are an essential part of a whole-food, plant-based diet. Beans are an excellent source of the amino acids that we need to make protein. It is important to understand that grains and vegetables are also important protein sources, a fact that many people are unaware of. See Figure 5.

As far as protein is concerned, more is definitely not better. According to nutritional authorities we should be getting

FIGURE 5

PERCENTAGE OF CALORIES AS PROTEIN

VEGETABLES		LEGUMES		NUTS & SEEDS	
Spinach	49%	Tofu	43%	Peanuts	18%
Broccoli	47%	Lentils	29%	Sunflower	17%
Cauliflower	40%	Split peas	28%	Walnuts	13%
Mushrooms	38%	Kidney beans	26%	Almonds	12%
Parsley	34%	Navy beans	26%		
Lettuce	34%	Chick peas	23%	FRUITS	
Green peas	30%			Lemon	16%
Zucchini	28%	GRAINS		Canteloupe	9%
Green beans	26%	Rye	20%	Orange	8%
Cucumbers	24%	Wheat	17%	Grape	8%
Celery	21%	Oatmeal	16%	Peach	6%
Tomatoes	18%	Buckwheat	15%	Pear	5%
Onions	16%	Barley	11%	Banana	5%
Potatoes	11%	Brown Rice	8%		

Source: USDA

anywhere from 2½ to 10 percent of our calories from protein. The National Research Council gives the figure of 8 percent, noting that this figure is not a minimum daily requirement, but contains a substantial safety margin.[18] Human breast milk derives only 5 percent of its calories from protein at a time when human beings are growing at an unprecedented rate. Beans of various sorts and bean products are recommended to help meet our protein requirements:

aduki beans	navy beans
black turtle beans	pinto beans
chickpeas	soy beans
kidney beans	split peas
lentils	soybean products such as
lima beans	tofu, tempeh, miso

Legumes also contain valuable components that can protect against cancer growth in various ways.

Protease Inhibitors

Soybeans contain protease inhibitors which have been shown to cause irreversible suppression of the process of carcinogenesis.[19] According to Ann Kennedy, Ph.D., a researcher at the University of Pennsylvania School of Medicine, by blocking the action of proteases (enzymes that promote tumor growth) soy beans can prevent and inhibit a wide range of cancers, including breast cancer.

Soy contains a unique protease inhibitor—the Bowman-Birk Inhibitor (BBI)—which in animal studies shows impressive success in suppressing tumor formation Dr. Kennedy is conducting human cancer prevention trials using BBI in people at high risk for developing cancer.

Isoflavones

Isoflavones are found in legumes and are converted in the body to phytoestrogens (plant estrogens). These hormone-like compounds have been shown to inhibit or block estrogen receptors. By binding to estrogen receptor sites on breast cells these physiologically less potent phytoestrogens prevent more potent estrogens from binding and entering cells, thereby helping to prevent hormone-dependent cancers from developing.[20] Isoflavones also directly inhibit estrogen.

Isoflavones have been shown to destroy certain cancer gene enzymes that can propagate and transform normal cells into cancer cells.[21] *Genistein* is an isoflavone that is found only in soy foods. It has been shown to specifically inhibit the enzyme tyrosine kinase, thus preventing activation of epidermal growth factor (EGF), an enzyme which regulates cell growth and division. Test tube and animal experiments have shown its ability to block the growth of breast cancer cells. Genistein also promotes the differentiation of cancer cells which, by definition, would render them less aggressive. Researcher Theodore Fostis of Children's University Hospital in Heidelberg investigated another mechanism by which genistein may prevent the spread of breast cancer. In his laboratory, genistein blocked angiogenesis, the process by which a tumor promotes the growth of new blood vessels to support its own growth.[22] These additional mechanisms support a non-hormonal effect of genistein on breast cancer, and indeed researchers at the University of Alabama[23] showed that genistein blocked the growth of nonestrogen dependent human breast cancer cells *in vitro*. Genistein also has the ability to act as an antioxidant, which may also confer additional anti-cancer properties.[24]

Other soy-derived phytoestrogens are *equol* and *daidzein*. Women eating the traditional Japanese diet high in soy foods excrete high levels of these phytoestrogens. It is clear that diets with an abundance of soy products confer protection against breast cancer. This is evidenced by the low rates of this disease in women eating traditional Japanese diets, by animal studies and by the latest research on these natural soy protector substances.[25]

Research indicates that soy foods are rich enough in isoflavones to be of potential preventive and therapeutic use in the treatment of breast cancer. (see Chapter 1). Soybeans also contain phospholipids and glycolipids, saponins, which function as immune modulators, and anticarcinogens. Learn to love soyfoods. Include at least one serving of tofu, tempeh, miso or soy milk in your diet each day. Health foods stores and supermarkets carry many soy products which are delicious and easy to prepare. I frequently eat Lemon Marinated Grilles—tempeh burgers by Lightlife.

EXCESSIVE PROTEIN, MORE BREAST CANCER

To put the protein myth to rest the late Nathan Pritikin said, "... I don't know any nutrition expert that can plan a diet of natural foods resulting in a protein deficiency, so long as you're not deficient in calories ..."[26] As long as a person is taking in sufficient calories, not as processed or refined foods or in junk food, but in whole foods such as grains, legumes, vegetables and fruit, there is no reason to worry about protein deficiency.

On the other hand there is a good amount of epidemiologic evidence that total protein intake correlates with the incidence and mortality of breast cancer.[27] [28] A high protein diet is not desirable. A high protein diet promotes the growth patterns that result in early menarche and which are associated with an increased risk for the development of breast cancer.

For both the treatment and prevention of breast cancer a low protein diet is more desirable, with the protein being derived primarily from plant sources. Colin Campbell, M.S., Ph.D., author and researcher of one of the most ambitious nutrition research projects ever conducted, *The China Diet and Health Study,* commented in an interview with Neal Barnard, M.D.:

Our study suggests that the closer one approaches a total plant food diet, the greater the health benefit. . . . Animal protein is about as well-correlated with overall cancer rates across different countries as is total fat. Of course animal protein is tightly coupled with the intake of saturated fat, so a lot of these associations between saturated fat and various cancers could just as easily be accounted for by animal protein. Whether it is the immune system, various enzyme systems, the uptake of carcinogens into the cells, or hormonal activities, animal protein generally causes only mischief. High fat intake still can be a problem, and we ought not be consuming such high-fat diets. But I suggest that animal protein is more problematic in this whole diet/disease relationship than is total fat.

Many Americans are switching from beef to skinless chicken breast and other animal-based foods, simply to reduce their intake of fat. However, it is my opinion that the existing evidence suggests that this makes little or no sense. It may reduce fat intake a bit, but even lean cuts of meat or poultry still contain around 20 to 40 percent of total calories as fat, or even more. This is not going to get us very far. It might get our fat intake down a bit, but our protein intake is not going to change, if anything, its already high level may go even higher. *One really has to change the total diet. Anything less than that is a cruel hoax on the population at large. It doesn't make sense.* (Emphasis mine).[29]

Quality, Not Quantity

With protein foods, as with all foods, quality is the key. While we don't want to eat too much protein, the protein we do eat should be satisfying and of high quality. During the year I underwent cancer treatment, the diet I was comfortable with had much less protein than I am currently eating. While my very low protein intake was appropriate for me at that time and was a necessary adjustment in the acute phase of my illness, years later I began to feel fatigued and knew my diet had to be modified. We need to be sensitive to changes in our condition: illness, age, lifestyle, taste, so that we can adapt our diet to our changing needs. The gauge is how we are responding and how we are feeling on a day-to-day basis; seek consultations when necessary. Pure vegetarianism may contribute to fatigue for some women. Adequate but not excessive protein intake will help women feel better. We need to be aware of our body's response to our food choices and be open to making necessary adjustments over time.

Legumes, nuts and seeds are nourishing protein-rich food choices. Tofu and tempeh can be prepared in a variety of ways. Organic eggs provide high-quality protein. Fish such as salmon, mackerel and sardines can provide both protein and the essential fatty acids that are so important. Small portions of organic meat (about two ounces) are also options. Our dietary needs reflect who we are and our health status. Protein needs are different if we are on a healing vs. a prevention diet. Children, adolescents, adult women and menopausal women all have differing needs. Where we live, the climate, the season, our occupations, our ethnic background and our individual tastes all impact on our needs and, ultimately, what will satisfy us as we attempt to achieve optimal health.

The Fat Connection

Research is abundant linking breast cancer to a high-fat diet. The standard American diet includes 40 percent of its calories from fat. Dietary animal fat, which is found in all red meat, poultry, dairy products and eggs, promotes, and with its toxic residues of pesticides and toxic chemicals, very likely initiates carcinogenesis.

Epidemiologic studies have repeatedly shown an association between dietary fat and the occurrence of breast cancer. The evidence is not new. The executive summary of the National Research Council's publication, *Diet, Nutrition and Cancer,* published in 1982, refers to the fact that both the high incidence and the mortality from breast cancer in various populations around the world correlates strongly with high per-capita fat consumption. Several international epidemiologic studies are cited in their report.

Seventh-Day Adventists, who have a breast cancer mortality one-half of that seen in the general U.S. population, have provided an interesting group for the study of breast cancer and diet. About half of them follow a vegetarian diet and nearly all avoid pork.[31] In one case-controlled study Phillips showed that five food categories significantly increased the risk of breast cancer: fried foods, fried potatoes, hard fat used for frying (butter, margarine, shortening), dairy products and white bread. How many Americans lunch on a grilled cheese sandwich on white bread with a side of fries! Another investigator found a significantly increased risk of breast cancer for women who consumed beef and other red meat, pork and sweet desserts.[30] Women who ate large amounts of meats had two to three times the risk of having breast cancer.

A recent and highly-publicized case-controlled study of American nurses from Harvard found no significant difference in breast cancer incidence between women in the lowest and the highest quintile of fat intake. This study has been challenged on methodologic grounds and calls into question the potential benefit of modest reductions of fat intake. As Dr. Neal Barnard commented, "Willett's study was brief—only four years—but it supports what most have suspected: to prevent cancer, fat intake must be reduced to the low levels found in China, Japan and other countries which enjoy low cancer rates."[31]

Japanese women eating traditional diets low in fat and protein and high in soy products have one quarter of breast cancer rates of American woman. Japanese immigrant studies show a dramatic increase in breast cancer rates as the diets of Japanese women are westernized. The same phenomenon occurred with the immigration of Polish women to the United States; a dramatic rise in their breast cancer rates occurred within one to two generations. Reflecting a rapid assimilation to the American diet/lifestyle, breast cancer rates increased from the relatively low rates characteristic of native Poles to the high rates experienced by American women.

Migration studies are critically important. Keeping genetics a constant, they point out the key role of environment, particularly diet, in the etiology of breast cancer. In *Save Yourself From Breast Cancer,* author Robert M. Kradjian, M.D. makes reference to more than 11 migration studies. He says, "In every one of these studies, a higher fat and lower fiber diet resulted in a loss of what was previously thought to be a genetic protection. Higher levels of breast cancer invariably followed. Migration studies alone are sufficient to convince me of the importance of lifestyle change."[32]

Kenneth K. Carroll, a biochemist from the University of Western Ontario, constructed a graph (Figure 6) that correlates estimated dietary fat intake (in grams of fat per day) with breast cancer death rates in various countries. The graph very dramatically shows the relationship between breast cancer deaths, fat in the diet and geographical distribution.

Evidence supports that a low-fat diet slows the progression of breast cancer. At the Japan Cancer Institute six of ten patients survived ten years past diagnosis as compared to three of ten for a similarly matched group in the U.S., at Vanderbilt University Hospital in Nashville, Tennessee.[33] The patients were otherwise matched for age, stage and treatment. Survival differences between Japanese and American breast cancer patients have been observed in other studies dating back to Dr. Ernst Wynder's work in the 1960s, attributing the lower fat content of the Japanese diet to the enhanced survival.[34]

Obese women have been shown in a number of epidemiologic studies to have a greater chance of early recurrence and shorter survival than nonobese patients. In one study the risk of death from breast cancer increased 1.4 fold for each 1000 grams of monthly fat intake.[35]

FIGURE 6.

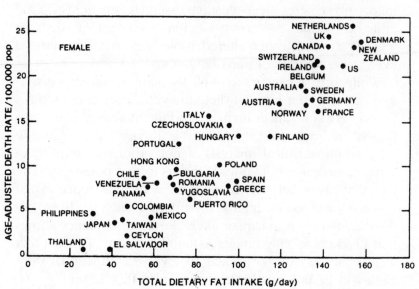

Laboratory findings also support the dietary fat/breast cancer link. As early as 1942, in his pioneering investigations, Tannenbaum showed that dietary fat significantly affected the development and growth of breast cancer in laboratory animals.[36]

Processed Fats Pose Health Risks

Fresh oils have characteristic flavors and fragrances. Freshness imparts distinctiveness as well as health benefits. The oil industry through the mass production of refined oils has created oils that are tasteless, devitalized, chemically changed and toxic. The destructive processing steps include technologies for seed preparation, distillation at 300 degrees, degumming, alkali refining, bleaching at 230 degrees, deodorizing at 450 degrees, artificial additives, carcinogenic preservatives (BHT, BHA, TBHQ) and hydrogenation. Perhaps, worst of all, processing creates trans fatty acids, a major group of altered molecules which interfere with many bodily processes including immune function. These treatments also destroy heat-sensitive essential fatty acids (EFAs) and the natural, protective vitamin E content of seeds as well as creating other altered molecules that are perhaps even more toxic than trans fatty acids.

While breast cancer, as well as many other cancers, is associated with a high-fat diet, an even closer correlation is found between cancer increase and the increased consumption of hydrogenated, trans fatty acid-containing vegetable oils. While statistical analysis is not proof that trans fatty acids cause cancer, it should alert us to that possibility. The fact that trans fatty acids interfere with vital functions of essential and other highly unsaturated fatty acids makes their involvement in cancer likely. Research evidence shows that EFAs (especially omega 3s) inhibit cancer. The fact that at least some cancers appear to involve a functional deficiency in EFAs lends further support to this theory.[37]

Not All Fats Are Bad

Now that the results of these convincing studies have filtered down through the media to the public, fat has become the villain in the standard American diet. However, it is far too simplistic to say cut all fat out of your diet. Some fats are essential to good health. Too much of the wrong kind of fat is certainly bad—but too little of the right kind is also detrimental. As Udo Erasmus notes, there are fats that heal and fats that kill.

Fats and oils are not just the padding on your hips and thighs, or a dietary no-no that can elevate your risk of breast cancer or heart disease. Fats and oils, in addition to their role in the storage of food energy, are the building blocks of our body, forming the structural core of each individual cell wall and providing the raw material for the creation of crucial hormones.

The prostanoid hormones or prostaglandins are short-distance messengers that are made by every cell of the body. As Dr. Sidney Baker describes it, when a cell wants to communicate with other nearby cells,

> it reaches for its own membrane, grabs a fatty acid (oil) molecule, makes it longer and more unsaturated, puts a loop in it, and launches it—all in less time than it took you to read this sentence. The "hole" left by the removal of a fatty acid molecule is left to be repaired by another derived from food. The hormones that are launched in this process are hot stuff. A cell cannot keep a pile of them lying around. Instead, it waits till the need for communication arises and then fashions the instruments for communication on the spot and out of its own cell membrane. Some are used for very short-distance communication among a few local cells. Others are released into the blood to send a general alarm or otherwise reach a large audience of cells . . . their effects are understood better in terms of a kind of orchestration of the balance among them than from trying to recognize the singular effects of any one of this large group of substances.[38]

We can understand how incredibly important the quality of our fat and oil intake is when we realize that at every moment our cells are rebuilding and repairing themselves, as well as speaking to one another, with these very substances. Prostaglandins are the language of our cells and essential fatty acids are the sole precursors.

Dr. Leo Galland writes that the whole spectrum of diseases that have become 20th century epidemics, including breast cancer, have a consistent prostaglandin (PG) pattern: the PG1 and PG3 series or their precursor fatty acids are deficient and one or more of the PG2 series are present in excess. Our intake of appropriate amounts of fresh, essential fats and oils can help restore our prostaglandin balance and our health. The primal human diet was lower in fat, however a larger part of the fat was in the form of EFAs. Today, the standard American diet is high in fat with just a small percentage consisting of these EFAs. The more non-EFAs in the diet, the more EFAs are required to balance them. EFAs control the production of about 50 prostaglandins, which are vital to the balance between health and disease.

The two families of EFAs are linoleic acid (LA) and alpha-linolenic acid (LNA). Linoleic acid is part of the polyunsaturated omega 6 family. Sunflower and safflower oils are the richest sources, but sesame, hemp, soybean, walnut, pumpkin, chestnut, flax and corn oils also contain LA. The new genetic varieties of high-oleic safflower and high-oleic sunflower oils have only small amounts of LA. Other sources of fatty acids in this family are borage, black currant seed oil, evening primrose oil, mother's breast milk and animal products. All of these can be utilized in the formation of series 1 and series 2 prostaglandins (PG1 and PG2).

Alpha-linolenic acid is part of the superunsaturated omega 3 family. Flax seeds are the richest source of LNA which is also found in hemp seed, canola, soybean, walnut, pumpkin seed, chestnut and dark green leafy vegetables. Other sources of fatty acids in this family are black currant seeds and the oils of cold water fish including salmon, trout, mackerel and sardines. All these can be utilized in the synthesis of series 3 prostaglandins (PG3). Omega 3 fatty acids decrease the risk of breast cancer.

Soybean oil, walnut oil, and hemp oil contain both omega 3 and omega 6 EFAs.

Flaxseeds also Contain Substances Known as Lignans

High levels of lignans have been associated with a low incidence of breast cancer. Like soy isoflavones and the drug tamoxifen, lignans bind to estrogen receptors and act both as a weak estrogen and an anti-estrogen. Lignans may also increase production of sex-hormone-binding globulin (a carrier molecule) which transports estrogen through the bloodstream, effecting its *in vivo* activity and elimination dynamics. Through its function as a carrier molecule, sex-hormone-binding globulin (SHBG) regulates the amount of biologically active estrogen. Women who develop breast cancer have lower levels of SHBG. In the definitive text, *Clinical Gynecologic Endocrinology and Infertility,* by Drs. Speroff, Glass and Kase it is noted that, "Perhaps SHBG measurements should be added to our screening efforts."[39] Flax contains the highest levels of plant lignans. It has 100 times the amount of lignan as does its closest competitors, wheat bran, rye, buckwheat, millet, soy beans, walnuts and oats. Flax oil contains only a small amount of lignans compared to the seeds or seed cake from which it is extracted.

Udo Erasmus discusses the importance of the balance of omega 6 to omega 3 fatty acids in achieving optimal health. He suggests a ratio of approximately three parts omega 6 to one part omega 3. He believes that the standard American diet is too rich in omega 6 fatty acids, which encourages the overproduction of the PG2 series leading to breast cancer and other health problems.

Obviously we cannot start counting fatty acid molecules, so how can we apply this information in a practical way? I recommend a blend called "Udo's Choice" formulated by Erasmus to achieve a physiologically optimal balance of these essential oils. The blend is an omega-3 rich dietary oil that supplies both EFAs and contains a variety of minor ingredients with major health benefits. It is available in most health food stores.

One could also incorporate flaxseed oil into the diet through supplements or by using it in a salad dressing. Flaxseed oil must not be heated or exposed to light. Flax seeds, valuable for lignans and fiber as well as oil, absorb five times their volume in water, so take them with adequate fluid. Try sprinkling freshly ground flax seeds on your cereal. I use an already prepared granular product formulated by Erasmus called "The Missing Link" which contains flax seeds and a number of other foods and food concentrates rich in essential nutrients, fiber, enzymes and friendly bacteria (see Resources).

Our bodies cannot synthesize LA and LNA, the two essential fatty acids that are the exclusive raw material for PG synthesis. They are an absolute dietary requirement for our health and they must be derived from the foods we eat. In order to turn EFAs into PGs we also need the following minerals: magnesium, iron, selenium and zinc, as well as the following vitamins: biotin, B3, B6, vitamin C and vitamin E. The following substances and processes block the conversion of LA and LNA to beneficial PGs: sugar, stress, alcohol and non-EFAs. Non-EFAs come from saturated animal fats, saturated tropical vegetable oils, heat-damaged fats from deep-frying and synthetic fats. These substances favor the formation of unbalanced, excessive and therefore damaging levels of PG2. The process of partial hydrogenation used in the production of margarine and too many of our processed foods turns LA and LNA into the synthetic fatty acids called trans fatty acids which are harmful to our health.

Taking Care of Essential Fatty Acids

Heat used in hydrogenation, commercial frying and deep-frying destroys EFAs by twisting their molecules from a natural *cis* configuration into an unnatural *trans* shape. The results of this twist are far-ranging: cis and trans molecules have different melting points, different chemical activities and different enzyme fits. Biologically, these processed trans fatty acids do not fit properly into our enzymes and membrane structures. However, they do incorporate well enough to effectively block the cis forms from binding yet they cannot do the job required. When they are incorporated into membranes, permeability is impaired and the membranes leak. On a molecular level trans fatty acids are disruptive.

Avoid these altered fats, specifically margarines (both hard and soft), shortenings and partially hydrogenated vegetable oils (used in processed, convenience and junk foods). Fried and deep-fried foods should be avoided because of the heat-damaging effects. When you read labels you will find that the supermarket shelves are packed with products containing partially hydrogenated oils. Herbert Dutton, one of the oldest and most knowledgeable oil chemists in North America said, "If the hydrogenation process were discovered today, it probably could not be adopted by the oil industry ... the basis for such comment lies in the recent awareness of our prior ignorance concerning the complexity of isomers formed during hydrogenation and their metabolic and physiologic fate."[40]

Light is also very destructive to EFAs, producing free radicals and speeding up the reaction of the oil with oxygen. This breaks down EFAs and results in rancid oil.

Nature knows better and therefore packages her oils in seeds that keep heat, light and oxygen out. Fresh raw seeds and nuts contain no altered fats. They are good choices in small quantities to provide us with EFAs. Although frying destroys all oils, some are damaged less than others. Frying produces free radicals that start damaging chain reactions in oil molecules, trans fatty acids and other more toxic oxidation products.

Butter Is Better

The butter vs. margarine question has received a great deal of media attention. Organic butter is the winner on taste, naturalness, digestibility and usefulness for frying. Margarine contains dozens of non-natural toxic molecules from the process of partial hydrogenation and is unsuitable for frying or for any purpose, for that matter. Neither butter nor margarine provides a good source of EFAs. In order to make your butter more healthful, try blending it with flaxseed oil. The addition of herbs such as garlic or parsley can also enhance the taste and health benefits of butter.

To recap this important point: our bodies depend on optimal quality and optimal quantity of fresh oils for both our structural and functional integrity and to protect us from a wide range of disease states.

Guidelines for a Healthy Oil Balance

1. Which Oils to Choose

When on a healing diet, it is best to avoid heating oils altogether. The best choice is sautéeing in water or vegetable broth. If, on occasion, you choose to sauté with oil, add a few drops of water to your pan first, heat and then add a teaspoon or two of oil; this will keep the temperature down and protect the oil from heat damage. Organic butter and organic sesame oil are reasonable selections for cooking and can be used sparingly by those in good health. Olive oil can be used for lower temperature cooking; however, some of the health-enhancing minor components of olive oil are not heat-stable.

We can dip our breads in fresh olive or flaxseed oil as is the custom in Mediterranean countries, eliminating the need for manufactured spreads. Those populations that consume high levels of olive oil have relatively low breast cancer rates. They use more unheated olive oil and also use fresher oils, very important components of the healthy oil equation. Fresh flaxseed oil can be mixed with other ingredients and used on salads or on vegetables after cooking; a small amount of these oils may be added to organic eggs after cooking to both enhance the taste and the nutritional value. In order to get my two tablespoons per day of EFAs, I use an oil blend called Udo's Choice on my pasta, with organic tomato sauce and garlic. I also use it on my morning cereal—white or yellow corn grits, rolled oats or barley flakes along with a dollop of maple syrup.

Walnuts, chestnuts, fresh raw sunflower, pumpkin and sesame seeds are also good sources of EFAs, but contain mostly omega-6s.

2. How to Process, Transport and Store Oils

"Oils should be mechanically pressed (as opposed to chemically, solvent-extracted) from pesticide-free seeds at low temperatures with light and oxygen excluded; they should remain unrefined and unheated; and should be stored in completely opaque, inert metal, earthen, or glass containers, kept frozen in storage, and refrigerated or frozen in our homes," according to Udo Erasmus. Fats and oils are best used when fresh and need protection from light, oxygen and heat. Proper packaging and storage can maximize their nutrient value and minimize damaging changes in the form of light-induced free radicals, heat-induced trans isomer formation and oxygen-induced rancidity. Spoiled or rancid fats contain oxidants, some of which are powerful promoters of cancer.

It is interesting to note that the oils on supermarket shelves are most often packaged in clear bottles with no protection from light or heat. If they are packaged in plastic containers, chemicals may leach into the oil. Perhaps most indicative of their nutritional inertness is the fact that commercial oils can stay on supermarket shelves indefinitely. High quality oils have a pressing date, an expiration date and must be refrigerated just as any fresh food would be.

3. How to Get the Most from Your EFAs

Reduce sugar, alcohol, saturated fat (animal foods, dairy, tropical oils) and synthetic fats which interfere with our ability to utilize essential fatty acids. As noted above, vitamin and minerals levels also need to be optimal in order to synthesize prostaglandins from EFAs.

4. A Word about Enzymes

The importance of pancreatic enzymes in the digestion, absorption and utilization of essential fatty acids and other micro and macronutrients cannot be overstated. The pancreas pumps nearly half a gallon of pancreatic juice into the small intestine daily. This juice is a blend of amylases, lipases and proteases which break down, respectively, starches, fats and proteins. Mild insufficiency of the pancreas is thought to be quite common, particularly among the elderly. Symptoms of this insufficiency include gas, indigestion, abdominal bloating and discomfort as well as the nutrient deficiencies that arise from impaired digestion. Lipase, in particular, can be a beneficial supplement in the digestion and utilization of EFAs.

At a lecture I attended in New York City in 1995, Nicholas Gonzalez, M.D. a well-known alternative cancer treatment practitioner, discussed his belief that a combination of deficient pancreatic enzymes in the presence of excessive estrogen sets the stage for the uncontrolled growth of breast cancer. His beliefs and treatments are based on the work of embryologist and author John Beard, who studied mammalian placentas. Beard noted that mammalian placental growth was limited in time and that the fall-off in placental growth coincided with the beginning of pancreatic enzyme production. He theorized that it was pancreatic enzymes that controlled the growth of the placenta and further, that primitive cells throughout the body are kept dormant by adequate pancreatic enzymes. Beard thought that an inadequate supply of pancreatic enzymes released primitive cells from their inhibition and was responsible for the development of tumors. Dr. Gonzalez also studied and developed protocols based on the work of Dr. William D. Kelley, who used pancreatic enzymes in the successful treatment of his own cancer. Dr. Kelley believed that protein-digesting pancreatic enzymes are the body's first defense against tumors and that the pancreas secretes enzymes into the bloodstream, where they digest cancer cells. Digestive enzymes are used extensively in Eastern Europe for the treatment of various cancers.

In the Introduction to *Enzyme Nutrition* by Dr. Edward Howell, a physician and biochemist who devoted a lifetime to pioneering research on food enzymes, medical writer Linda Clark comments, ". . . Dr. Howell exposes the crippled attempts of modern medicine to heal disease and its failure to attack the root of the problem. His conclusion is that many, if not all, degenerative diseases that humans suffer and die from are caused by the excessive use of enzyme-deficient cooked and processed foods."[41]

CONNECTING NOURISHMENT WITH NURTURANCE

In a culture that is obsessed with food it is important to clarify our connection to food. Americans spend $33 billion a year on losing weight. Twenty million women have eating disorders, and 50 percent of all women are constantly dieting.

"Because our patterns of eating were formed by early patterns of loving, it is necessary to understand and work with both food and love to feel satisfied with our relationship to either," writes Geneen Roth in her eye-opening book *When Food is Love*. It is easier to comprehend the principles of healthy eating discussed in this chapter than it is to incorporate these same principles into our daily living. In order to effect optimal changes, adjustments must be made in shopping patterns and meal plans; moreover, specific foods need to be eliminated, some of which may be associated with love on an unconscious level. For women who have used food as a substitute for love, making significant changes in eating patterns and food choices can be frightening and difficult.

We must address our emotional issues along with changes in our diet. The path to healing will be incomplete if we focus solely on food choices and ignore the role food plays in our emotional lives. Pain that was blotted out by assuming unhealthy eating patterns in the first place will reemerge if not addressed.

Our task is to:

- Connect eating nourishing foods with taking care of ourselves.
- Uncover and work with the emotional issues that are connected to unhealthy eating patterns.

It is important to find your own comfort level with these guidelines. If there are too many rules for you and you find yourself turning your focus outside rather than inside, simplify the guidelines. Pay attention to what feels right for you, physically and emotionally. When you can validate the experience of healthful living on the inside you are on the way. You will begin to know on a gut level what is healthy. Then your eating patterns can really change, your relationships can change and your health will change.

> When my mom got sick I
> felt scared but you shouldn't feel scared because you
> can do things to help your mom like
> asking your dad to visit your mom spending alot of
>   time with
> her and you can help yourself by not eating meat or
> alot of dairy products but eating occasionally fish
>
> —by Zachary, age 8

SUPPLEMENTS—A REASONABLE APPROACH

Cancer as a Deficiency Disease

The concept of cancer as a deficiency disease is an interesting notion worth considering. In an article on the subject of food and cancer prevention in *Cancer Causes and Con-*

Important Food Guidelines

1. Eat whole grains. Unrefined, unprocessed grains will maximize nutrient density and naturally provide fiber, which eliminates carcinogens and excess estrogens from the gastrointestinal system quickly. Avoid nutrient-depleted processed and refined foods.
2. Eat organic produce. Organic vegetables have substantially more nutrients and fewer toxic residues. Substantially increase your consumption of a wide variety of organic vegetables. Eat five or more servings of vegetables each day. Include fresh vegetable juices, rich in enzymes, to enhance digestion.
3. Get a balance of the two essential fatty acids by incorporating fresh oils and fresh nuts and seeds into your diet. Avoid margarine, shortening and partially hydrogenated oils which contain dangerous trans fatty acids.
4. Remember the value of high quality protein: legumes, nuts, seeds, tempeh, fish, organic eggs.
5. Incorporate soy products including tofu and fermented soy products such as tempeh, miso and shoyu (soy sauce).
6. Decrease dietary animal fat substantially. This includes red meat, poultry, luncheon meats and dairy foods. This will decrease excessive protein intake, unhealthy fats, toxic residues and synthetic hormone additives.
7. Eliminate junk food. What you eat is as important as what you don't eat. Avoid sugar, artificial sweeteners, soft drinks, candy, commercial chips and processed foods. Eliminate alcohol, drugs and caffeine.
8. Always read the ingredients on all packaged foods.
9. Pure water is vital for drinking and cooking.
10. Don't underestimate the power of your emotional connections to food.

trol[42] the authors view cancer as a response to nutritional deficiencies. They point out that the cancer patient's diet may lack the nutrients needed to create detoxification enzymes, stop the formation of cancer cells, dilute and bind cancer-causing substances in the digestive tract, supply antioxidant activity and generally support the body's defense.

The fact that breast cancer has been increasing in frequency over the past 50 years is testimony to the fact that no matter what our high-technology treatments have to offer they have no bearing on the rising tide of increased incidence. And the corollary is that in spite of all the publicity surrounding early detection, age-adjusted mortality rates have not shown the hoped-for decline.

In the natural course of events a healthy immune system can remove the cancer cells that develop throughout our lives. However, our 20th century lifestyle, with its exposures to chemicals, radiation, free radicals, viruses, unbalanced hormones, emotional stresses and a nutritionally depleted food supply, has rendered our immune system dysfunctional.

What, in addition to eating nourishing foods, can we do to bolster our immunity and increase our resistance to breast cancer? Supplemental nutrients can and have been proven to enhance the immune system. The antioxidant vitamins A, C and E, the antioxidant mineral selenium, and other vitamins and minerals are all part of a complex interactive system. With adequate levels of nutrients many key enzymes such as superoxide dismutase, catalase and glutathione peroxidase can be produced in adequate quantities and will assist in attaining optimum immunologic functioning.

ESSENTIAL NUTRIENTS

There are approximately 50 essential nutrients—substances that our bodies need but do not have the ability to make, at least in sufficient quantity. These include the vitamins and minerals, other micronutrients, essential amino acids from protein foods and essential fatty acids from oils. Gov-

ernment studies have shown that most Americans are deficient in one or more of these essential nutrients, nutrients
that our bodies have no way of making and cannot do
without. Whole foods are the best way to obtain them; nutrient supplements can be supportive and restorative.

Two government surveys—the Health and Nutrition Examination Survey (1971–1974) and the Nationwide Food
Consumption Survey (1977–1978) measured the intake of
13 essential nutrients in tens of thousands of people. Of the
13 nutrients only sodium was present in adequate amounts
(actually some people suffer from sodium toxicity from the
overuse of table salt). The following chart summarizes these
findings and the findings of similar studies:

FIGURE 7

NUTRIENT	% WHO GET LESS THAN RDA	NUTRIENT	% WHO GET LESS THAN RDA
Calcium	68%	Vitamin B$_1$	45%
Folacin	10+%	Vitamin B$_2$	34%
Iron	57%	Vitamin B$_3$	33%
Magnesium	75%	Vitamin B$_6$	80%
Phosphorus	27%	Vitamin B$_{12}$	34%
Vitamin A	50%	Vitamin C	41%
Biotin	10%	Silicon	30%
Chromium	90%	Vitamin D	10%
Copper	85–90%	Vitamin E	20–40%
Manganese	20–30%	Vitamin K	15%
Pantothenic acid	25%	Omega 3 fats	95%
Selenium	50–60%	Zinc	35–60%

There are a number of reasons why it can be difficult to
obtain adequate nutrients from our food:

- "Let food be thy medicine and thy medicine food."
  Hippocrates taught that food was the foundation of

health nearly 2,500 years ago, but health is not a priority when Americans go to the grocery store today.

- As a culture we have not been educated regarding the
  basics of a healthful diet. The average training in nutrition received during four years of medical school by
  U.S. physicians is 2.5 hours.[43]
- The quality of our food has declined; as a result of
  the topsoil erosion induced by the farming practices of
  modern agribusiness there are progressively diminishing nutrients in the soil, and thus in our food.
- There are real obstacles in the quest for nutritious food;
  it is difficult to obtain a wide variety of fresh local
  organic foods with a full complement of nutrients without the depletion that is inevitable with transport and
  storage.

For these reasons, most people can benefit from nutritional supplements. There is substantial evidence that food-
based supplements can have preventive as well as therapeutic benefits. For women acting to prevent cancer as well
as for those undergoing treatment for and recovering from
cancer, a program including balanced supplementation in
addition to a healing diet will assist the body in many ways.

The development of cancer suggests a depleted internal
environment, a lack of natural resources. Supplements can
help replenish the body; they can assist in the healing from
surgery and promote the detoxification and excretion of
chemotherapeutic drugs, thus easing their serious side effects. Supplements can also assist the body in the recovery
from radiation injury sustained in the course of treatment
and can be helpful in renewing the emotional energy necessary to embark on a healing path.

Physicians specializing in nutritional biochemistry and/or
environmental medicine can scientifically measure antioxidant systems and vitamin and mineral levels intracellularly
and thus target supplementation for each individual patient.
By measuring cell growth in specific media we can investi-

gate how well each nutrient functions as opposed to just measuring levels of vitamins and minerals in the blood, urine or hair. The bottom line in nutrient status is really how well nutrients function within our cells, reflecting not only the food we eat but how it is absorbed and utilized. Biochemical individuality is the overriding principle.

However, getting insurance reimbursement for nutritional investigations and therapy can be difficult if not impossible. Even more unfortunate is the fact that most doctors are not motivated to know more about nutritional adequacy and its role in cancer. Before I got ill, I was programmed so negatively from my medical school and residency training that even I thought people who took supplements were hypochondriacs!

∾ *Remember...*

The energy and love present in a whole food cannot be bottled. Vitamins and minerals are best absorbed through a healthy diet. However, when a cancer patient is depleted, supplements can make a life-saving contribution. Supplements are just that—they *add to* a nutrient-rich whole foods diet.

SUGGESTED SUPPLEMENTS FOR WOMEN UNDERGOING TREATMENT FOR BREAST CANCER

Women undergoing treatment for breast cancer need to meet and exceed the normal nutrient requirements of a body in good health. After treatment for breast cancer, your body is spending extra energy and essential nutrients in mending physical wounds and processing toxic chemicals and radiation. You are also physically processing the hormonal counterparts of the emotional stress associated with your diagnosis.

The recommended daily allowances (RDAs) are meaningless in the context of treatment for breast cancer. RDAs are intake standards that the government has set to prevent deficiency states in otherwise healthy people. These levels are minimal, not optimal. While normal human weight and height may vary by 200 percent, their biochemical requirements may vary by more than 2,000 percent.

The concept of Optimal Daily Allowances put forth by nutritionist Shari Lieberman, Ph.D. is more to the point. In *The Real Vitamin and Mineral Book* Lieberman writes:

We have gradually expanded our knowledge and our thinking to include the notion that health should no longer be negatively defined as the absence of disease. Our current concept of real health is not one of mere survival—it is a positive state of total mental and physical well-being . . . In order to attain this state of optimal health and disease prevention, we must take into our bodies *optimum*—not minimum—amounts of vitamins and minerals. To distinguish them from the lesser amounts characteristic of the RDAs, I have called these amounts the *Optimum Daily Allowances,* or *ODAs.*[44]

Dr. Andrew Weil reiterates this point in the premiere issue of his newsletter, *Self Healing,*

Another action of some vitamins and minerals in higher than recommended doses is as natural preventive agents. I consider the antioxidants I take to be in this category, for example. If you think of vitamins and minerals only as vitamins and minerals—that is, as essential nutrients needed in small amounts to prevent deficiency states—then it seems that we should be able to get them from our diets . . . But if I want to use these substances as natural preventive agents to reduce oxidative damage to my cells and tissues, then I believe I need to use them in supplemental form to achieve the necessary doses.[45]

The concept of vitamins, minerals and other food substances as natural preventive, and in some cases therapeutic, agents is fairly new. The term nutraceutical was coined by Stephen L. DeFelice, M.D., chairman of the Foundation for Innovation in Medicine to indicate "any substance that may be considered a food, or part of a food, and provides medical or health benefits, including the prevention and treatment of disease."[46] The boundary is very thin indeed between foods and medicines; in fact, botanicals are currently the source of 25 percent of our pharmaceuticals. We all have unique biochemical requirements and will serve our bodies well by trying to meet our unique needs in the context of our current health conditions.

All the essential nutrients are important for optimal functioning. I want to bring attention to those supplements that have particular relevance to breast cancer. This will not be an exhaustive review, but a starting point for you to explore further.

THE ANTIOXIDANT STORY

In all of nature what can be valuable, essential and healing in one dose and form can be dangerous in another. Even oxygen, which is essential to all life, has the potential to do harm. Oxygen has a predilection for creating free radicals, which are unstable molecules with unpaired electrons that can cause damage in the body. Free radical damage to DNA has been directly linked to breast cancer. Yet all of life is a balancing act; pro-oxidants are actually a useful component of our immune system, part of our self-defense mechanism. White blood cells are capable of producing oxidative bursts of superoxide free radicals and hydrogen peroxide when detecting and detoxifying harmful bacteria. So the point isn't that oxidants are bad, but they must be carefully managed. Antioxidant vitamins and minerals do just that: they precisely control the body's ability to oxidize and see that this function remains well-regulated.

Antioxidants function within a system that also includes other nutrients, enzymes and bacteria. Intestinal bacteria decompose substances that can otherwise develop into oxidants leading to uncontrolled damaging oxidation. The gut, as such, actively interacts with our environment, it is not a passive passageway. Once oxidants form, the enzymes, superoxide dismutase and glutathione peroxidase, break them down. Coenzymes and cofactors assist this process. These include selenium, copper, vitamin B2, glutathione, coenzyme Q10, cysteine, manganese, zinc and bioflavonoids. If oxidants are forming at too fast a rate, nutrient antioxidants are available to restore balance.

Vitamin A, Beta-carotene and Other Carotenoids

Over 30 years of research have linked vitamin A, beta-carotene and lycopene with a decreased risk of cancer. Vitamin A has anticancer properties. The growth of human breast cancer cells is decreased by vitamin A.[47] Vitamin A appears to lower the incidence of breast cancer in women and to slow the spread of breast cancer in animal studies. Low dietary levels of vitamin A have been associated with increased risk of breast cancer. In a study of women with metastatic breast cancer, when vitamin A was combined with chemotherapy there was a significant increase in complete response rate.[48]

It is estimated that 25 percent of the population has a diet that supplies less than the recommended daily allowance, which is surely less than what is necessary for optimal functioning and considerably less than what is needed for a healing regime. Vitamin A requirements increase with illness, infection, trauma, anxiety, stress and alcohol use. BHT, a common food additive, depletes vitamin A, underscoring the importance of integrating a whole-food approach along with vitamin therapy.

Vitamin A is vital for normal growth, good vision, and healthy skin and hair. It is essential for normal immune function. Vitamin A protects the external skin and the body's "internal skin" or mucus membranes, thereby help-ing the body fight infection and environmental pollution. By protecting the gut lining we can then absorb other essential nutrients. Vitamin A's ability to neutralize free radicals is one of the ways it protects membranes. By protecting the endoplasmic reticulum, the intracellular membrane where detoxification occurs, vitamin A protects the function of de-toxification. We all need to detoxify the environmental con-taminants that contribute to the formation of cancer. Vitamin A is not only important in detoxifying chemotherapy; it en-hances the effectiveness of chemotherapy. Ralph Moss, member of the Alternative Medicine Advisory Council of the National Institute of Health writes, "Beta-carotene and other retinoids improved tissue tolerance of animals undergoing both chemotherapy and radiotherapy with no adverse ef-fects on the tumor-killing ability of these methods."[49]

Vitamins act in concert. Vitamin A works best with adequate zinc levels, adequate protein levels and adequate vitamin E levels. Zinc is needed to release stores of vitamin A. Vitamin E is necessary for proper absorption of vitamin A. When vitamin A is deficient, vitamin C is lost more rap-idly from the gut. Stress and alcohol deplete vitamin A; alcohol also interferes with the absorption of vitamin A.

Beta-carotene has its own function in addition to precursor activity. Several carotene pigments can be con-verted into vitamin A. Beta-carotene is one of about 500 colorful food pigments, 50 of which are of biological impor-tance. Beta-carotene is the most available of these pigments and is called provitamin A. Beta-carotene acting as a precur-sor is converted to vitamin A as the body requires it. In decreasing cancer risk, beta-carotene has an important role independent of this conversion. Intact beta-carotene has been shown to have anti-tumor activity and may also detox-ify carcinogens. It is an excellent defender against singlet oxygen free radicals. Breast cancer tissue shows decreased levels of beta-carotene.[50] Decreased levels of beta-carotene in the blood of breast cancer patients may indicate a role for this provitamin in the development of breast cancer.[51] Whereas vitamin A can be toxic in high doses over extended periods of time, beta-carotene is quite safe.

Beta-carotene increases a group of substances known as cytokines, which help the body work against cancer: interferon, interleukin, tumor necrosis factor. All of these substances have been used within the scientific community as adjunctive treatments. It makes intuitive sense to me to allow the body to make these substances through its own mechanisms, given adequate dietary and supplemental precursors, trusting that a more physiologic balance will be achieved.

In a small study at the University of Pavia in Italy, beta-carotene given to decrease breast cancer recurrences resulted in an increase in disease-free survival.[52] Various studies show that women who consume more vitamin A and beta-carotene decrease their risk for breast cancer. A review article showed 10 of 14 studies supporting the link between beta-carotene and protection from breast cancer.[53] In a number of dietary studies around the world the increased consumption of foods high in beta-carotene has been associated with dramatic reductions in breast cancer rates both for pre-and post menopausal women. Diets high in orange and dark leafy green vegetables offer a host of other important nutrients in addition to beta-carotene.

Some dietary researchers have concluded that supplements are helpful in the prevention of breast cancer only for those suffering from outright deficiency states. The implication is that here in America, in the land of plenty, we could not possibly be suffering from nutrient deficiencies. In fact, the truth is that many of us are malnourished; we are starving for essential nutrients as we eat processed foods. The medical community is unaware of the scope of the problem. I believe that cancer in many cases develops out of a deficiency state caused by a diet of depleted foods and exacerbated by our highly polluted environment. It is very likely that many women in this country suffer from nutrient deficiencies. Optimization of our nutrient status should be a high priority in health care even if we are not in outright deficiency states.

Examination of beta-carotene's effects reveals that this supplement is very promising for breast cancer prevention and adjunctive treatment. A group of leading nutritional researchers from all over the United States wrote in the publication *Nutrition Reviews* that the data clearly supports the claim that antioxidant nutrients may decrease the risk of cancer.[54] It never ceases to amaze me how the FDA and conventional medicine, with its poor success rates in the treatment of many cancers and the well-known side effects of chemo, choose to point accusingly at the use of supplements as if their efficacy was being put forth in a deceptive manner. I see the situation very differently: I see many patients blindly faithful to conventional treatments who are unable to take advantage of the wealth of nutritional research because of our culture's inborn suspicion of complementary nutritional approaches and the medical community's inadequate validation of the importance of nutrition.

David Kritchevsky, Ph.D. states in the journal *Cancer* that, "Breast cancer might be prevented if more women were to get sufficient amounts of vitamin A, beta-carotene and the other carotenoids."[55] Active vitamin A is found only in animal sources. It is especially high in the fish liver oil from cod, halibut, salmon and shark; it is also found in eggs. Good food sources for the carotenoids are leafy greens and yellow vegetables. Seaweed, broccoli, kale, parsley, Brussels sprouts, Romaine lettuce, mustard greens, peas, dandelion greens, beet greens, collards and asparagus are good green sources. Carrots, sweet potatoes, winter squash, yams, corn and pumpkins are good yellow sources. Red cabbage, cauliflower and turnips are also good choices. Apricots, peaches, cantaloupe, tangerines, prunes, nectarines, mango, papaya and watermelon are good fruit sources.

Be advised that beta-carotene in produce is easily destroyed in storage and when exposed to light, oxygen and processing. Therefore, it is important to buy and eat fresh, local produce when possible. Planting your own vegetable garden is worth considering, yielding food for both body and soul.

What are reasonable supplement dosages?

- **Vitamin A - 5,000 IU daily.**
- **Beta-carotene - 25,000–50,000 IU daily.**

Carotenoids are best assimilated if taken with fat. Take these supplements at mealtime or with your essential fatty acids. Supplements containing a full range of carotenoids are closer to the spectrum found in food sources. The latest research shows that other carotenoids present in food may work with beta-carotene and offer additional health benefits. As these mixed-carotenoid formulas come on the market we can take advantage of their greater range of activity.

Vitamin C and Bioflavonoids

Among its many functions, vitamin C is a cofactor in various important enzyme-mediated chain reactions. It regenerates vitamin E, helping the immune system to function optimally. Adequate vitamin C prevents other antioxidant vitamins such as A and E from being oxidized in the body. Vitamin C is required by the adrenals to synthesize hormones that regulate stress. Vitamin C has been shown to impact favorably on the cancer-causing effects of more than 50 common pollutants.[56] Vitamin C given to guinea pigs whose cancer was being treated with adriamycin effectively prevented the drug-induced damage.[57] One of vitamin C's mechanisms of action is free radical scavenging. It functions in other ways as well.

Nobel laureate Linus Pauling believed vitamin C may turn out to be the most important of all nutrients in the control of cancer. Pauling claimed that large amounts (greater than 10 grams/day) inhibit the growth of cancer. Linus Pauling took 18,000 mg of vitamin C per day. In 1990 Pauling teamed up with Dr. Abram Hoffer and published a study of women with cancer who received high doses of vitamin C. The "good responder" subset of patients who received vitamin C lived 16 times longer than those who did not get the treatment.[58] Although the role of vitamin C in the treatment of cancer is debated, its immune-enhancing abilities are certainly valuable in a cancer prevention program and in mitigating the side effects of chemotherapy. Pauling noted that "vitamin C . . . controls to a considerable extent the disagreeable side effects of the cytotoxic chemotherapeutic agents, such as nausea and loss of hair, and that benefit seems to add its value to that of the chemotherapeutic agent. We now recommend a high intake of vitamin C, in some cases up to the bowel-tolerance limit, beginning as early as possible."[59]

After reviewing over 90 studies on the relationship between vitamin C and cancer, Gladys Block, Ph.D., of the University of California at Berkeley, concludes, "There is overwhelming evidence of the protective effect of vitamin C and other antioxidants against cancer of the breast."[60] And Geoffrey R. Howe of the National Cancer Institute of Canada reviewed 12 case-controlled studies of diet and breast cancer and noted that vitamin C had the most consistent statistically significant inverse relationship with breast cancer risk.[61]

Humans are unique in the animal kingdom in their inability to produce or store their own supply of vitamin C. Other animals produce generous amounts of vitamin C and do not require dietary sources.

Fresh fruits and vegetables are good sources for vitamin C. The foods that are the highest are leafy greens (kale, parsley, collards), broccoli and Brussels sprouts. Citrus fruits (oranges, grapefruits, tangerines, lemons), tomatoes, strawberries, cabbage, cantaloupe, cauliflower, asparagus and potatoes are good choices. Vitamin C is very perishable and can be diminished by cooking—especially in water, or by heat, oxygen and time. Vegetables should be eaten raw or lightly steamed to retain most of this vitamin. Juice sold in bottles or cartons have almost no vitamin C.

Bioflavonoids are a family of substances thought to enhance, protect and increase the absorption of vitamin C. Bioflavonoids detoxify carcinogens and may inhibit the development of cancer. The best known bioflavonoids are rutin, citrin, hesperidin and quercetin. Bioflavonoids are found in the white pulp of citrus fruits, in grapes, plums, black currants, apricots, buckwheat, cherries, blackberries and rose hips.

How much is a reasonable supplement dosage? Dr. Emanuel Cheraskin believes that most Americans need between 2 and 10 grams of vitamin C daily, although the RDA is only 60 mg for an adult. Dr. Robert Cathcart developed a technique of taking vitamin C to bowel tolerance. What he found was that the sicker the patient, the more vitamin C she could tolerate before getting diarrhea. For cancer patients he found that 15 to 100 grams every 24 hours in four to 15 divided doses was a safe and effective range. Diarrhea indicates the need to back off on the dosage. If taking vitamin C to bowel tolerance, be sure not to cut back too quickly, but to reduce the dosage over time. I suggest:

- **3–5 gm per day for breast cancer prevention and general health maintenance.**
- **5–10 gm per day for breast cancer treatment phase.**

Vitamin C is best taken in divided doses throughout the day.

Vitamin E

One of the body's most potent antioxidants, this lipid-soluble vitamin protects fats in areas of high oxygen concentration like the bloodstream as well as cell walls and within cells from free radical damage. In this same way, liquid vitamin E added to salad and cooking oils will protect them from rancidity. Vitamin C is useful in regenerating and extending the life of vitamin E.

Vitamin E is actually a family of compounds called the tocopherols—alpha, beta, delta and gamma and the tocotrienols. The alpha forms are the most active; d-alpha-tocopherol is the name given to the form of tocopherol found in vegetable oils; dl-tocopherol is the synthetic analog. Tocotrienols are more potent antioxidants than tocopherols. Supplements usually contain only alpha-tocopherols. Supplements can be purchased as "mixed" tocopherols, as they exist in food. The structural variety of tocopherols in food sources is likely related to a full range of vitamin E activity. Some of the roles of vitamin E in the body are:

- Antioxidant—working with selenium against free radicals.
- Helping in the production of the antioxidant enzyme superoxide dismutase.
- Protecting the body from carcinogens, heavy metals and chemicals.
- Protecting vitamin A and vitamin C from oxidation.
- Decreasing side effects from chemotherapy.

Vitamin E and estrogen/progesterone ratios.

It is clear that our estrogen/progesterone balance has a major impact on the development of breast cancer. Doctors at the North Charles General Hospital in Baltimore, MD studied the effect of 600 IU vitamin E daily on women with nonmalignant breast disease and controls. They monitored clinical response, measured hormone levels of estradiol, estriol and progesterone as well as blood levels of vitamin E. Eighty-eight percent of the women showed a clinical response to vitamin E administration; the ratio of progesterone/estradiol increased favorably in those who received vitamin E. According to these doctors, "Results of this study indicate that vitamin E therapy may correct an abnormal progesterone/estradiol ratio . . . with implications on reducing future risk for malignant breast disease."[62] A large-scale study in Finland which followed women over an eight-year time period showed that women who had the lowest blood levels of vitamin E had more than a one-and-half times greater chance of developing cancer than the women with the highest levels of this vitamin.[63]

Vitamin E is found in unrefined safflower and other vegetable oils, in the inner oil-rich germ of wheat, barley and other whole grains, in dark green leafy vegetables such as kale, collards, broccoli, mustard greens and lettuce, in egg yolks, legumes, seeds and nuts. The more refined the oil, the lower the natural vitamin E content. The more refined supermarket polyunsaturated oils that one consumes, the more vitamin E is required to protect your body from the oxidative damage that can follow. Choose cold-pressed oils from your health food store. High consumption of processed polyunsaturated fats, refined grains and white flour products which are depleted of vitamin E puts one at a high risk for deficiency of this vitamin.

A suggested dose for general health maintenance is 400 IU daily. For those undergoing chemotherapy or radiation a dose up to 1,200 IU daily may be more appropriate. This dose offers protection against the unpleasant side effects of chemo such as nausea, vomiting, loss of appetite, mouth sores, hair loss and fatigue as well as the more life-threatening effects of bone marrow toxicity and cardiac failure.

Selenium

Selenium is a naturally occurring mineral of the sulfur family. Selenium, acting in concert with vitamin E, activates the key antioxidant enzyme glutathione peroxidase. Acting together with vitamin E and also independently, selenium is a powerful antioxidant.

Selenium is found in the soil and is taken up by plants. We get selenium in our diet directly from plant food or via animals who have eaten selenium-containing plant food. Despite the small requirements, selenium levels have been found to be consistently lower than normal in patients with a variety of chronic diseases including breast cancer. Dr. Raymond Shamberger found a geographic correlation between cancer death rates, blood selenium levels and selenium levels in the soil.[64] Researcher G. Schrauzer studied the dietary selenium intake in 27 different countries and 19 different states in the U.S. and concluded the higher the blood selenium content the lower the cancer incidence.[65]

In the laboratory selenium has shown a variety of anticarcinogenic effects. Harold Ladas, Ph.D. reviewed dozens of studies on these effects. The statistics for breast cancer are striking. He observes, "The higher the selenium, the lower the breast cancer."[66] A study in Yugoslavia revealed women with breast cancer had half the blood levels of selenium when compared to healthy controls.[67] These researchers discussed serum selenium levels as a potential noninvasive screening modality.

Grains and vegetables grown in certain areas are naturally deficient in this important mineral. If you live in a selenium-poor area and consume local produce, then supplementation may be advisable. The areas of the United States with the lowest soil selenium are Florida, the Pacific Northwest, the Northeast and the Great Lakes region. Women living in South Dakota, Wyoming, New Mexico and Utah have high selenium levels in their local produce.

Good vegetarian sources of selenium, depending on the selenium content of the soil in which they are grown, are mushrooms, garlic, whole grains and asparagus. Fish and organ meats can be rich in selenium, if the animals of origin ate a diet high in selenium. Selenium, more so than any other trace minerals, has a narrow therapeutic margin. A safe supplemental dosage is 50–400 mcg per day.

Coenzyme Q10

CoQ10 is a vitamin-like substance synthesized in our cells which promotes the production of energy at the cellular level. It is similar in structure to vitamin E and also functions as an antioxidant. CoQ10 is a potent immune stimulator, scavenging free radicals and strengthening cell membranes.

At the Eighth International Symposia on CoQ10 researchers reported that breast cancer patients had lower than average blood levels of CoQ10. Karl Folkers, M.D., Ph.D. of the University of Texas at Austin reported partial tumor regression with CoQ10 treatment in a number of cases and complete regression in two case studies.[68] Women on chemotherapy will benefit from CoQ10, which can help prevent adriamycin cardiotoxicity. Many animal studies have indicated that CoQ10 protects the heart tissue from adriamycin

CoQ10 is abundant in tuna, sardines, peanuts, spinach and organ meats. The recommended dosage for women on chemotherapy is 100–300 mg per day.

N-Acetyl Cysteine (NAC)

NAC and glutathione (GSH) are the two major intracellular antioxidants and work together. NAC is a precursor for GSH as well as having its own specific antioxidant properties. By increasing GSH levels we can take advantage of one of the most important antioxidants and anticarcinogens. NAC is liver-protective and is also well-known for its mucolytic properties. I recommend NAC for women on chemotherapy as well as during and after radiation. I have personally found NAC to be extremely helpful for the pulmonary complications that I have had following radiation. After including this supplement in my regimen I went through the first winter since my treatment without any troublesome chest complications. Before taking NAC, I experienced multiple bouts of pneumonia and bronchitis. I take and recommend a maintenance dose of 500 mg per day for women who

have had radiation. When I have acute chest symptoms—
excess mucus production with or without a cough—I take
this dose up to six times per day.

For a multi-vitamin preparation I recommend: Epresat by
Floradix or New Chapter Every Woman, available at many
health food stores. It's a good idea to alternate between
different brands.

∾ *Remember...*

Because vitamins, minerals and other supplements
work in concert it is impossible to design meaningful
studies that evaluate isolated nutrients. As individuals
trying to create health, we don't need to have all the
studies. We need to value our innate common sense
and use both our knowledge and our intuition to create
our own healing programs.

HERBS: MOTHER NATURE'S PHARMACOPOEIA

Herbal medicine has a very rich heritage. Native cultures
throughout history made use of plant medicines, long before the advent of pharmaceuticals. Currently, approximately 25 percent of prescription drugs are derived directly
from botanicals and, to a large extent, modern-day plant-
derived pharmaceuticals are used for the same indications
as the botanicals from which they are derived. Because
herbs are complex combinations of substances rather than a
single specific molecular substance, the validation of herbal
medicine by scientific methodology is similarly complex.
However, extensive scientific documentation does exist
concerning the use of herbs for health conditions, including
cancer. Herbal medicine is the meeting point of science and

nature, of experimental data and folklore usage, perhaps the ultimate synthesis of the traditional and the modern.

An herb may refer to a whole plant or a plant part (leaf, flower, stem, seed, root, fruit, bark) used for its medicinal value. Naturally occurring chemicals that are found in herbs may be isolated and are in part responsible for their biological activity; however, of equal or more importance is the undefined synergism between the multiple chemical constituents that, taken together, make up the herb. Here, as elsewhere, the whole is greater than the sum of its parts. Herbs can be prepared and used in a number of different ways, as teas, tablets, tinctures, essential oils and ointments.

Therapeutically, herbs can be important inhibitors of the growth and spread of breast cancer as well as valuable adjuncts in the prevention of this disease. Herbs, like supplements, work on many levels:

- Healing plants can enhance overall immune function by supporting adrenal function, soothing the nervous system and boosting vital energy.
- Herbs can enhance the detoxification of carcinogens and hormonal metabolites via beneficial and facilitating effects on the digestive system and hepatic function.
- For women undergoing chemotherapy, herbs can help clear these agents.

The herbal tonic that I currently take is a custom-made preparation formulated by my herbalist, Donny Yance, to strengthen my immune system. The tonic takes into account my history of breast cancer, pulmonary scarring secondary to radiation as well as other unique personal health factors. My current tonic includes the following herbs: astragalus, burdock root and seed, celandine, essential oils of clove and camphor, hyssop, licorice, poke, red root, schizandra, sundew, thuja and turmeric.

Susun Weed's *Breast Cancer? Breast Health! The Wise Woman Way* discusses the use of many herbal remedies.

Consult an experienced herbalist for guidance in formulating a personal program. Like a diet and a supplement regime, an herbal program needs to be dynamic—to change with your changing needs and condition. The herbal formula that I used while I was getting radiation and chemotherapy treatments was chosen for my needs and condition at that time and included astragalus, echinacea, goldenseal, mistletoe, red clover, reishi, orange peel, poke, propolis, stillingia, sundew, thyme and una de gato.

The following herbs have been found to be particularly effective for the treatment of breast cancer:

- **Red clover**, rich in isoflavones, is specifically active against breast cancer.
- **Poke** has anti-cancer activity and is particularly helpful with breast tissue. It is a general immune stimulant that has protective effects on the lungs and lymphatics.
- **Goldenseal** and **thuja** are used specifically for the treatment of breast cancer.
- **Mistletoe** inhibits tumors and has been used in Europe for many years in the treatment of breast cancer.

The following botanicals are also noteworthy:

- **Astragalus** is a valuable immune enhancer which strengthens natural killer cell activity, protects the lungs and relieves lymphedema.
- **Sundew** is another immune activator.
- **Burdock**, **echinacea** and **una de gato** all have anti-tumor effects.
- **Reishi**, a mushroom with antitumor effects, was part of my original herbal tonic. I now take it as a supplement for its overall immune enhancement and energizing effects as well as to counteract the stress of a cancer diagnosis, conventional cancer treatments and 20th century living.

- **Thuja** and **schizandra** protect against the side effects of chemotherapy and radiation.
- **Turmeric**, a popular culinary herb, is a strong antioxidant with liver protecting qualities. It is helpful for women on chemotherapy and tamoxifen. Season your food with it.

Fu Zheng, which means "restoring and supporting normality," is a particular system of traditional Chinese herbal medicine which utilizes ginseng and astragalus, among other herbs. Fu Zheng is used in Chinese hospitals as an adjunct to conventional cancer treatments. The *Journal of the American Medical Association* reported on significant improvements in survival and better toleration of conventional treatment when this particular herbal support was utilized.[69]

Essiac is an herbal formula that a Canadian nurse, René Caisse, formulated based on information derived from an Ojibwa medicine man. It contains burdock, sheep sorrel, slippery elm and turkey rhubarb. The core formula has been combined with a number of potentiating herbs (watercress, blessed thistle, red clover and kelp) and is marketed as FlorEssence. I have used this preparation from time to time to strengthen and detoxify myself.

It is available in health food stores and through Flora (see Resources).

4

The Mental and Emotional Aspects of Breast Cancer

SUPPRESSED EMOTIONS ARE TOXIC, LOVE HEALS

I went to an overnight workshop with Dr. Bernie Siegel shortly after I began chemotherapy. I needed his help. It was pouring when I arrived. I put my flashers on, left the car in the entryway and brought my luggage in. There were some youngish boys in the hallway smoking cigarettes. Carcinogens were not yet part of their vocabulary. Small groups of people were conversing in the lobby. Who were the cancer patients? I wondered as I looked around.

Later, in my room, I stared at myself naked in the full-length mirror. I looked into my eyes—very red, a few tears. I examined my loose stomach, three pregnancies in four years. But still I felt beautiful. I had an urge to call home. I missed my children. At that moment, it struck me like a thunderbolt. Why did I have to be here? Was this really happening to me? I just couldn't believe it. More tears rolled down my cheeks. I yearned for forgetfulness, for some magical transport from this nightmare. I looked at my breasts, not quite believing that deep inside my left breast was a mass of cancer the size of a tennis ball. Had my body betrayed me? I prayed. I prayed to an outside power and I prayed to an inside power. My heart cried that I had to leave my three children (Oliver only weeks old) to do this work. I was so frightened—what happens next? Can I do it?—do what? Live, live serenely, without fear. One of my associates had warned me: as long as you live, he said,

177

every ache and pain will remind you that a recurrence is possible. We all die, that's true, but it's how you live that counts. I knew I had to calm my inner being—that is the only way.

Grace descended. The workshop began and, although there were over 100 participants, I felt a sense of intimacy as we went around the room and briefly told our stories. My attention was more focused than ever before. I was so present. The threat of annihilation had catapulted me into the present moment as never before. Later, when Bernie asked, "With whom would you like to switch places?" no one raised a hand.

Our journey is our own. I accepted this with an open heart.

∾

The work of emotional processing is that of facing ourselves. Once we do this, we have embarked on the journey that we were born for. We can walk through all our fears, but first we need to recognize them.

Our Emotions Are Physical

Physicians and philosophers of antiquity accepted the link between mind and body. Up until 1900, the fact that cancer and a patient's emotional life were linked was fully accepted in medical circles. The 18th and 19th century medical literature contains various references to this association, including repeated observations made by eminent physicians of the time:

Case One: Mrs. Emerson, upon the Death of her Daughter, underwent Great Affliction, and perceived her Breast to swell, which soon after grew Painful; at last broke out in a most inveterate Cancer, which consumed a great Part of it in a short Time. She had always enjoyed a perfect state of Health.

Case Two: The Wife of the Mate of a Ship (who was taken some Time ago by the French and put in Prison) was thereby so much affected that her Breast began to swell, and soon after broke out in a desperate Cancer which had proceeded so far that I could not undertake her case. She had never before had any complaint in her Breast.[1]

After this time the mind and body began to be viewed as separate entities. Surgery was developed and made its bid as the treatment of choice for cancer patients: radiation came shortly thereafter. Both focused attention on cancer as a local disease, a disease of a specific body part and not of the organism. So for half a century the idea that cancer was related to the life history of a patient disappeared. It is only in recent years that physicians are once again coming back to the understanding that mind and body are one, that psychological factors play an integral role in the health equation and that the emotional life history often plays an important part in the resistance to and the development of cancer.

When I first got sick, it thrilled the scientist in me when I stumbled upon the field of pyschonueroimmunology (PNI). I had barely heard of it previously, so focused was I on my practice of obstetrics and gynecology. As an obstetrician, I did recognize the enormous impact of attitude on a woman's course in labor but I did not have any ideas about how to harness this power in labor or in life. I was too busy. Unless there are compelling reasons (like when one's own life is at stake!) doctors often become very narrowly focused on their specific field. In order to become the specialists we think we need to be, that the public demands, that the insurance companies reimburse to, we lose sight of the big picture.

The basic concept in PNI is that our emotions manifest themselves physically. There are actual messenger molecules called neuropeptides that correspond to our emotional states and which have far-reaching effects throughout our bodies. Incredibly, these molecules and their receptors are located not only in our brains, but diffusely throughout our bodies. Thus our entire body including our immune system responds quite concretely to our emotions, both positive and negative.

In the early phase of my illness I was following all leads that might bring to light reasonable therapeutic advantages in my struggle with breast cancer. Thus I wrote to Sandra Levy, Ph.D., who was at the forefront of clinical research on the mind-body connection and its particular application to breast cancer. Dr. Levy was kind enough to reply personally and sent me published and unpublished scientific research[2] that she had been involved with, documenting the complex relationship between natural killer cells (immune system cells that can kill the blood-borne malignant cells that become future metastases), specific emotional reactions, lymph node involvement and the eventual course of the disease. Her investigations gave me additional evidence that my mind, my attitude, my reactions and how I would choose to cope with my diagnosis were going to affect my survival. It reassured me greatly to know that putting my emotional life into better balance could have a positive physical impact on my illness.

In 1991, shortly after my contact with her, Dr. Levy left the Pittsburgh Cancer Institute where she had been working for over a decade in collaboration with Dr. Ronald Herberman, the man who in 1972 discovered the existence of these natural killer cells. I learned she had left to pursue training as an Episcopal priest. I don't know her personal reasons for pursuing this career change, but through my own work with breast cancer I myself have experienced the close connection between science and the spiritual.

Suppressed Emotions Are Toxic

Sandra Levy found that the women who complained the most, who had difficulty adjusting to having cancer and who had good social support had stronger killer cells. Those women who adjusted well to this diagnosis, who were apathetic, fatigued and had poor social support had more lymph node involvement, weaker natural killer cell activity and tended to have earlier recurrences. The women who complained more have the same coping style as Bernie Seigel's exceptional cancer patients,[3] those people that refuse to become statistics—*listen, doctor I'd like to be a nice patient but I just can't die right now, I have other plans* as opposed to those patients (the "good girls") who die six months to the day after being given six months to live.

Lydia Temoshok, Ph.D. writes:

. . . I never thought I had stumbled upon a tragic psychological blueprint whereby a person's character led him inexorably toward malignant disease. The cancer patients did not share similar personalities or life histories. What they shared was a manner of handling life stress. . . . they displayed most or all of the following behaviors:

1. They were nonexpressors of anger. Often, they were unaware of any feelings of anger, past or present.
2. They tended not to experience or express other negative emotions, namely anxiety, fear, and sadness.
3. They were patient, unassertive, cooperative, and appeasing in work, social, and family relationships. They were compliant with external authorities.
4. They were overly concerned with meeting the needs of others, and insufficiently engaged in meeting their own needs. Often, they were self-sacrificing to an extreme . . . These are the essentials of a behavior pattern I would soon name 'Type C.'[4]

∾

I was so nervous about telling my Dad I had breast cancer, and our meeting took place on Father's Day, no less. He cried. The last time I saw him cry was when I was eleven and he told me my mother was dead. I reassured him that I was okay, that the treatments were going well and about all the positive things I was doing. He immediately focused on the past; comparing me to my mother he said, "She too felt great a year before she died." He reflected on how he had succeeded in hiding her diagnosis of ovarian cancer from her.

After talking to Tullia, my therapist, about some of the things that were said I confronted Dad at our next visit together. Cancer had finally allowed me to tell him that secrecy didn't work. That, in fact, the secret had tragically prevented my mother from facing her own death. Moreover, it had robbed me of my chance to say good-bye. How I still ached for that final parting in love, for those few intimacies that would have made the memory of her parting so very different. I knew that in order to heal and live I had to confront my past and I was finally able to do it directly.

∽

Dr. Temoshok drew on the work of many researchers before her who described certain consistent traits in breast cancer patients. In 1952, Bacon, Rennecker, and Cutler described breast cancer patients as women who "had no techniques for discharging anger directly or in a sublimated fashion." In 1975, Steven Greer, M.D. studied women with breast lumps prospectively; 50 percent of those who were diagnosed with malignancy were found in their screening interviews to be "extreme" suppressers of anger.[5] Only 15 percent of the women with benign disease had such a profile. Drs. Scherg[6] and Wirsching[7] conducted similar studies concluding that "adequate expression of feelings was not observed in *any* of the women with cancer . . . who tended to an extreme degree to avoid trouble and conflict . . . and who put off their own wishes in favor of more socially desirable behavior . . ."

> I was angry with my friend:
> I told my wrath, my wrath did end.
> I was angry with my foe:
> I told it not, my wrath did grow.
>
> —William Blake

I have learned that suppressed anger is lethal. Anger, unlike other emotions, does not lie dormant waiting until we are ready to deal with it. Anger is an active emotion that, if not processed in a conscious, timely and productive manner, will process itself destructively in many areas of our lives. If anger is not given clear, conscious expression it will manifest in various ways:

- Relationship difficulties, both personal and professional.
- Erosion of our self-respect and self-love, if we don't give voice to our true feelings.
- Deeply through our physical bodies in the form of discomfort and disease, breast cancer included.

℘ *Remember...*

Anger itself is not destructive; it is the suppression and repression of anger that can harm us. Our culture has taught us at home, at school, in our religions and in the media, directly and more often indirectly, that women must not express anger. Women that freely express anger are seen in this culture as bitchy, pushy, domineering, aggressive, offensive, hostile, castrating, emasculating.

We need to go beyond the self-limiting cultural stereotypes of women and give our anger expression. Express it. Direct it appropriately. Release it. Be done with it. If we deal with anger honestly, it can be a powerful tool in the creation of self-esteem, success and health.

Dr. Greer and his colleagues, Tina Morris and Keith Pettingale, did a ground-breaking study on women with breast cancer focusing on the relationship between mental and emotional adjustment to breast cancer and outcome.[8] Greer divided the women's coping styles into four groups.

1. **Fighting spirit:** Accept the diagnosis with optimism; gather all relevant information; determined to fight the disease.
2. **Denial (positive avoiders):** Reject the diagnosis or minimize the magnitude of the disease.
3. **Stoic acceptance:** Accept the diagnosis with a fatalistic attitude and a pretense that all must still go on as normal.
4. **Helplessness/hopelessness:** Patient's life is totally disrupted, and the predominant thoughts are of dread and doom.

After 15 years of study, the fighters and deniers remained more than twice as likely to be alive than the stoic and helpless/hopeless women. The women with the fighting spirit had the best outcomes; they actively took charge of their care, were in touch with their needs on many levels and were able to express their emotions. The deniers also fared well. Even though they were unable to acknowledge their illness and gather information in the interest of their recovery, they were able to direct their energy toward living and were able to function reasonably well. The stoics were passive and unemotional, profoundly disempowered. The helpless/hopeless were the women who had the poorest outcomes. Completely unable to gather their resources and cope like the fighters, unable to deny and carry on like the positive avoiders, unable to repress their negative emotions and carry on like the stoics. All coping mechanisms completely broke down for these women.

Another prospective study by Morgens Jensen found a cluster of psychological traits including an inability to express negative emotions, helplessness-hopelessness, chronic stress and repressive personality styles in those women whose breast cancer progressed. The psychological profiles were significantly predictive of the disease outcomes.[9]

> "Fools" said I, "you do not know—silence like a cancer grows."
>
> —Simon and Garfunkel

Silence, Sexuality and Motherloss

Women with breast cancer may well be *Women of Silence,* the title of Grace Gawler's book about the emotional healing from breast cancer. "Women with breast cancer often appear to have developed a way of coping that involves the 'bottling up' or withholding of emotional energy of some kind. Usually this emotional energy centers around painful experiences which these women have felt personally incapable of resolving effectively. So, silence instead of expression . . . Often withholding is the only means of maintaining oneself through crisis . . . inner pain and its containment is a feeling common to many women . . . Emotions of repressed anger, resentment, unhappiness and discontent are veiled by a passive silence . . ."[10]

The exploration of how certain women develop these silent coping mechanisms holds many answers to the puzzle of why breast cancer occurs. The adolescent breast is extremely sensitive, and emotionally stressful events at this time of life may, in fact, set the stage for breast cancer. In her book, *The Silent Wound,*[11] Dr. Peggy Boyd talks about the similarities between two critical time periods in a women's development: adolescence and menopause. She notes that many of the tasks that the adolescent girl must accomplish are revisited in the years leading up to and culminating in menopause. She believes that there is a connection between the manner in which these tasks are resolved and the development of breast cancer later in life.

According to Dr. Boyd, the adolescent girl responding to the rising hormone levels of puberty must:

- Come to terms with her developing body's changes, her breasts, her new womanly shape, other secondary sexual characteristics.
- Establish her identity as a woman—the girl/virgin becomes the woman/mother.
- Cope with sexual feelings and the corresponding emotions as well as develop an appropriate code of behavior in response to these feelings.
- Begin to make education and career choices that are consistent with her emerging identity as a woman.
- Establish her independence from her family.

The way an adolescent responds to these tasks has long-term psychologic and physiologic consequences. It seems reasonable that the successful establishment of a solid female identity would impact positively on her health in general and specifically on her ability to later healthfully negotiate menopause when identity issues reemerge.

The presence of a strong mother or mothering person is crucial to a young woman's healthy resolution of these issues. An absent mother figure due to any cause—whether it be premature physical death or the emotional neglect of a dysfunctional mother—can set the stage for eventual breast cancer.

In *Motherless Daughters,* Hope Edelman writes:

> Without a mother or mother-figure to guide her, a daughter has to piece together a female self-image of her own. While most girls separate from their mothers during the teen years to create an individual identity and then spend the later years trying to return as an autonomous adult, the motherless daughter moves forward alone. Adulthood is a significantly different experience for the woman who travels through it with a maternal void and the memory of a dramatic loss.[12]

As daughters and women who travel alone, physically or emotionally, we must take care not to fill the void with fear, anger, resentment and silence.

If, when the time comes to do this work, the tasks are

too fraught with conflict, if the necessary support networks are not in place and the issues are silently tucked away, then a sense of dis-ease is fostered that may later give rise to actual disease. The active working through of these very basic female issues vs. the silent wounding induced by the inability to move with these challenges can have psychologic, nueroendocrine and immunologic consequences which in turn can impact on a woman's risk for breast cancer.

When a woman arrives at menopause, the challenge is once again to find appropriate solutions to the developmental tasks that come up and which mirror the previous tasks. Dramatic hormonal changes once again set the stage as the menopausal woman must:

- Come to terms with the physical changes her body is undergoing as she ages and her menstrual cycle ends; beauty must be redefined.
- Establish her identity as a wise woman—the mother becomes an elder.
- Reorganize sexuality and sensuality in her life now that the possibility of pregnancy is past.
- Make new choices regarding creative outlets with more internally generated goals, establishing, reestablishing or furthering a career as her grown children become more independent.
- Reassess primary relationships and make the necessary shifts.

At the critical times of puberty and menopause dramatic changes in hormone levels form the backdrop of the struggle to create balance in a field of multiple physical, psychological and social stressors. Dr. Boyd designed a questionnaire to elicit information on these two critical times. By isolating differences in sisters who had similar genetic and family history, the analysis was able to focus on psychologic and social predictors of breast cancer risk. The Boyd Project found that, in fact, the women who had developed breast cancer were likely to have had significantly more psychological and social conflict during adolescence and menopause than their unaffected sisters . . . and revealed that a woman's attitude toward her own body, her feelings about the other women in her life (her mother in particular), her degree of satisfaction with her first sexual experience and her current sex partner, and her ability to come to terms with the way becoming a woman has influenced her life all have a far greater impact on her susceptibility to breast cancer than does genetic history or social and economic circumstances. In fact, a woman can have almost exactly the same genetic, economic, and social risk factors as her own sister and still be at many times greater risk of developing breast cancer! . . . The woman who lives with the silent wound—resulting from her adolescent conflict between the experience of her physical maturity and her psychological and social immaturity—is, in general, more than twice as likely to develop breast cancer as her own, less conflicted, sister. In some cases, she is more than 20 times more likely to do so![13]

∾

I remember the shock of my first menstrual blood. I didn't have a mother to tell me what to do. It wasn't a celebration, a time of female bonding or a rite of passage, it was only an embarrassment. I didn't understand what my body was up to any more than I understood my emerging sexuality. I longed to be caressed by good-looking young men but somehow I was ashamed of the body I was in, the body I didn't understand. My mother wasn't there to explain.

∾

Boyd emphasizes that the emotional factors that are so much a part of our daily lives are but one of the determinants in the multi-causal model of breast cancer. The power in this, however, is that as Boyd suggests, a woman who is already at statistically increased risk by virtue of ethnic/racial background, family history, early onset of puberty, economic status, urban location, childlessness, etc., may, "want to look at her own adolescent experience and the resulting attitudes toward her sexuality that are right now influencing the way she thinks and behaves. Experience cannot be changed, but attitudes can be."[14]

∾ *Remember...*

We cannot change the past but we can change its influence on us here and now. Our adolescence is accessible to us through our thoughts, feelings, dreams and memories. We can free ourselves by opening to, acknowledging and releasing the past; as we grant ourselves great respect for our holdings we can let go and move on. When we begin to think about the development of our illness, we may feel guilty. However, self-blame is a mind trap that has no useful application in healing. The development of self-compassion is the key to growth and healthy change.

CHANGE

A feeling hardened
into a belief. It was
heavy and solid
and immovable.
Cold as ice.
hard as steel. Tight
as a clenched jaw.
It was so deep, so long, so old.
Talking about it reinforced it
like earthquake proofing,
making my throat bloody and sore.
I brought it, like a sculpture,
out into nature and set it
in the garden

underneath a tree.
Feelings change unless they harden.
Wind in your leaves, teach me.[15]

—Jnani Chapman, R.N.

FINDING A VOICE

As I learned more abut the profile of women with breast cancer I became determined to give voice to my feelings and let my emotions out as they arose. So in August of 1991 I sent a note to Dr. Hirt, one of the doctors who had given me a second opinion on my initial treatment options. In my note I explained how isolated I felt after our consultation. Perhaps because I was a physician he felt obliged to stick to the facts and quote statistics. I wanted him to be aware that his assumptions about the nature of my disease and my uncertain fate did not promote a healing partnership nor engender hope.

Dr. Hirt had very strongly advised me to get an immediate radical mastectomy and quite openly shared his view on my poor prognosis. His opinion was that there really were no other acceptable options in the optimal management of my case. I sensed on a deep level that the pathology specimen, the large mass of fresh tumor tissue that had formed in my breast was something that he as a research scientist very much wanted in his laboratory.

I never did get a response to my letter but that wasn't important; with the expression of my emotions came the healing. I felt empowered by understanding and naming the feelings our meeting evoked. I knew the forthright expression of these feelings, which was not a skill I had learned in my upbringing or in my medical training, would serve me well.

Dr. Hirt recommended immediate radical mutilating surgery. He marched into the examining room with an entourage, spoke *at* me rather than *to* me and made it clear that he viewed his recommendation as the only suitable option. In contrast, Dr. Love, another doctor with whom I consulted, explained the various options and spoke at length with me in a quiet, private setting. Her heart was open as she assured me I had choices. Dr. Hirt, Dr. Love—the absurdity of the obvious.

℃ℐ *Remember...*

Resolving feelings doesn't necessarily mean walking up to someone and telling them what you think, nor does it exclude that approach. Direct confrontation is not always necessary and is not always possible or advisable. There are many ways to release emotions. Write letters, send them or burn them, write in your journal, write a book, talk to your counselor, join a group, bring the person you are in conflict with up in a forgiveness meditation and do the work on that level. The person who forgives is the one who truly heals. See page 323 for a forgiveness meditation.

FACING THE TRUTH IN OUR SITUATION, AS WOMEN, AS PATIENTS

I remember being told that I had cancer. It was so confusing. In practically the same breath, the surgeon who did the diagnostic incisional biopsy told me I had cancer but that I had nothing to worry about. Much later, as I reflected on it, I realized that when he said the diagnosis was not life-threatening he was rather clumsily trying to protect me and perhaps himself from the truth. But as a physician I knew too well that this diagnosis certainly was threatening my life ... invasive ductal carcinoma, nuclear grade 3 with extensive necrosist ... I had to answer back, I couldn't ignore my feelings anymore; my life depended on it and I knew it.

Expressing my appreciation for his surgical expertise, I

also sent a letter to this doctor emphasizing my need to confront honestly the life-threatening nature of my diagnosis and to be involved in the decision-making process every step of the way. Sensitized to my own mortality, every decision became important, every detail worthy of my consideration. My physicians would have to be comforting yet cognizant of my need to fully participate. While honoring my knowledge, I began to trust more in my instincts; while developing my ability to make informed decisions, I was always conscious of my gut feeling. I knew I needed to create my own healing path.

∾

It took me a while to realize how I had been treated, how my fears had been minimized and how close we can come to being shuffled through the medical system without asserting ourselves. It felt good to write this and literally get it off my chest. Express the truth in your situation; we have been quiet for too long.

∾　*Remember...*

All our feelings are appropriate including the fears that surface with a diagnosis of cancer. Let your fear of death surface. Breast cancer gives us the opportunity to scrutinize our fears as they freely come up, thereby allowing for the possibility of transformation.

Don't let anyone minimize your feelings and fears. Your fears are there to help you work out issues and to help you through. Feelings validate our experiences; believe them and go with them.

When looking back I try to understand why the surgeon who performed my diagnostic biopsy chose to minimize the seriousness of the diagnosis. I immediately recoiled at his attempt to shield me even momentarily from the truth. For it is only in the truth of our situations that we can be healed.

My feelings about my surgeon's approach were colored, both then and now, by my mother's death in her early forties from ovarian cancer. The diagnosis was hidden from my mother because of my father's misguided attempt to protect her from the fear and to allow her to live the rest of her days "happily." The working through of our emotions and the lessons we learn are so much more important than a false "happiness." True happiness can only emerge from honesty and truth.

∾

As my mother was getting progressively more distended from the intra-abdominal spread of her ovarian cancer, drinking ginger ale to help with her feelings of indigestion, we drove back and forth, checking in and out of the hospital with an invented diagnosis that seemed more palatable to my father and her doctor. I had no idea that my mother's life was drawing to a close. I now believe that she must have known but that she, too, was caught in a web of silence. The message was clear: her doctor, my father, her brother were all in cahoots—no one wanted to discuss the truth with her and for her to speak through that wall of denial was not possible. So the fear stayed hidden. It was stuffed back into her abdomen and it killed her along with the cancer.

∾

With that in my background I recoiled from the pretense that my cancer might be anything else than what it was. Having been through medical school I knew that the communication skills of physicians were not adequately addressed. It is difficult, if not impossible, for many physicians to communicate with frankness either in privacy or as part of a team approach.

One has only to read Bernie Siegel's books to know the pain the traditional medical education system promulgates. The pain he talks about is the pain that each individual physician experiences in his or her life as well as the pain of institutionalized medicine in a larger sense. Dr. Siegel writes: "We M.D.s deny our sadness at a patient's misfortune, our anger at a patient's resistance, even our joy at a patient's recovery . . . Playing God leads to self-destruction . . . No wonder our rates of suicide, drug addiction and middle-age death are way above average . . . The denial of empathy benefits no one. As mechanics, we doctors always fail in the long run, but as counselors, teachers, healers, and care givers we can always contribute . . ."[17] As physicians, we need to address the real goals of our profession.

A panel set up by the Association of American Medical Colleges concluded that technological specialization is driving out the "exquisite regard for human needs" which is the essence of healing. Albert Schweitzer said "Medicine is not only a science, but also the art of letting our own individuality interact with the individuality of the patient." Subspecialization encourages the use of medical jargon which serves to isolate the physician from authentic interaction. Specialists spend little time with patients, deferring discussion to primary care physicians. Patients gets lost in the shuffle. This dualistic atmosphere encourages the worship of facts without feeling and promotes the intellectual detachment that physicians use to keep their own emotions out of the picture.

∾

In the journal, *Psychosocial Oncology,* the following scenario points out the irony of the physician's uneasiness in using the word cancer even when the patient is perfectly comfortable with this word:

The wife of a young couple asked me one day, with a mischievous look at one another, if she had cancer; I laughed with them; it was so preposterous; she had cancer of the spine and the word had been used freely in all our discussions and we had discussed many aspects of it and the effect that it was having on their lives, and I asked "Why?" They then said they had counted up all the different terms that had been used by doctors in place of the word "cancer;" the list was extensive. One might ask why this word had to be replaced in the various discussions between this patient and her doctors, ostensibly and in other circumstances it might be said that the word "cancer" is avoided in order to protect the patient, but that could not be the case here. She and her husband used the word freely so in this instance one surmises that it was not to protect the patient, but to protect the doctor who had put himself in their shoes.[18]

In order to make himself feel better, my doctor told me that my cancer was not really cancer, it wasn't life-threatening. I find that to be the ultimate irony. Here I was coping with the diagnosis of breast cancer and I had to tiptoe around the terminology so that I didn't upset my doctors! It was clearly time for me to stop trying to endlessly nurture and comfort everyone else. As Bernie Siegel writes,

Many colleges are now trying to teach compassion through courses in humanistic medicine . . . The best physicians are those who can find both the "masculine" and "feminine" virtues that exist within their personalities—the ability to make tough decisions and yet remain compassionate and caring. Neither extreme makes a good physician. You can become too involved to make good decisions, and you can also make decisions based on diseases and think nothing of the patient. Combining both is the best way. This has been borne out by studies showing that those who combine both aspects become more effective doctors and also remain happier amid the stresses of their profession.[19]

MY INVOCATION

May my patients know how much they teach me
that they help me as much as I help them
May we both become whole

——B.J.

With breast cancer comes the necessity and the permission to begin to nurture yourself. The pain our doctors feel in admitting to themselves that the conventional diagnosis and treatment protocols are very much deficient can be a meeting point. Do not take upon yourself the pain of this hurting profession. Many physicians are wounded and most are not conscious of their wounds. In their woundedness they may be unable to be frank, open and clear in their communications. Our lives depend on clarity. We need to meet with our health caregivers and acknowledge the truth in our particular situations. Demand no less. Now, if ever in your life, is a time for honesty, privacy and partnership; accept no less.

HEALING THE EMOTIONAL MESSAGES OF BREAST CANCER

Candace Pert, Ph.D., a well-recognized expert in the field of mind-body medicine, had this to say about the link between suppressed emotions and breast cancer:[20]

> It's clear to me that emotions must play a key role, and that repressing emotions can only be causative of disease . . . there is a growing body of literature, much of it European, that suggests that emotional history is extremely important in things like the incidence of cancer. For example, it appears that suppression of grief and suppression of anger, in particular, is associated with an increased incidence of breast cancer in women. . . . We're sold on high-tech, incredibly expensive medicine that is bankrupting the country. Why not try a little prophylaxis? Let's begin to appreciate simple, less expensive therapies that deal with releasing emotions, and let's get some sound scientific studies to see what works better. For example, the Spiegel study shows that women with breast cancer who met with other women in a support group live twice as long as women who had the same chemotherapy, but didn't get together to talk. I think in Western medicine, we have come to the point where we're ignoring what is obvious.

The Spiegel study Candace Pert makes reference to is a study all women with breast cancer should be aware of. Dr. David Spiegel's study[21] on women with metastatic breast cancer, published in the prestigious medical journal, *Lancet,* in 1989, has been widely quoted and its scientific methods undisputed. After ten years of follow-up these researchers found that the women with metastatic breast cancer who were randomly assigned to a group therapy program lived almost twice as long as those receiving the same medical treatment but who did not participate in the group therapy. In group therapy these women were able to express their fear and in so doing lessened its grip; they supported one another which became an empowering experience for both the self and the other. These women bonded to one another and in their connection experienced love, commitment and healing.

Sandra Levy also demonstrated the role of positive emotions in terms of prolongation of life in a group of women with recurrent breast cancer.[22] After a seven-year follow-up it was discovered that the survivors differed from the two-thirds of the original group who had died in that all had expressed more joy in the initial evaluation. Joy was a powerful positive predictor of prognosis. Expression of our full range of emotions is healing.

❧ *Remember...*

Your body's wisdom, encoded in the mechanism of its immune system, is the primary force behind your healing. Medical treatment is secondary. The mind-body work we do both to heal and prevent breast cancer is scientifically based in the enhancement of immune function. Boost your immune function by expressing and releasing emotions.

WHY THE BREAST?

Cancer was my body's call to attention. My body informed me that my life was not in order by calling attention to my breast. What were the messages? Why were the messages stored in my breast?

In *Women of Silence*[23], Grace Gawler writes, "Breast cancer could be described best as an illness characterized by the misdirection or damming up of nurturing energies within breast tissue." Generally, the breasts are physical metaphors for giving and receiving love and nourishment. Are we able to freely give and receive love? Can we nurture? Can we allow ourselves to be nurtured? Women with breast cancer tend to be caretakers of others but not of themselves. Women often hold emotional pain inside their bodies in their breasts.

In trying to understand the emotional messages of breast cancer I became aware of another way of looking at the human body. The Eastern spiritual traditions teach that each person is really a system of energy. Here the physicists and mystics see eye to eye. The term chakra is the Sanskrit word used for each of the seven major energy centers in the human body, which correspond to the major nerve centers of Western medicine and also to specific organs and their functions. Each chakra center is associated with specific life issues. Certain patterns of emotional, psychological or spiritual stress will manifest in disease in a particular chakra if the energy is blocked there. Caroline Myss, who co-authored *The Creation of Health* with neurosurgeon C. Norman Shealy, says,

> We are not carelessly designed creatures. Everything about us has purpose, logic, and intelligence built into it, including how and why we become ill. The emotional, psychological and spiritual stresses present in our minds travel, like oxygen, to every part of our bodies. When stress settles in a particular area of the body it is because that part of the body corresponds to the type of stress we are experiencing.[24]

All the chakra centers interact in much the same way as the components of our nervous system exchange information. Each of us is unique and, therefore, what is a motivating or tolerable situation to one women may be overload and traumatic to another. With this in mind I list below some of the emotional issues and dysfunctional behavior patterns cited in *The Creation of Health* which are common settings for the eventual development of breast cancer.

- Fear of not being loved or the belief that you are not worthy of being loved.
- Fear of showing or sharing affection.
- Resentment that develops from seeing others receive more love and attention than yourself.
- Feeling emotionally paralyzed by experiencing too much loneliness.
- Experiencing emotional contamination as a result of holding on to old hurts and past resentments.
- Developing emotional fears and bitterness as a result of believing you cannot forgive or directly refusing to forgive.
- Continually creating relationships that are emotionally unfulfilling or abusive.
- Doing something or being with someone when your heart is not in it.
- Too much grief and sorrow.

The fourth chakra which emcompasses both heart, lungs and breasts is about learning to give, receive and share love and nurturance. The breasts are the symbol for nurturance in every culture. If love is associated with pain, as it is in children who are raised in abusive or neglectful families, then participation in healthy love will not be possible without first healing this association. Fear, anger and resentment are part of that emotional setting. If one is brought up in an atmosphere of conditional love then the emotional body will suffer insecurity until as adults we choose, with humility and self-acceptance, to alter the lessons that grew out of our previous perceptions. Early emotional neglect can lead to the self-protective development of bitter, insensitive and even cruel qualities of the personality which isolate women from the inborn ability to interrelate and nurture. If, as children, we learn that the way to please is by diminishing our excitement and enthusiasm for life, then our vitality will suffer.

I had to find out what my messages were and how I had processed the emotional events in my life to my detriment. I had to learn how to allow the wall of repressed anger, grief and unacknowledged fears to melt into the more primary pain. I had to learn how to feel that pain and transform it into new ways of relating to the world, new and clearer emotional responses and behaviors consistent with this new way of being. How could I free the blocked energy and harness this powerful force for healing?

∾

I always wondered why I had so few memories of my mother. After all I was just about 11 when she died. Why do I have only a few snapshots of her in my mind? Why can't I remember her laughing? I only remember the bad times, the day she yelled at me for taking so long picking out new shoes, the day I was so jealous when she played the piano with my friends and finally the awful trips back and forth to the hospital. I still can see the view of the East Side Drive from the backseat . . . For years after she died I did everything and anything to avoid the subject of moms. Of course, in my house that was no problem; after the funeral we never spoke of the loss. My father paced around for years, lost in his grief. Only when I was alone in the room I shared with my sister Peggy did I dare to cry. I wrote a song about my mother that I would sing ever so softly, with a lump in my throat, choking back the tears. And always there was the shame—I couldn't bear for anyone to know I was motherless.

෬

Being mothered is an essential human need. Without nurturing in one's early life there is sure to be emotional pain. As a reaction to this many women nurture others to excess. The result is that everyone else's needs are met. Breast cancer tells women that the nurturer needs nurturing. I began to pay attention to the deep wounding that resulted from being a motherless daughter. I started to nurture myself through meditation and visualization. The emptiness still remains but I have begun to respect the depth of the wound. In this way I can begin to let go of the pain.

HOW CAN WE PROCESS OUR EMOTIONS IN ORDER TO HEAL?

How can we, moment to moment, consciously process emotions whose expression is so vital to our healing? How can we utilize the blocked emotional energy from the past to our advantage? This is what I set out to do to enlist my own emotions to heal breast cancer:

- Release the emotional blocks from my past.
- Live my emotions in the present tense.
- Create a new way of being by transforming the strength of withholding to the power of living passionately.

How to begin:

- Be honest with your life story.
- Recognize the need to make changes in your emotional style.
- Stop what you are doing during the day and ask, "How do I feel about what I am doing right now?" Listen for an answer.
- Be gentle with the blocked feelings.

- Immediately identify negative emotions, both mentally and where you feel them in your body.
- Become a nonjudgmental witness to unproductive emotions: breathe deeply, let them go.

A therapist can help

SESSION

You tell me of your mother's fear,
the great navigator of your life.
It whispered to you,
"Follow me, don't go away to school."
You followed it.
It whispered to you,
"Follow me, don't marry him"
You followed it.
It whispered to you,
"Follow me, the lump will go away"
You followed it.
You lay it down between us
on the rug.
We look at it together.
now, with one breast
and nothing left to lose.
Finally, you can begin.[25]

—RACHEL REMEN, M.D.

Meet Tullia Forlani Kidde, my spiritual counselor

I knew I needed someone to help me through the crisis of breast cancer; all my life I prided myself on my ability to make it alone. After my mother died, 11 years old and with no way to mourn but silently alone, I cracked, then hardened. I was unable to reach out then and no one in my world could openly share the devastation of her death upon my life.

From this pain I learned to take care of myself; I bonded

with my friend Elaine whose mother had abandoned her in a different way. I did well in school, always straight As, became a hippie, befriended Jill who radiated hope and dubbed me BJ, made love to long-haired boys, experimented with hallucinogens, studied art, fell in love with Maurice, my motorcycle-riding art teacher, modeled in the nude at the Brooklyn Museum Art School, studied astrology, waitressed to save money, dated my biology instructor at Hunter College, traveled around the world alone for a year with a backpack and travelers' checks, worked on a kibbutz in Israel, thought about marrying my wealthy Israeli boyfriend until I found out he was cheating on me, swam in the cool clear exquisitely blue waters of Paleokastrista on the island of Corfu, rode the gondolas in the waterways of Venice, immersed myself in organic chemistry, enrolled in medical school, used amphetamines and coffee to get through the courses and exams, married my best buddy Les, completed an obstetrics and gynecology residency in New Jersey, moved to Connecticut, never understanding why I entered into a marriage without passion, divorced Les, got pregnant, married again to a medical school classmate with more passion but no intimacy, two more children were born.

I spent half a lifetime yearning for my mother's sweet nurturance, and through it all I was alone with the pain. Now it was different. I knew I needed to reach out to someone and ask for help and that someone turned out to be Tullia Forlani Kidde . . .

The moment I heard her voice I felt better. I felt a physical sensation—a pain in my breast—and I knew she was going to help me. Through her compassion I developed more compassion for myself. She helped me to articulate my needs and to be with myself as I experienced the intense roller coaster of feelings that I was to go through as my diagnosis and staging were completed. She empowered me to make the choices that felt most comfortable. As my treatment unfolded, she helped make sense of the images that were pour-

ing through my dreams nightly; she suggested books to read, taught me exercises in visualization and meditation, shared valuable resources, pointed me in directions that she had not traveled. She encouraged me to express myself in letters to significant people and in my own journaling. She supported necessary confrontations with my doctors, my father, my husband. She provided valuable advice on helping my children through this crisis, a shoulder to cry on, an ear to listen without judgment, a heart to hold me, a calming influence, a refuge. Tullia, my therapist, my friend, my dear one. . . . We are all here to support one another and I encourage you to find a therapist, a friend like Tullia to be there with you. Reach out, together you can confront the pain and remember the love.

☙

There can never be a substitute for personal experience in any area. I believe this wholeheartedly. There's no substitute for being there, or at least in the vicinity! And that's part of what made Tullia so special; she'd been there. At about the same age as I, she was diagnosed with a terminal malignancy, given six months to live and here she was 15 years later.

In honor of Cancer Survivor's Day in 1994, Tullia, a therapist affiliated with ECaP (Exceptional Cancer Patients, founded by Bernie Siegel, M.D.) made the following remarks:

I have been part of ECaP for several years and have explained to people what being exceptional means in our understanding. To be exceptional doesn't necessarily mean that we learn to heal our body and live forever. Our exceptionality comes from the courage, the strength, the acceptance that we master along the way, taking responsibility for our lives in our struggle, learning to conquer fear each day, learning to resolve the conflicts in our hearts and in our lives.

To be exceptional means willingness to change whatever

is not working well for us any longer, learning to live in the moments of our lives, understanding the preciousness of each moment, as difficult as it may seem at times. To be exceptional means willingness to look into our heart and our spirit and understand that there is a whole dimension that goes far beyond our body; a dimension that transcends the physical, but that can affect the physical as we are finally accepting.

To be exceptional means that we are not helpless or hopeless in spite of our diagnosis, but that maybe we need to learn to look at life through different eyes, through a different understanding of our value system, our priorities and purpose. To be exceptional at times means to learn that we count, that we are as important as anyone else, that we have to address our needs, and often take better care of ourselves in a loving way.

So here I am tonight, not because I belong to the Cancer Club, but because I am exceptional. I am here to honor all of you and myself for the struggle, the courage, the endurance, the ability to live and laugh and overcome in spite of our tears, in spite of the many challenges.

Cancer has been a true teacher for me. My cancer, as I said, was diagnosed terminal. But I have learned and learned, and I am still learning about the preciousness of life in the moment. My physical pain has taught me that I can endure, that I can tap into my inner resources for strength. My heart has taught me to forgive, love and accept people and circumstances as they are presented to me, without becoming a victim. My spirit has taught me that I am a limitless being, that I am so much more than my physical self, that I can learn to find peace and joy even within my challenge if I keep my mind and my heart open.

I have also learned that I don't have to compare myself with anyone else, that I can embrace my humanness with understanding and humility, for my journey is my very own. Life has many seasons, each unique and special. I have learned about gratitude, and taking nothing for granted and this, of all, has been my greatest lesson. In conclusion, my exceptional friends, let's celebrate life, live in the moment knowing that, no matter the experience, we can never be defeated.[26]

Tullia taught me all that and more. Because she went through the pain her words were more than words; her soul talked to my soul. Find a therapist who resonates with you.

One of the important things that I learned in the course of therapy was to accept rather than fight who I was. The past cannot change but its influence on the present can be modified. Although we know our emotional patterns have contributed to the development of breast cancer and are no longer serving us well, we can still appreciate and respect why these patterns developed. The way we view the world and the way we behave are influenced by early experiences. At these early points in our development we do the very best we can, sometimes under adverse conditions. By understanding and honoring dysfunctional behavior patterns as the essential coping mechanisms they are, we loosen their hold. By accepting the child who had limited abilities we open the door to change, to productively choosing the behavior that is in our best interest. As adults we can choose our responses.

Be Open—Become Yourself

Breast cancer can allow you to be open with the world. Go ahead, say what's on your mind, say what lies heavy on your heart. Living close to the possibility of death, the day takes on new meaning.

The issues of a wig or no wig, a prosthesis or a breast reconstruction are really metaphors for more profound issues. One of our initial reactions to the diagnosis of breast cancer may be to hide from it. Hiding from breast cancer, we hide from the other issues in our lives that we have been thus far afraid to deal with. There is an element of shame about breast cancer, shame that we are not perfect. Whoever said we were.

So I learned from my own reaction to this crisis of impending baldness. Faced with the likely possibility of walking around bald, a testament to my imperfection and the brutality of the treatments I was receiving, I felt I had to hide. I prepared for the act and readied my costume. As I became considerably more gentle with myself, continuing to release my emotions and working on the issues of my life, I found to my own and my doctor's surprise that I had nothing to hide from. My fear of what I might look like, what others might think, lost its power. The waiting and anticipation of this bareness became the divine play of growing into who I am.

I am sure that fewer people will suffer side effects from cancer treatments if they can work on the emotional settings in which they receive their treatments. At the very least, being gentle with yourself will feel better. Losing your hair, if it does happen, is not a failure; use the experience to become even gentler with yourself and have some fun along the way.

THE SHAME OF BREAST CANCER

Do You Really Need a Wig?

After I was told that I was going to lose my hair sometime during the course of chemotherapy, I was determined to be prepared. I went to a fancy salon in the next town before I went bald so I could be ready for this upcoming event.

∾

I suppose I was doing all I could to be nonchalant. Oh yes, I need a wig or two, uh huh, sure, no problem, yes, no, not to change my look; I'm going to be losing all my hair, probably next month, oh well, la de dah, probably after the next chemotherapy, uh huh, yes, I have breast cancer. (Don't you dare feel sorry for me . . . My God, you poor dear. I saw it in their faces.)

I remember the owner of the salon, a kind of slimy character, black, greasy hair. Had I been in my right mind I would have run right out of there. But I couldn't walk around bald—or could I? How absurd, my life hanging by a thread and I was worried about what I would look like; what would the world think if I walked past with a shiny head! A bleached blond lady helped me, you know the 50's type, her hair all teased and sprayed, with black eye make-up. The place stank of cigarettes.

I tried on a few wigs. It was hard to stuff my still shoulder-length hair up and picture how I would look.

Why did I have cancer, I wondered? These two people looked like characters out of an environmental disaster movie—sprays, fumes, peroxides, bleaches, hair colorings, cigarette smoke. Why not them?

A few days later I went back with my husband and mod-eled a few of the wigs for him. Lovely? What was he think-ing? He said they looked fine. I think he tried to make some jokes. I think I tried to laugh. They charged me $500; as my Dad would say, they laughed all the way to the bank. Later I found out those wigs were only worth about $40. I didn't dare think about the price until much later; there was no time to wait for a sale.

I put the wigs up in my closet on the mannequin heads they gave me and I waited. I waited and waited. I cut all my hair off. I'd had some really short styles before and I figured it would look better real short when it started to fall out. I waited and waited. In the morning I would scratch my head and watch some hairs fall into the sink but when I looked in the mirror I still had a full head of hair.

Throughout the nine months of chemotherapy I had an ongoing relationship with those wigs. I kept looking at them on the high shelf in my closet, wondering when I would need them, and they kept staring back at me, faceless.

∾

We don't have to let everyone know we have breast can-cer, nor do we have to hide. There is a middle ground. Don't let the discomfort of others dominate the way you conduct yourself. If you want to walk around bald, go ahead. If anyone has a hard time looking at you, they've got their own issues to deal with. If you want a wig, by all means buy one, but please shop around! If you buy one for security, as I did, before your hair falls out, just buy one. Reputable salons will fit you for a wig without the necessity of a purchase, then if you need it quickly, you can get the one you've chosen.

As the months went by I made peace with those mannequin heads. The real me would just walk around bald when the time came. With some heavy eye make-up, perhaps, and big hoop earrings, one could look quite stylish bald, making quite a fashion statement and bank the money saved on wigs!

My hair thinned a bit but I never did go bald.

On Being Bald

Bernie Siegel said he kept shaving his head because people treated him differently.

> A year before I began ECaP, I shaved my head. Many associates thought it was a message of empathy with those who lose their hair during chemotherapy, but it had nothing to do with that. I later realized that it was a symbol of the uncovering that I was trying to make, baring my own emotions. The reactions were often revealing. Many people began to talk to me in a different way, as though I were handicapped. They shared their pain readily. . . . I realized that what I meant to uncover was my love and spirituality, not my scalp.[27]

Uncovering ourselves in a physical way can put us in touch with our humanness, our basic emotional vulnerability. Uncovering, unmasking, revealing, exposing, baring, we peel away the layers that shield us from our pain and our depth. In *The Power Within* author Wendy Williams tells of one woman who pushed the boundary of her disfigurement to allow self-love in:

> Bald from five months of chemotherapy prescribed after a recurrence of ovarian cancer, Lisa was discouraged, depressed and angry. She still had the cancer, which had failed to respond to the chemotherapy, only now she had no hair. Her baldness symbolized her separateness from other young women—her cancer. Lisa fought her depression using her favorite weapon: the practical joke. She flaunted her baldness down Newbury Street, self-conscious yet laughing all the way. . . . Instead of my bald head making people look away from me, pitying me and feeling ashamed of their good health, the baldness drew people to me, either to glare at me or to smile indulgently. This was fun. And I just had to get some fun out of the chemo. The limbo of existence, the discouragement from chemo's failure, threatened to overwhelm me. Cancer might touch parts of my body, might even disfigure me, but my spirit could survive if I chose to let it.[28]

On the Loss of a Breast

Breasts are symbolic of our feminine identity. Our breasts are soft, beautiful, sensual, erotic. We receive and impart life through our sexual nature. Our breasts are full and nourishing. They produce, contain and deliver nature's perfect food. Our breasts are divine metaphors for our roles as women, lovers, mothers, caregivers and nurturers. The breasts embody the female in the dance of life, they give nourishment and they are open to receive. Female energy receives, contains and transforms.

How then do we let go and allow the sacrifice of our breasts? If we need to make the sacrifice, we can. Out of suffering and conflict, we grow. We die to one part of our life and we are born to the next. Let the suffering be experienced with great awareness. Let us sacrifice, if we must, the container for the essence. And let us always remember why.

Deena Metzger reflects on the sacrifice: "I have made a decision. I will sacrifice my breast. Barbara says it's a proper sacrifice, that it will please the gods. This bit of flesh for life. I wish that there were another way."[29]

One-Breasted Women: Our Doctor's Worst Fears or Our Own?

Dr. Patricia Brandenberg's dissertation examining the social support network for women with breast cancer examined the feelings of the men who treat women for breast cancer for fresh insights. "Men regarded mastectomy as the most prominent feature of breast cancer. . . ." Sixty-nine percent of the male surgeons surveyed stated that "mastectomy was the worst thing that could happen to a woman. . . ."[30] Only 28 percent of the women surgeons interviewed agreed.

I think it is clear then that information is not just information isolated from the context in which it is given. We are being informed about breast loss and the reconstruction issues in an emotional milieu, often by male physicians who have very strong feelings about the meaning of breast loss. Remember, our lives are at stake, not just our vanity. We need to be clear on whose needs and fears we are responding to when we make our decisions about mastectomy and reconstructive surgery. If we choose to create the illusion of a new breast it will be in our best interest that this act be born out of self-respect and not out of an attempt to hide. Our own deepest needs should be addressed and respected in the process of making this decision so that we can become whole even as we lose an honored part of us.

> Your grief for what you've lost
> lifts a mirror up
> to where you're bravely working . . .
>
> —RUMI

THE POWER OF THE FEMININE

In facing the crisis of breast cancer we come into a new relationship with our female identity. Perhaps the roles we have undertaken as female caregivers have not served us well. We are called upon to both sacrifice a part of our femaleness and at the same time to nurture ourselves through this experience. It is at this time that we need strong women in our lives. We need the wise women of old that can hold us, love us, show us what we must learn in this situation in order to heal and remind us that in our womanhood there is the strength we need.

Breast cancer can empower us to reach out to other women, to acknowledge the negativity we've absorbed in this culture as women and to release our pain in the presence of other women. Holistic gynecologist Christiane Northrup, M.D. writes,

> Since Everywoman's problem occurs in part because of the nature of being female in this culture, which programs us to put the needs of others ahead of our own, we need to make radical changes in our minds and lives to get and stay healthy. . . . Our culture gives girls the message that their bodies, their lives, and their femaleness demand an apology. . . . Our culture habitually denies the insidiousness and pervasiveness of sex-related issues. I first learned in my medical practice that abuse against women is epidemic, whether subtle or overt. And I saw how abuse sets the stage for illness in our female bodies.[31]

The well-known fruit fly experiment is illustrative of how mindset creates reality. Flies placed in a jar with a lid on it will not leave the jar even when the lid is removed. The premature cognitive commitment has in effect limited their choices and their reality. Similarly, the experiences of our childhood and the beliefs we have inherited from our families and our culture can become the lid on our lives. The nature of reality and the creation of health are more fluid than we have been led to believe. Healing from breast cancer can remove this lid as we confront the negative beliefs we have inherited.

We are not alone. The power of women is enhanced in community. The essence of woman is a natural ability to listen, to receive, to unite and to allow change and transformation. All this is facilitated when women allow other women in. Author Grace Gawler speaks of the role of women of wisdom:

> . . . the appearance of wise and understanding women in your life will be a blessing. These women can help you to revive your creative life, show you the way with a gentle and guiding hand and help you to reconnect with your inner self. . . . Seek the company of such women on your healing journey for they will help you speak your truth. They are survivors themselves who can teach you how to creatively deal with major life issues. . . . For regular support I recommend also that you seek the company of a woman's circle. Such circles are once again rising in popularity as women recognize the importance of sisterly bonding in their lives and understand their feminine nature and needs. Basically women need women with whom they can communicate, trust, and share the experience of living a passionate life.[32]

ALL THAT WE CAN DO

We can open to the many truths in the experience of breast cancer:

- The physical truth is that we can be gentle with our body and help it heal by feeding it clean and nourishing food. There is an incredible power in our daily food choices which can affect personal and planetary healing. The Earth reflects our current health crisis and she is ill. As consumers of food, medicine, goods and services women can be an effective political and economic force.

- The emotional truth is that we can hold ourselves in our own hearts and see where in our body we hold our emotions and how we can now in our best interest let them go.

- The spiritual truth is that healing is only possible when we live, experience and acknowledge the truth as it is in the present moment. Once we let go of our worries about the past and our preoccupation with the future, we can open to the power of the universe and align with our highest purpose. Prayer in this sense is a very personal communication with this power and our purpose.

Intimacy is another way we can open ourselves to healing. Stephen and Ondrea Levine write in *Embracing the Beloved*, "Few recognize the enormous power of a relationship for physical, spiritual and emotional healing."[33] A breast cancer experience can deepen the bond in a committed relationship.

In our culture there is a great deal of fear surrounding sexuality which is then compounded when a women is diagnosed with breast cancer. A woman who has faced surgery and disfigurement, whose sex drive has been wiped out by chemotherapy and radiation may not only feel undesirable, she may also feel guilty about not being there sexually for her partner. Couples touched by breast cancer desperately need help with sexuality issues. Author Ken Wilbur writes, "The men are frightened of having sex with their mates because they fear they might hurt them. In the men's support group at Cancer Support Community, when the men were offered an outside expert, they chose a gynecologist. They just needed simple information . . . and that helped enormously with their fears."[34] Sexual intimacy can be a powerful healing force for women. If commitment is there, allow yourself the gift of embracing your beloved and being embraced.

THE POWER OF PRAYER

Prayer is paying attention. Merida Wexler writes in her cancer journal, "Yes. This is what I try to do. I attend. I stay with myself. This is the gift of cancer: to be present with myself, to not abandon myself, no matter what. To be present with the 3 A.M. terrors, present for the loving touch, present under the daily radiation. I stay with her, with me . . . "[35]

In *Healing Words, The Power of Prayer and the Practice of Medicine* author Larry Dossey, M.D. notes that there are easily 130 studies that show that if you take prayer into the laboratory under controlled situations it has remarkable effects. And these effects are not limited to human beings and certainly go beyond what the medical community disparagingly refers to as the placebo effect. In an interview, Dr. Dossey commented,

One of the things that intrigued me about the studies was how this material has been marginalized. You certainly don't hear anything about these studies in medical school. But after considering the evidence, I decided to incorporate prayer rituals into my medical practice. It seemed to me that not to do so was the equivalent of withholding a potent medication or a needed operation . . . I think most physicians in medical science won't even look at prayer because it doesn't fit their theories . . . at some dimension of the psyche, we are living in perfection. Utopia is here and it's now. The recognition of this has been called, in various spiritual traditions, enlightenment, which means waking up to what is, to what is already present. Although I'm much in favor of using prayer to achieve some nice outcome, I think the best lesson is that it can help us get in touch with what is already present. That's the starting and ending point of *Healing Words*.[36]

If we allow ourselves the belief in the power of prayer and pray for our highest good in the way that comes most naturally to us and with the utmost compassion for ourselves, we can support our healing.

BREAST CANCER PRAYER

May
breast cancer open our hearts to our deepest pain.

May
the fear we face through this experience make us stronger.

May
we walk through this together, holding each other within our hearts.

May
the power of Woman be renewed.

——B. J.

❧

PART THREE

Who We Are From the Outside In

5

Out There and In Here: Breast Cancer and Pollution

This we know: The earth does not belong to us. We belong to the earth. The earth is our mother. What befalls the earth befalls all the sons and daughters of the earth.

This we know: All things are connected like the blood that unites us. We did not weave the web of life, We are merely a strand in it. Whatever we do to the web, we do to ourselves.

—CHIEF SEATTLE

THE EARTH IS OUR BODY

One of the problems with the concept of pollution is the perception that the environment "out there" is being polluted and that even though we are deeply concerned about this problem, still it is happening out there. Nothing could be farther from the truth. Everything that happens out there also happens in here. The chemicals we have created in our laboratories and thoughtlessly scattered about are now concentrated within our bodies. We look out there and join in the cry to clean up Mother Earth but we do not realize that the chemicals we are fighting against are also accumulating within our own breasts. Our bodies in the most literal sense are in equilibrium with the contamination that we have collectively allowed on this earth, our planet, our home.

∾

Women's bodies, especially the breasts, are composed of a greater percentage of fat and are therefore more susceptible to the deleterious effects of fat-soluble contaminants. Our bodies have become the dumping ground for a variety of chemicals. In 1962 Rachel Carson warned:

> The most alarming of all man's assaults upon the environment is the contamination of air, earth, rivers, and sea with dangerous and even lethal materials. . .chemicals are the sinister and little recognized partners of radiation in changing the very nature of the world—the very nature of its life . . .
>
> Since the mid-1940s over 200 basic chemicals have been created for use in killing insects, weeds, rodents, and other organisms. . .These sprays, dusts, and aerosols are now applied almost universally to farms, gardens, forests, and homes—nonselective chemicals that have the power to kill every insect, the "good" and the "bad," to still the song of birds and the leaping of fish in the streams, to coat the leaves with a deadly film, and to linger on in the soil. . .[1]

Because they are outside the limits of biologic experience, we have no means of detoxifying and eliminating many chemical contaminants. Carson issued her prophetic warnings nearly 30 years ago when the effects of these chemicals were first noted in wildlife. The situation is even more desperate today. We are a culture of women dying of breast cancer amidst a toxic environment of our own creation and born of our silent complicity. Crazed cancer cells that know no limits mirror a culture gone wild in its unconscious war against Mother Nature, which is in fact a war against ourselves. There seems to be no limit to the destruction.

People are both blind and insensitive to the damage. Mother Earth appears to absorb it all, but in reality there is nowhere for these toxins to go. They are processed through the earth and then come back out of the earth into our bodies via the air, water and food.

Xenobiotics are foreign chemicals, chemicals the body cannot recognize or which confuse the body on some level. Xenoestrogens are a subset of these foreign chemicals that in some way mimic estrogen. They are perceived as estrogens and stimulate the cascades of reactions that estrogens initiate, but when they are introduced into our delicately balanced hormonal feedback system, their effects are dangerous, unbalanced and unpredictable.

XENOESTROGENS WREAK HAVOC WITH OUR BIOCHEMISTRY

Dr. Devra Davis, Senior Fellow of the World Resources Institute in Washington, D.C. and Visiting Scientist at the Strang-Cornell Cancer Research Laboratory in New York, pinpoints pesticides, household chemicals, drugs, fuels and common plastics as estrogen imitators, substances that are long-lived and that amplify the effect of estrogen in our bodies. Few of these xenoestrogens existed before World War II when researchers developed the first synthetic organochlorine compound—DDT. It has been theorized that women who already have a genetic susceptibility to breast cancer may be exquisitely sensitive to the proliferative effects of xenoestrogenic materials from the environment.[2] These substances are ubiquitous in our 20th century world.

One well-accepted hypothesis for the development of cancer is that there are two distinct stages. The first is initiation, the second is promotion. It has been suggested that in the initiation phase our genetic material is irreversibly altered by a number of agents and/or processes including:

• Chemicals such as xenoestrogens.
• Radiation.
• Infectious agents such as viruses.
• Inherited mutations.

The promoters which further damage the cell include:

- Prolonged exposure to estrogens or xenoestrogens.
- High dietary fat intake.
- Tobacco.
- Alcohol.
- Certain food additives such as nitrates.
- Radiation.
- Other chemicals.

An initiated cell may lie dormant until regularly bathed by one or a series of promoters over a long period of time. After 10, 20, 30 or even 40 years of promotion, the initiated cell will begin to reproduce uncontrollably. This is cancer. However, the good news is that the proper diet, supplements, herbs and a healthy immune system can act as antipromoters.

How Do We Process the Pollution?

The body has a detoxification system which cleans up accumulated toxins (xenobiotics) so they do not harm the body. The detox system is found in every cell of the body; some of the reactions occur in the membrane system known as the endoplasmic reticulum and some occur freely in the substance of the cell known as the cytosol. In order to get rid of xenobiotics, we need to have an intact detox system. The problem is xenobiotics damage the very system required to transform and excrete them. This creates a vicious cycle whereby the damaging agents contribute to their persistence in our system.

We are not biologically equipped to handle the steady flow of chemicals in our environment. In her book, *Tired or Toxic*[3], Dr. Sherry Rogers cites a breath analysis of 355 urban residents in New Jersey that showed that chemicals such as chloroform, trichloroethane, benzene, styrene, xylene and carbon tetrachloride were actually circulating in their bloodstream and being expelled from their lungs. These chemicals and many others are the "normal" constituents of the air we breath everyday and as such are being incorporated into our internal milieu. Our bodies have no means to eliminate many of the poisons that are wreaking havoc with our environment. As the face of the earth is being changed, so too are the blood and tissues of our bodies; breast cancer is just one of the horrendous results.

The human detoxification system is not programmed to eliminate all of these chemicals or their metabolic by-products. Moreover, we are continuously weakening the system by the non-stop ingestion, inhalation and absorption of these pervasive agents. The 20th century has been the breeding ground for a brand new disease: Environmental Illness (E.I.). Those who suffer from E.I. have become too sensitive to chemicals to even venture out of doors. In order to function at all some of the people suffering from E.I. need to be isolated in environmental units such as those run by William J. Rea, M.D. in Texas; here their bodies are given a break in the toxic exposure cycle. By gradually building up their immune and detoxification systems they can again become functional, although they may need to continue to exercise a host of environmental controls in order to maintain their health and return to the world. On the cover of Dr. Rogers' book is a person wearing a gas-mask. Is this our fate?

How does this all relate to breast cancer? What lies ahead for those of us who venture forth daily into a sea of chemicals? Radiation and chemical damage take their toll differently in each person—that is the essence of biochemical individuality. Yet no one can completely escape unharmed. Breast cancer is one serious manifestation of the ongoing damage that we are subject to as our bodies attempt to process the pollution.

The Whole Exposure is Greater than the Sum of Its Parts

Chemicals alone, radiation alone or both taken together in deadly synergism have the power to damage our genetic material. In our worship of technologic advancement, research proceeds to isolate the genes that are "causing" breast cancer. In our unwillingness to foresee the scope of our environmental damage and therefore our inability to effectively halt it, we, in effect, contribute to the creation of more abnormal genetic material.

The evidence is accumulating that our breast cancer epidemic is in part caused by environmental agents. We must resist the lull of complacency. Mainstream education campaigns such as Breast Cancer Awareness Month focus almost exclusively on mammography—yet another technology that *detects* breast cancer but does not prevent it. The role of heredity as well as certain reproductive and personal historic factors have been explored in the quest to understand the cause of breast cancer. The focus has not been on carcinogens in our food, air and water. What about the role fat plays in the etiology of cancer? Is it the fat itself or what is stored in fat? Fat is the vehicle by which fat-soluble contaminants get into our bodies and fat is the place where contaminants are stored in our bodies.

It is much too easy to point a finger at the profile of a "typical" breast cancer patient: an overweight middle–aged woman or a woman who had children too late or not at all. Wait a minute; I got breast cancer at age 36. I had three children. I've never been fat—there's a lot more going on than the powers that be would have us know.

∾

Breast cancer is very personal and, at the same time, breast cancer is very political. Had I not been diagnosed with breast cancer I would no doubt be continuing along in my practice of Obstetrics and Gynecology, advancing my

knowledge along the party lines: learning new laser tech-
niques to treat cervical dysplasias, advising women to get
mammograms in accordance with the American College of
Obstetrics and Gynecology guidelines and, in general, giv-
ing advice within the limits of my experience. But now life
is different; life will never—can never—be the same. To say
it could would be a lie. The truths I've uncovered are not
mine—they belong to all of us. Rachel Carson did some of
the work for us by writing Silent Spring *in 1962, two years*
before she died of breast cancer. Audre Lorde uncovered
these same truths in The Cancer Journals. *She too died of*
breast cancer. We uncover and affirm the same truths. I
compile the evidence in my own way. I present it to you
anew with my own story.

∾

CHEMICAL PROPAGANDA

The industries largely responsible for chemical pollutants
hide behind simplistic notions such as:

- There are only trace amounts of harmful chemicals
  going into the environment, therefore your chance of
  developing cancer from the exposure is equally small.
  Untrue. The extent of damage is not always related to
  the amount of exposure; it depends on the toxicity of
  the agent. Moreover, chemical exposures are not always
  small; as organisms acquire resistance, more frequent
  and greater pesticide applications are necessary. Many
  classes of these compounds accumulate in the food
  chain at levels much higher than that in the environment.

- There is a safe dose or an acceptable risk. Untrue.
  Rachel Carson warned there may be no safe doses.
  And after all, just what is an acceptable risk? A risk
  assessment that concludes that someone has to be sac-
  rificed for the benefit of technology and profit is a

questionable conclusion—one that may indeed be a human rights abuse. There are no studies on the carcinogenicity and long-term chronic toxicity for the majority of these agents. Just what do we mean by safe? The World Health Organization International Agency for Research on Cancer concluded that there are no valid human data which can possibly justify the conclusions of safety claimed by the chemical industry.[4]

- The exposures are isolated events. Untrue. Harmful chemicals undoubtedly interact, and exactly what the combined effect of all these diverse chemicals is, no one can possibly know. We can only guess at the deadly synergism as breast cancer rates continue to climb. Apples alone have residues from as many as eight pesticides, according to the Washington, DC-based Environmental Working Group.[5]

- Exposure of fetuses, infants and children is in no way different than the exposure of an adult. Untrue. There is evidence that organochlorines freely cross the placental barrier; thus, we are exposing fetuses to these chemicals while they are developing in utero. Exposure begins at conception. Infants and children whose immune and detoxification systems are immature, who distribute these chemicals differently because of their smaller body mass, and who may eat large quantities of fresh fruit are particularly susceptible to the risks of multiple chemical exposure. Dr. Heuper of the National Cancer Institute suggests that congenital cancers and infant cancers may be related to the actions of these *in utero* exposures acting upon rapidly developing tissue. Experiments show that the younger an animal is when it is subjected to a carcinogen the more certain its effect. This holds true for chemical, radiation and hormonal exposures. We must use extreme caution when establishing safe levels of chemical exposure for infants and children.

THE PESTICIDE CONNECTION

Since the 1940s when the large-scale production of synthetic pesticides began, the effects of one major group, the organochlorines, have been implicated in the causation of breast cancer. DDT is in this group as are PCBs (polychlorinated biphenyls) and dioxin. In the 1979 exposé, *The Politics of Cancer,* Samuel Epstein, M.D. listed 25 organochlorine pesticides in use at that time, 19 of which were proved carcinogenic in animal studies.

Although DDT was banned in the U.S. in 1972 it's still very much around. Its half-life is 60 years so it remains in the soil, finding its way into vegetables, into our bodies and into the next generation through mothers' breast milk. Organochlorines currently in use are found on produce and many are particularly concentrated in fat as they move up the food chain, both in animal fat and in milk fat, where their effects are biologically magnified.

Dr. Mary Wolff of the Mt. Sinai School of Medicine in New York wrote in the *Journal of the National Cancer Institute* that the 32 percent increase in breast cancer incidence between 1973 and 1980 in women over 50 ". . . is consistent with the historical pattern of accumulation of organochlorine residues in the environment; i.e., older women who had the greatest potential cumulative exposure to DDT between 1945 and 1972 may now experience a higher risk of breast cancer than women much older or younger who were not similarly exposed.[6]

IN VIVO EVIDENCE—PESTICIDES LINKED TO BREAST CANCER

In 1990 Finnish researchers linked high levels of the pesticide beta-hexachlorocyclohexane, with 10 times the normal risk of breast cancer.[7] A 1992 study at the University of Connecticut School of Medicine[8] analyzed tissue from suspicious breast lumps in 40 women and found that those with cancer had increased levels of PCBs, DDT and DDE (a DDT by-product) residues compared to those with benign lumps. At Mount Sinai Medical Center[9] this was taken a step further: blood was analyzed from 14,000 women and it was found that the women with the highest blood levels of DDE had a four times higher risk of breast cancer than those with lower levels. Not all studies have confirmed these findings,[10] but evidence is accumulating. From a public health standpoint it would be sensible to implement alternatives to pesticide use.

Pesticides Masquerade as Hormones

Since the 1940s, when estrogenic pesticides were first widely used, the incidence of breast cancer has doubled. The Environment Protection Agency (EPA) does not classify, regulate or require tests for estrogenicity. Estrogenic pesticides should be classified as such and phased out.

Some organochlorines are xenoestrogens, that is, they exert some of their damaging effects via hormonal mechanisms. DDT has an estrogenic effect. A 1994 Canadian study[11] found a relationship between breast cancer and a DDT breakdown product in women who were estrogen-receptor (ER) positive and therefore more likely to be sensitive to the exposure. Estrogen-sensitive breast cancers have comprised a larger and larger portion of the increase in breast cancer in recent years. The EPA announced in October of 1993 that there was evidence that the insecticide, endosulphan, and other chemicals that imitate estrogen, may be associated with breast cancer.[12] The FDA found endosulphan in 21 of 22 fruits and vegetables heavily consumed by children.

Ana Soto, M.D. and Carlos Sonnenschein, M.D. found in their studies that when mixing small amounts of the estrogenic pesticides endosulphan, dieldrin and toxaphene together, the combined lower concentrations induced the same estrogenic response as large amounts of each pesticide individually. Dr. Soto warned: "By looking at the effects of only one chemical, we won't find the link between xenoestrogens and breast cancer, we should look at the cumulative effects."[13]

Women are at greater risk than men when exposed to the same amount of pesticides because of their smaller weight and greater percentage of breast tissue. The government calculates the Allowable Daily Intake for pesticides based on a 70-kilogram man. Politicians have also shortsightedly allowed substantially higher levels of pesticide residues on imported produce. The General Agreement on Tariffs and Trade passed in December of 1994 allows 5,000 percent higher levels of DDT on certain imported fruits and vegetables than current U.S. standards.

OUR PRUDENT ACTION CAN HAVE AN IMPACT

From 1976 through 1986 Israeli breast cancer rates dropped. In 1978 Israel banned the organochlorines DDT, BHC and lindane. In the mid-1970s pesticide use had elevated BHC levels in Israeli milk to 100 times the levels present in US milk; lindane levels were 17 times higher and were being found in extraordinarily high concentrations in other dairy products and human breast milk. Within two years of the ban lindane levels in breast milk decreased by 90 percent, DDT by 43 percent and BHC by 98 percent. By 1986 the breast cancer death rate for Israeli women under 44 years old had dropped by 30 percent. Overall, breast cancer rates had dropped almost 8 percent.[14] Some scientists argue that a direct connection between the pesticide ban and Israeli's falling breast cancer rate is unlikely because the dramatic effect on deaths within a decade is not consistent with the natural history of breast cancer. If these agents act as promoters in an already at-risk population, however, this relatively short time frame does make sense.

Organochlorines Are Not Only in Pesticides

In addition to the manufacture of pesticides, the balance of 40 million tons of industry-produced chlorine per year is combined with petrochemicals by the plastics industry to make PVC (polyvinyl) plastic, solvents and refrigerants. Organochlorines are also the by-products when chlorine is used in the paper manufacturing industry to bleach pulp and paper, in wastewater disinfection and in the manufacture and incineration of various chlorinated chemicals. According to a study by Greenpeace at least 177 organochlorines have been identified in the fat, breast milk, blood, semen and breath of the general populations of the U.S. and Canada.

Danger: Plastics Are Not Inert

In an accidental discovery at Tufts University Dr. Ana Soto noticed that cells in plastic dishes were growing as if they had been exposed to estrogen. Dr. Soto and her associate, Dr. Sonnenschein, identified the contaminant, nonylphenol, a chemical used to prevent plastic from cracking, as xenoestrogen. Research at Stanford University has shown that certain plastics, when heated, release estrogens. Dr. Soto thinks that heating plastics in microwave ovens may have a similar effect, resulting in the additional ingestion of xenoestrogens. Dr. Soto also thinks that estrogenic nonylphenols that leach out of the plastics used to package dishwashing liquids and toiletry products could be dangerous.[15]

Polycarbonate plastics which constitute molded products such as baby bottles and water jugs also contain xenoestrogens. Heated polycarbonate plastics release bisphenol-A which in concentrations of two to five parts per billion can induce noticeable estrogen effects in the laboratory.[16]

DIOXIN: A DEADLY BY-PRODUCT

Dioxin, a by-product of chlorine bleaching is present in the water supply of most industrialized nations. The newsletter[17] of the Connecticut Public Interest Research Group Citizen Lobby (ConnPIRG) cites a new EPA report documenting that even minute exposure to dioxin can cause serious health damage including breast cancer. The EPA study notes that small amounts of dioxin have been found in nearly everyone who has been tested including 99 percent of the breastfeeding women tested in milk studies. Dioxin, also a xenoestrogen, works some of its damage by imitating estrogen in the body. Dioxin may also be passed through the placenta. The EPA estimates that by the time a child is one year old he or she may have accumulated 4-12 percent of his or her lifetime exposure to dioxin.

DON'T DRINK YOUR MILK

Since early 1994, when recombinant bovine growth hormone (BGH) was approved by the U.S. Food and Drug Administration and went on sale by Monsanto under the trade name Posilac, the milk in this country has been tainted. BGH was approved for the sole purpose of boosting milk production for the $64-billion-dollar national dairy industry. Genetically engineered BGH, also known as bovine somatotropic hormone, in effect forces cows to produce up to 25 percent more milk. The FDA Veterinary Medicine Advisory Committee recommended approval of BGH despite a variety of health hazards that have been associated with its use. For example:

- The use of BGH dramatically increases the rates of udder infections; BGH milk contains more pus and bacteria than non-BGH milk. Residues of the antibiotics used in the attempt to combat these infections are found in the milk we consume. Infected cows that don't respond to antibiotics are slaughtered and sold as beef, serving as reservoirs for the growth of fatal E.coli bacteria.

- Milk from cows that receive BGH has greater amounts of saturated fats.

- The cows that receive BGH are pushed into metabolic overdrive; they require more energy-dense food and, despite the fact that they are ruminant vegetarians, they are being fed the ground-up flesh and bones of cattle, sheep and other animals. Reports of a fatal disease known as bovine spongiform encephalopathy have surfaced and may have health consequences for humans. Great Britain's beef industry is in crisis at this writing because of "mad cow disease."

- The use of BGH has been associated with breast cancer.

In a letter written by Dr. Samuel Epstein to Dr. David Kessler, the Commissioner of the FDA, the following point was made: BGH administration induces a sustained increase in levels of an uncharacterized insulin growth factor (IGF-1) in milk, IGF-1 is not destroyed by pasteurization. Furthermore, IGF-1 is not inactivated in the human gut; in fact, casein (the principal protein in cow's milk) has a protective effect on IGF-1. The dangers for children and infants may be even greater as their more permeable gut walls may allow for even greater absorption of this molecule. BGH absorption may increase IGF-1 production by breast epithelium. In human breast epithelial cell cultures IGF-1 induces rapid division, multiplication and malignant transformation of normal cells.[18] Despite this warning the FDA has approved BGH for use in dairy products.

Rachel's Environment and Health Weekly notes that "According to the *Statistical Abstract of the U.S.* (1994 edition), Americans in 1992 consumed an average of 564.6 pounds of cow's milk and milk products, or about 1.54 pounds per person per day; this includes milk, cream, ice cream, ice milk, buttermilk, cheese, cottage cheese, various 'dips' and yogurt. . . . Because milk is consumed in such large quantities an increase in growth-promoting hormone in milk is of potentially great public health interest."[19] Yet, labelling to indicate which products contain BGH and which do not is forbidden due to the pressures put on the FDA by the dairy industry.

FOOD ADDITIVES

In 1957 Dr. Francis Ray warned that "we may be initiating cancer in the children of today by the addition of chemicals [to food] . . . We will not know, perhaps for a generation or two, what the effects will be."[20] Well, here we are that generation later. From 70-80 percent of food is packaged in polymers, some of which contain potential carcinogens that migrate into our food daily.[21]

The National Research Council found that toxicity data were either inadequate or nonexistent for 80 percent of 8,600 food additives. Long-term toxicity assessment continues to be a problem. Establishing long-term safety for additives that have their effects on a disease that develops over 10, 20, 30 or even 40 years is difficult at best. Just as with pesticides the interactions between the various food additives as well as between food additives and the over 63,000 other chemicals in common use is another area of concern.

RADIATION

Ionizing radiation in the environment plays a role in the etiology of breast cancer. Atomic bomb survivors show the effect of radiation: they develop breast cancer at higher rates than the unexposed. Medical exposures for both therapeutic (flouroscopy for the treatment of tuberculosis, radiation of the thymic gland in infants, X-ray treatment for mastitis, radiation treatment of Hodgkins disease) and diagnostic exposures (multiple series of x-rays on adolescents for scoliosis, x-ray studies in the radiosensitive carriers of the ataxia-telangiectasia mutant gene) have been implicated in the elevation of breast cancer rates. Dosages and age at exposure are both significant variables.

What has not been adequately explored is the effect on breast cancer of nuclear fallout from the open air atomic bomb testings and the continued exposure to nuclear fission products that remain and accumulate from both nuclear accidents and emissions from nuclear power facilities. Jay Gould, author of *Deadly Deceit,* counters the assumption that only the high doses of radiation from atomic bomb blasts seriously injure our health and that the smaller doses of radioactive fallout, known as "low-level" radiation, do little harm. Dr. Gould, a former member of the Environmental Protection Agency Science Advisory Board cites the work of a Canadian radiation biologist, Dr. Abraham Petkau, whose laboratory findings show that the destruction of cell membranes actually occurs much more efficiently at low-dose levels. The upshot is there is no level of radiation that is "safe."

Rosalie Bertell, director of the Canada-based International Institute of Concern for Public Health, suggests that the exposure to nuclear fallout from testing in the 1950's has contributed to the current breast cancer epidemic. The volume of fission products released into the atmosphere from this testing was equivalent to the explosion of some 40,000 Hiroshima bombs; baby-boomers were exposed to this *in utero*. Fission products that were released into the atmosphere, in particular radioactive strontium, enter the food chain, concentrate in the bone marrow and effect immune function. The exposures still continue as Brookhaven National Laboratory has documented hundreds of accidental civilian reactor releases since the mid-60s, including emissions in 1975 from the Millstone reactor in Connecticut and the largest civilian disaster which occurred at Three Mile Island in 1979. Dr. Gould maintains that the baby-boomers born into the nuclear age have sustained immune system damage having ingested fission products *in utero,* at birth and in their early childhood and are therefore being disproportionately affected by a range of immune disorders. This low-level radiation exposure, coupled with a long latency period, is a reasonable contributing mechanism accounting for the rising incidence of breast cancer.

SMOKING

Thirty-five percent of all cancers are related to smoking. There are 4,000 chemical carcinogens (cancer promoters) in every puff. A study of more than 600,000 American women showed that women who smoked were 25 percent more likely to die from breast cancer than non-smokers or ex-smokers. For women who smoked more than two packs a day there was a 75 percent greater risk of breast cancer death.[22] In a Danish study[23] women who had smoked for 30 years had a 60 percent higher risk of developing breast cancer and developed the cancer at a significantly younger age.

ALCOHOL

Women who consume alcohol regularly increase their risk of developing breast cancer. In a recent study[24] involving 6,662 breast cancer patients and 9,163 healthy women, researchers found that the risk increases with the amount of alcohol consumed: those who drank one drink per day over the course of a lifetime were 39 percent more likely to develop breast cancer than those who did not drink; two drinks a day put a woman at a 69 percent higher risk of breast cancer and three drinks increased her risk to 230 percent.

Daniel Hayes, M.D., medical director of the Breast Evaluation Center at Dana-Farber, noting the increased risk for women who drink alcohol regularly, commented, "spread over a large population, it could account for a substantial number of breast cancers." Shockingly, he followed his observations with, "Because of the substantial benefits associated with moderate drinking, to suggest to women that they not have a glass of wine a day is premature."[25] It is unfortunate that we have come to a point where our medical establishment views alcohol intake as a means of reducing one's risk of heart disease rather than approaching it sensibly through diet, exercise and stress reduction. My advice is to have an occasional drink at a party if you want to, but let's not delude ourselves about our addictions and call them healthy.

Age-Related Sensitivity to Pollutants

Our degree of sensitivity to the entire range of environmental pollutants is affected by our age. The adolescent breast is more sensitive to environmental exposures. The survivors of the atomic bombings of Hiroshima and Nagasaki showed a marked increase in the risk of breast cancer 10 years after the bombings. The survivors who exhibited the greatest risk were those who were adolescents or younger at the time of the bombings. Similarly, women who have undergone flouroscopy treatments for tuberculosis showed an increased risk of breast cancer 15 years after the treatments, with exposed adolescents having the greatest risk.

The Enormity of the Problem

Coming face to face with the enormous impact of environmental pollution on the epidemic of breast cancer is not a popular focus for the petrochemical, pharmaceutical, tobacco, meat and dairy industries.

Malignant Neglect, a comprehensive report on the environmental aspects of cancer written by members of the Environmental Defense Fund, states: "Cancer is not caused by some inexplicable miasma, although it may seem that way to the uninformed. *Instead, most scientists now agree that the overwhelming majority of cancers are environmentally caused.* As such they are largely preventable, but failure by the public, industry and government to recognize this fact and *act* on it is why we have a cancer epidemic today . . ."[26] One of the most ignored facts is that breast cancer has a significant environmental component and that the incidence of breast cancer can be reduced by diminishing environmental carcinogens.

Consider the following statistics from the 1989 Toxic Release Inventory National Report:[27]

- 551,034,696 pounds of industrial chemicals were dumped into public sewage storage.
- 1,180,831,181 pounds of chemicals were released into the ground, threatening our natural aquifers.
- 188,953,884 pounds of chemicals were discharged into surface waters.
- The total amount of air emissions pumped into the atmosphere was 2,427,061,906 pounds.
- The Environmental Protection Agency estimates that a grand total of 5,705,670,380 pounds of chemical pollutants were released into the environment in 1989.

The list of toxic chemical exposures in a typical day is phenomenal; it would fill nearly five pages of this book. From the mattress with flame-retardant chemicals in the bedroom to the chlorinated tap water in the bathroom, from the food additives in the pantry to the auto emissions from our cars, from the pesticides on our lawns to the commercial cleaning solutions used at work and school, we are exposed from morning to night, in our homes and offices, in our food, air and water. Many chemicals are stored in fatty tissues. Many are known carcinogens.

> ## ∽ *Remember...*
>
> Total environmental load is one of the key concepts in understanding environmental stress. The environment is dynamic. What we take in from the outside world changes daily—air quality, vitamin and mineral content of our foods, toxic residues and, of course, the mental-emotional stress in our lives is in constant flux. Our ability to process our environmental load also varies; it fluctuates with our enzyme levels, nutritional status and any previously sustained toxin-induced damage to our biochemical machinery. Because of inborn differences the damage from chemicals, radiation and other pollutants takes different forms. For some it might be environmental illness, for others, breast cancer and for others, who can predict?
>
> The pervasiveness and subtleties of the environmental impact on breast cancer must be made known. We need to investigate and make the safer and sometimes less convenient choices. Our lives, indeed life on earth, lies in the balance.

WHAT YOU CAN DO

Eliminate toxins as best you can from your environment in every aspect of your life. Educate yourself about the alternatives.

- **Food.** Avoid agricultural chemicals by purchasing organic foods. When possible, buy locally grown organic produce. Peeling and scrubbing help only a little as chemicals typically permeate the entire food. Try to purchase beverages in glass containers. Store foods in glass or ceramic containers. Use only BGH-free dairy products.

- **Clothing and furnishings.** Purchase the least chemically contaminated clothing and furnishings. Buy clothes of cotton, wool, linen, ramie and silks; eliminate synthetics. Reduce or eliminate items that need conventional dry cleaning. Buy solid wood, metal, glass or cotton furnishings.
- **Smoking and alcohol.** Stop smoking. Stop drinking.
- **Water.** Avoid chlorinated and otherwise contaminated water for drinking, showering and swimming. Investigate and get an appropriate water filtration system (see Resources).
- **Paper goods and household products.** Stationery, facial and toilet tissues, disposable diapers, tampons, coffee filters, and milk and juice cartons are some of the products that may contain dioxin and other toxic organochlorines and for which alternatives exist. Do not buy chlorine-bleached paper; use peroxide-bleached or unbleached paper products. Paper products that have not been chlorine-bleached are widely available. Companies like Seventh Generation offer chlorine-free toilet paper, tissues and napkins. Avoid chlorine bleach; use non-toxic cleaning products.
- **Feminine hygiene products.** Seventh Generation also offers ecologically safe sanitary napkins and tampons. On a deeper level our preference for disposable pads and tampons may be related to negative feelings about our menstrual cycle and a desire to hide our menstrual blood. The Menstrual Health Foundation offers support and non-disposable products that encourage feminine ecology (see Resources).

Imagine this scenario . . . A 32-year-old pregnant woman eating the standard American diet consumes a host of potential carcinogens that are legally permitted as food additives. These affect both her and the developing embryo. Fat-soluble pesticides on her supermarket fruits and vegetables lodge and accumulate in her breast and cross the placental barrier to affect the fetus. This same woman is advised to eat a high-protein diet because she is pregnant. The meat and chicken she consumes are high on the food chain, and fat-soluble contaminants are more concentrated. Factory-farmed animals have been injected and fed estrogens which contribute to her estrogen load, affecting her future risk and the risk of her fetus to breast cancer. The quality of the mother's food affects the developing fetus and breastfeeding infant as surely as its DNA. Pesticide residues cross into the breast milk as the baby feeds. . . . At the pediatrician's advice, the older infant begins drinking cow's milk. Hormones fed to the cows accumulate in the child's body. . . . The child's school lunches, subsidized by the National Dairy Council, include milk daily. . . . The busy family frequents fast food establishments; rancid fat takes its tool. As a teenager the girl is put on the birth control pill at age 13 to relieve her severe menstrual cramps. Her gynecologist assures both her and her mother of the pill's safety record. By age 18 the sexually active teenager decides to stay on The Pill for birth control purposes. Without a break she stays on The Pill until she is ready to start a family in her 30s. Her periods are light, much less painful and are predictably convenient. The young woman develops breast cancer at age 35. . . . *This scenario, with many variations, is commonplace in our society today.*

PRESCRIPTION ESTROGENS

"It is interesting, and perhaps worrying, that we are trying, both with the pill and with HRT, to establish safe conditions of use while a generation of women are using them."

—DR. RONALD MANN
Royal Society of Medicine in London[28]

To appreciate the exquisite balance of our hormonal system is to appreciate the struggle we are in as our internal world becomes increasingly affected by chemicals and chemicalized foods that directly and indirectly shift this delicate balance. "It's truly amazing how very few hormone molecules are required to produce a major effect. Even at the top of the range, there is only one hormone molecule for every *fifty billion* molecules in your blood plasma. At the low end of the concentration sweep, there may be one hundred times fewer hormone molecules—one in every *five zillion* (that's five thousand billion!). *Keep this in mind when you consider intervening by using synthetic hormones in your own body,*" warns Betty Kamen in *Hormone Replacement Therapy Yes or No?*[29]

Studies have shown a link between estrogenic chemicals of many types and breast cancer. The diethylstilbestrol (DES) fiasco is a case in point. Starting in the 1940s until the early 1960s this potent synthetic estrogen was administered to between 2 to 4 million U.S. women to prevent miscarriage. The result of this experiment was an increase in a rare vaginal cancer in the daughters of women who used the drug and a variety of reproductive abnormalities, including undescended testes, in their sons. Twenty years later studies investigating the link between DES mothers and breast cancer found up to a 50 percent increased risk.[30] Additional follow-up years may show an even higher risk; time will also show whether DES daughters themselves are at increased risk for the development of breast cancer.

I'm very concerned about the links between birth control pills and breast cancer and between estrogen replacement therapy and breast cancer. The breast is an estrogen-sensitive organ. Of course there is always a weighing of risks vs. benefits whenever we choose any medical intervention. Women must understand that ultimately the choices and the consequences are their own. Physicians must take their responsibility to "first do no harm" seriously. They must offer their patients up-to-date information presented compassionately and then allow women to make the decisions that they are comfortable with. The question is one of individual comfort level. However, it is clear that The Pill and Hormone Replacement Therapy are risk factors for the development of breast cancer.

Birth Control Pills

"Worldwide use of birth control pills, in spite of conclusive evidence of carcinogenicity of estrogens in experimental animals, constitutes the largest uncontrolled experiment in human carcinogenesis ever undertaken." [31]

—Dr. Samuel Epstein
The Politics of Cancer

Approximately 60 million women[32] worldwide take birth control pills (also called BCPs, oral contraceptives, The Pill) for reasons of personal convenience or for the treatment of various minor gynecologic complaints and they often take them for extended periods of time. As early as 1978 the World Health Organization reported on the potential for increased risk of breast cancer in certain groups of women taking the pill: those with benign breast disease, those who used oral contraceptives before the birth of their first child and young women in general.

❧

I remember well the pharmaceutical lunches during my residency. After our morning Ob-Gyn clinic was over, a catered lunch was a welcome break from our labors. The drug rep would bring deli sandwiches, potato salad, cole slaw, coke and an assortment of diet sodas. While we ate and drank he or she would show us a film about a common gynecologic problem, one that could always be best addressed with a handy prescription for birth control pills. Then came the little perks: calendars, pens, penlights, notepads (with the name of products inscribed all over the item)

plus lots of free samples to start our patients on. Start them
on and keep them on. Drug pushers? Perhaps.

  So it was here, in groups with other residents, and later
privately in our offices, that we all learned the prescribing
practices that we had not been taught in the high-tech envi-
ronment of the hospital. Factual information (presumed un-
biased) about these contraceptives was being proffered by
the manufacturers themselves, those in a position to profit
by their sales. In the hospital the focus was on surgical
procedures and IV medications, but out in the world pa-
tients wanted birth control. What could be easier—pop out
a pill, start on the first day of your menses and never look
back. The 28-day pack was complete with seven inert pills;
no need to stop and restart or rethink—just stay with the
program: a pill a day. The focus was on simplicity of in-
struction and ease of administration rather than side ef-
fects, whether major or minor. Alternate methods were
viewed as cumbersome. The push in marketing was always
toward a state of blissful sexual freedom. Just take the pill.
Side effects? They'll go away in a few months, wait and see,
and if they don't you'll be so happy with the convenience
of the pill we'll just switch brands.

∾

When I read Dr. Epstein's description of pesticide sales
reps which follows, it brought these memories back to me.
In both cases, profit is the bottom line.

The greatest absurdity in contemporary pest control is the
dominant role of the pesticide salesmen who simultaneously
acts as diagnostician, therapist, nostrum prescriber, and pill
peddler. It is difficult to imagine any situation where society
entrusts so great a responsibility to such poorly qualified
persons . . .[33]

Just substitute "birth control" for "pest control" and, fellow physicians, ask yourselves, who we are allowing to

educate us and who we are putting in charge of guaranteeing the safety of our medications?

Birth control pills disrupt the hormonal ecology of women, yet under the prevailing system they are prescribed to millions of women and their safety is assured by unqualified salesmen who have vested interests in their distribution.

Reports on the safety of birth control pills have been so contradictory that both doctors and patients are confused. I cringe when I think of all the women I reassured about the benefits of the pill. When I was a busy gynecologist I didn't have time to read the FDA transcripts on oral contraceptives, nor do most practicing physicians. But, alas, even these transcripts don't hold the answers we are looking for. The original research upon which the FDA based its approval of Enovid, the first contraceptive pill in the 1960s, was based on the clinical studies of only 132 women in Puerto Rico who had taken it for a year or longer.[34] The scientists studying this first oral contraceptive did not even request autopsies on the three women who died while they were participating in the trials. This dismal state of affairs prompted Virginia Soffa to write:

> I wanted to conduct my own research, since no one else seemed to be doing the kind of studies we need to prevent breast cancer. . .I wanted to look at. . .the effects of oral contraceptives on risk of breast cancer. . . .Having a Ph.D. or an M.D. doesn't always open doors, and in fact can close doors, because in order to achieve professional ranking many women are being trained to conform to and advocate the party line. In essence they are silenced by the very system they wanted to help advance.[35]

There is an unnaturally close relationship between organized medicine and the drug industry.

∾

I, the gynecologist, was sure that oral contraceptives (OCs) could not be marketed if they were not verifiably safe. I, the woman, was not so sure. I, the breast cancer survivor, need to examine the possible complicity and false assumptions—my life and the lives of women who trust me are at stake. Looking back I was caught between the drug industry's assertions of safety and my patients' trust that I was the supreme authority who knew and could make sense of it all. I conformed; I pushed the drugs. I remember writing in the charts over and over after prescribing OCs, "Risks and benefits discussed." Over and over I wrote it: part of it was the training I received in residency, the importance of detailed and complete charting was ever emphasized, part of it was no doubt a result of my training in malpractice defensiveness, and I am sure some of this served to assure me that I was doing the right thing in dispensing these drugs. Risk/benefit ratios and safety are words that haunt us. Whose risk, and just what is an acceptable risk? Whose benefit? Whose safety assessment?

∽

"The Pill" is not one pill, but rather more than 150 different formulations marketed worldwide. In this country most brands have the synthetic estrogenic compound ethinyl estradiol or mestranol which is combined with a synthetic progestin. The long-term effects of OCs on breast cancer are poorly defined for many reasons. The constant revisions of formulations cloud the picture in the follow-up of women on specific formulas and dosages. The long latent period associated with breast cancer (10 to 30 years) is another factor that complicates the investigation of cause and effect. But these difficulties do not excuse the government or industry from its responsibility to design a system to detect and report an increased incidence of breast cancer in users of oral contraceptives. Unfortunately the difficulties in study design have been used to promote the pill's safety rather than to challenge us to adequately explore the long-term risks. Short-term statistical follow-up is misleading in a disease like breast cancer.

In 1989 Swedish oncologist H. Olsson published a review that stated, "All hormonal components of oral contraceptives have been found to be carcinogenic in animal models.[36] Olsson compiled studies that showed a statistically significant increase in the risk of breast cancer to OC-users. As author Virginia Soffa writes regarding the development of her breast cancer, "Essentially my generation—women who were in their late teens between 1967 and 1972—is the first generation that has used oral contraceptives long enough, and began early enough, to experience breast cancer as a consequence."[37] And we are only now in a position to find out the long-term consequences.

Initially the pill was introduced into the U.S. market in the 1960s without meeting long-term animal testing standards, and inserts were not included. In 1968 Kathryn Stuart Hoffman took the pill for months at the insistence of her husband (a medical resident, at the time). A profoundly unsettling account by her mother, Natalee S. Greenfield, entitled *First Do No Harm*[38] records the details of her daughter's diagnosis of breast cancer at age 22, her radical mastectomy, the ensuing complications, her divorce and her death from metastatic disease. Kathryn's determination to live long enough to uncover the dangers of the pill to women and to mandate package inserts make an incredibly moving story.

Ten years after the pill's introduction, inserts were finally included in the pill package. They stated, "There is no proof at the present time that oral contraceptives can cause cancer in humans." The inserts of today are written in jargon that is too technical for the lay public or even for a professional to understand. Our current prescribing practices, the pill's availability and our culture's general acceptance of this method of birth control all imply that the pill is safe and that the warnings on the tissue paper inserts are not meant to be taken seriously.

In the 70s, while women continued to take the pill, National Institute of Health's Roy Hertz criticized the unrestricted use of estrogen, publicly calling attention to possible long-term consequences including breast cancer. National Cancer Institute's John C. Bailar III concurred and stated in a review of the papers presented at the First National Conference on Breast Cancer in 1969, "In my opinion there is no sound basis for assuring any women that any dose of any estrogen given for any reason is safe."[39] In January 1970, Senator Gaylord Nelson convened a Senate panel to inquire into the safety of oral contraceptives a decade after the FDA approved their use. Although no definite conclusions were reached, the American Medical Association's Council on Drugs responded to the hearings cautiously, admitting ". . . the possibility that oral contraceptives might stimulate the growth of some existing tumors of the breast . . . and that those who have or have had a known or suspected hormone-dependent tumor should not use this method of contraception."[40]

In the early 1980s, Professor Malcolm Pike, former head of the Imperial Cancer Research Fund's Cancer Epidemiology Unit in Oxford, now at the University of Southern California in Los Angeles, created an uproar when he published the results of his investigations of the pill's long-term effects on younger women. Noting that the age at which a woman went through her first full-term pregnancy affected her risk of breast cancer, Pike believed that the adolescent and early adult years were a critical time for establishing breast cancer risk so that taking pills at this time could seriously increase the chance of developing early-onset breast cancer (breast malignancy prior to age 45). His findings indicated an increased risk of breast cancer to younger women (under 25) who used the pill for prolonged periods of time. He found that after one year on the pill a young woman's risk of early onset breast cancer was 30 percent higher than normal; after eight years, it nearly quadrupled.

These findings contradicted the early results of the largest investigation into this question, the Cancer and Steroid Hormones Study (CASH), a joint project of the U.S. Centers for Disease Control in Atlanta and the National Institute of Child Health and Development in Washington. Support for the association between the pill and breast cancer also came from a number of studies in Scandinavia, New Zealand and Great Britain; finally, in 1988, CASH investigators published a reanalysis of their data showing an increased risk of breast cancer, 5.6 times higher than the norm, in a subgroup of women who had started the birth control pill before age 20 and remained on it for more than eight years. In the *British Medical Journal* review, 8 of 13 studies linked premenopausal breast cancer with long-term (greater than eight years) oral contraceptive use. A new study published in the *Journal of the National Cancer Institute*,[41] and one of the few to include women taking the lower-estrogen pill, shows that women who start taking oral contraceptives before age 18 and continue to take them for more than 10 years increase their breast-cancer risk threefold.

Ꮬ*Remember...*

The oral contraceptive pill was never adequately studied. We are the experiment. For some women there are serious health risks associated with the use of the pill. In some women OCs may contribute to the manifestation of breast cancer; in others the long-term exposure to synthetic estrogens may initiate or promote the process in association with xenoestrogens from other sources and genetic susceptibility to these agents. The younger the woman is at the exposure and the longer the exposure the greater the potential risk.

Do not assume OCs are safe because they are on the market. Risk? Benefit? Sexual freedom? Breast cancer? Life? Death? Make the choices for yourself. Become informed. Consider non-hormonal alternatives such as diaphragms or condoms for birth control.

HORMONE REPLACEMENT THERAPY

The way we think about menopause has a great effect on how we think about hormone replacement therapy (HRT). Ultimately the ease with which we proceed through the menopause is determined by our physiology, our mindset and the cultural backdrop. Most women who are diagnosed with breast cancer are already menopausal or in the perimenopausal transition period. In fact, 77 percent of women newly diagnosed with breast cancer are age 50 or older.[42]

Others are thrust into a treatment-induced menopause as a side effect of chemotherapy and/or radiation or as a result of surgical removal of their uterus and/or ovaries. If the transition to menopause is abrupt as a result of bilateral oophorectomy or as a sequelae to chemo or radiation in a young woman there is a higher probability that menopausal symptoms will be an issue. If a woman is under 40 at the time she receives chemo or radiation, ovarian function may return after a period of cessation. In any case, bothersome menopausal symptoms need to be addressed whether on a short- or long-term basis; women may also want to address preventive strategies regarding cardiovascular and bone health.

In general, when we think of menopause as a deficiency state or a period of inevitable decline, we are much more likely to seek the cure for our situation in the form of hormones. When menopause is viewed as a natural transition to our wisdom years, then hormone *replacement* might actually be considered inappropriate. No one is so eloquent about the need for us to reframe the way we think about menopause than Dr. Christiane Northrup. She writes, "Many women know the menopause by the name 'change of life.'

Whatever we call it, no other stage of a woman's life has as much potential for understanding and tapping into woman's power as this one—if, that is, a woman is able to negotiate her way through the general cultural negativity surrounding menopause."[43]

Our bodies have been pathologized and medicalized by a deficiency mentality that seeks to manage and thereby control our natural transitions. Obstetrics and Gynecology, traditionally a male-dominated specialty, ostensibly cares for women by managing dysmenorrhea with oral contraceptives, managing dysovulation with clomiphene, managing the perimenopause with Provera and managing menopause with HRT. In an opinion column in the February 1, 1996 issue of Ob-Gyn News, a contributing gynecologist writes, "The most difficult problem with perimenopausal or post-menopausal women is convincing them to begin estrogens." At the end of the column Ob-Gyn News exhorts its readership, "If you have found the key to success in getting your patient on estrogen, we would like to hear from you."[44]

What is currently being marketed as "natural" estrogens is anything but. Premarin, the most commonly prescribed form of estrogen replacement therapy is extracted, as the name implies, from pregnant mares' urine. It is made primarily in Canada by the Wyeth-Ayerst Company. Among its 14 ingredients, Premarin contains estradiol and estrone, large amounts of equilin, a horse estrogen, as well as shellac for the nice shiny coating on the pill. Mares are impregnated to produce Premarin and, from the fourth month through the end of their 11-month pregnancy, they are confined and their urine is collected with a harness and surgical tubing. After giving birth the mares are then reimpregnated. If we decide to take exogenous hormones, the source of these hormones is a factor to consider.

Plant-derived estrogens, including estriol, are available and may be compounded in individualized dosages. In pharmaceutical dosages estriol has a safer track record than estradiol and estrone which are currently used by conventional physicians. Estriol is weaker and requires larger doses to ameliorate symptoms (see Resources). Jonathan Wright, M.D., a nutrition-oriented physician in Kent, Washington, has been using estriol with his patients since the early 1980s. He uses a formula which he developed called tri-estrogen which is a combination of 80 percent estriol, 10 percent estradiol and 10 percent estrone. The combination was developed because Wright found that in many cases the amount of estriol required to relieve symptoms caused excessive nausea. Tri-estrogen was designed to maximize benefits and reduce risk. Dr. Wright found that 2.5 mg of tri-estrogen is usually effective for the relief of menopausal symptoms and, according to Wright, is the therapeutic equivalent of .625 mg of conjugated estrogen (Premarin).

Instead of viewing the new energy available to meno-pausal women as they are freed from the challenges of the reproductive years as a positive, the medical establishment sees only the need to medically replace what is in fact no longer needed. We cannot fail to be affected by the media that portrays menopausal women as barren crones with atrophic vaginas and brittle bones and without the libido required to satisfy our potent men—unless we ingest phar-maceutical hormones. I was taught this both practically and philosophically in medical school and residency; I was propagandized by the pharmaceutical industry; my prescrip-tion pads had advertisements for hormones on every other page, the journal ads displayed hump-backed dowagers. In the fine print of the scientific articles I read supporting the use of these products I noticed that the corporate research grants came from these same pharmaceutical houses.

Unfortunately we don't have large-scale, unbiased studies on healthy women who opt not to take HRT. We have not done the research to elucidate why many women who *don't* take hormones *don't* get fractures, depression, thinned vagi-nal membranes or heart disease. The pharmaceutical re-search grants are not being used to compare heart disease in women who take HRT with heart disease in women who

eat the type of diet I describe, who exercise and who prioritize their own emotional health. The strength of the power
of belief is enormous. My own premature menopause was
reversed after years of hot flashes, amenorrhea and vaginal
atrophy when I allowed life-affirming sexuality to reenter
my life.

With the images we have been inundated with regarding
menopause is it any wonder that we reach for the fountain
of youth HRT promises? We need to dispel the myth that
decrepitude follows on the heels of menopause. A col-
league of mine, Dr. Ida Fisher Davidoff, who recently cele-
brated her 91st birthday, is writing a book about ageism in
our culture, *Youth: A Gift of Nature; Age: A Work of Art.*
She is my role model, lifting weights, counseling, writing
and lecturing; Ida Davidoff is the essence of the wisdom,
power, and *joie de vivre* that age can bring to women.

Here are some powerful words from Dr. Susan Love:

> There must be some reason menopause exists in the first
> place, and maybe our bodies really need to stop having these
> hormones at some point. I'm concerned because once again
> gynecologists are casually giving out hormones without suf-
> ficient research, and we may well end up with another DES-
> type situation on our hands.

The HRT-Breast Cancer Link

Meta-analysis of the studies on this issue have revealed that
HRT is associated with an increase in the risk of breast
cancer of 1 to 30 percent.[46] Although these increased risks
were not deemed statistically significant the association remains and may have profound implications. In August of
1989 a randomized controlled study done in Uppsala, Sweden involving 23,244 women showed an increase in breast
cancer after seven years of estrogen use.[47] Not all the studies
support this link.

After an extended follow-up of the participants in the Nurses' Health Study, Graham A. Colditz, M.D. of the Harvard Medical School showed that current estrogen-users were 32 percent more likely to develop breast cancer and current users of estrogen and progestin 41 percent more likely to develop breast cancer than women who had never taken hormones. Current users who had been on ERT/HRT for more than five years were 46 percent more likely to develop breast cancer than women who had never taken hormones, and the risk was even greater for older women. According to the Boston researchers, a 60- to 64-year-old woman who had been on therapy for more than five years was 71 percent more likely to develop breast cancer than a woman the same age who had never taken estrogen.[48]

Commenting on the results of this study, Louise Brinton, Ph.D., chief of the environmental studies section at the National Cancer Institute in Bethesda, MD said, "It's widely recognized that [hormone-replacement therapy] has major beneficial effects, but the risks have often been ignored in favor of the benefits. I think that most of us have been convinced that estrogen does have some adverse effect on breast-cancer risk, and this study reinforces that."

What about Estrogen after the Diagnosis of Breast Cancer?

Recently I read an article entitled *HRT After Breast Cancer: A Practical Approach,* endorsing the use of estrogens for women who had been treated for breast cancer. The article was written by Dr. Gloria Bachmann, a physician I knew in my residency training program. I was stunned. First, we increase the probability of getting breast cancer by over-prescribing OCs to women when they are young; then we do the same thing with HRT during menopause. As if that weren't enough, we are ready to prescribe even more hormones after women develop breast cancer. In fact some researchers have been sounding the horn for trials of ERT in breast cancer survivors. Dr. Melody Cobleigh of the Rush-Presbyterian-St. Luke's Medical Center, Chicago, said in an interview with *Ob-Gyn News,* "I believe we need to look at a series of pilot studies that will lay the groundwork for larger clinical trials. We need to address the issue of ERT on breast cancer recurrence and the concomitant use of tamoxifen and other interventions."[49]

At a panel of experts on breast cancer in New York City in 1994 Dr. Susan Love said, in her own inimitable way,

> For a long time, based on absolutely no data, doctors have said that no woman who has ever had breast cancer should take hormones. And now, within the last couple of years, based on absolutely no data, doctors are saying it's fine for women with breast cancer to take hormones. Women need to realize that having no data that shows hormones are harmful doesn't mean they're safe. It means we don't know one way or another.[50]

A few months after reading the article by Dr. Bachmann, I attended a lecture in New York City given by Nick Gonzales, M.D., a well-known physician offering alternative care to cancer patients. The topic of the night was hormone therapy. He, too, struggled with the risk/benefit of pharmaceutical hormones in certain situations. He told two heartbreaking stories about women in his practice who survived very aggressive chemotherapy for breast cancer and then went on to die not from their breast cancer, but from osteoporosis. Having successfully eradicated breast cancer, these women were left completely estrogen-deficient as a sequelae to the adjuvant triple chemotherapy that they had received. These stories really hit home because I am a survivor of the same type of aggressive chemotherapy that these women received and also because the concept of estrogen as a "dangerous" hormone had been floating around my consciousness (and I'm sure the collective consciousness of all gynecologists) and was sorely in need of some fine-tuning.

What we need to achieve is a balanced approach. Severe estrogen deficiency resulting from the complete cessation of ovarian function in premenopausal women who have been treated with aggressive chemotherapy for breast cancer certainly needs to be addressed. The women Dr. Gonzalez spoke of were in an artificially imposed chemical menopause that was clearly nonphysiologic and harmful. Under these circumstances hormones night be judiciously replaced in an individualized program. The program should also include dietary and herbal phytoestrogens, progesterone, estriol or perhaps the tri-estrogen formulated by Dr. Jonathan Wright which has a large amount of estriol.

What we must not do is confuse the situation of severe and complete estrogen depletion with the more common situation of progesterone deficiency and relative estrogen excess that most women manifest. As a responsible gynecologist it is important to explore the role of progesterone as opposed to synthetic progestins and to question studies using conjugated estrogen blends whose potency, metabolism and side effects are not understood and for which breast cancer has been shown to be an undesirable side effect. We have to overcome the notion of good and bad hormones and treat women in the context of their own very individual histories.

In postmenopausal women with a history of breast cancer estrogen therapy is an option that must be considered only with utmost caution and only after thorough exploration of the alternatives.

The medical community incorrectly warns us that the risk of breast cancer is the price that women must pay to prevent osteoporosis and heart disease through the administration of hormones. In fact, the fear of osteoporosis and cardiovascular disease are doctors' most powerful argument for the use of HRT.

HRT and Osteoporosis

Let me reassure you that we need not choose between breast cancer and osteoporosis. Osteoporosis is a multifactorial disease of progressive bone loss. Like breast cancer, there are many contributing factors and similarly, no magic bullet. Osteoporosis is associated with lack of exercise, high-fat, meat-based diets, smoking, alcohol, multiple vitamin and mineral deficiencies, genetics and estrogen and progesterone deficiencies, among other factors. We cannot attribute osteoporosis simply to a lack of estrogen, ignoring all the other factors, any more than we can attribute breast cancer simply to an excess of estrogen. However, estrogen dynamics do play a role in both diseases.

Bones are made of collagen and various essential minerals including calcium, phosphate, magnesium, silicon and boron; however, even with adequate nutrient intake, bones will not mineralize unless they are put under some physical stress. Weight-bearing exercise is thus essential for bone health.

Of course hormones also play a role in bone metabolism. Interestingly, although conventional medicine teaches us that estrogen is pivotal in maintaining bone mass, in reality the cells that build bone, the osteoblasts, are controlled by progesterone. During the child-bearing years progesterone production is cyclic, peaking after each ovulation. During the perimenopause, the years prior to menopause when ovulation ceases but bleeding continues, the production of first progesterone and then estrogen declines. The lack of progesterone in these years accounts for the observation that many women enter menopause with significant bone loss. The lack of estrogen causes increased activity of the bone cells known as osteoclasts, whose job it is to resorb bone, so bones thin further, in response. When menopause occurs estrogen production continues to decline. The effect of estrogen supplementation on restraining bone resorption is most noticeable for the first five years following menopause, after which bone loss proceeds anyway.[51]

Progesterone and Osteoporosis

Although for an estimated 30 percent of women no significant bone loss will occur at all, in those who do experience
a loss the decline begins in the mid-30s, accelerating for
three to five years after menopause, and then continuing at
a slower rate. If estrogen alone were responsible why
would osteoporosis begin 15 years before menopause? An-
ovulatory cycles with deficient progesterone production are
common in the perimenopause. While measuring estrogen
and progesterone levels in athletes, Jerilynn Prior, M.D. of
the University of British Columbia discovered that athletes
with low progesterone and high estrogen had signs of osteoporosis. Progesterone is clearly an important and overlooked hormone in bone formation.

The early studies on osteoporosis evaluating the use of
estrogen (without progesterone) had serious flaws in their
design, and the results lacked the substantiation afforded
by current bone density measurement technology. After reviewing 31 estrogen osteoporosis treatment studies,[52] U.S.
Barzel, M.D., concluded that unopposed estrogen has a host
of unacceptable side effects and complications including endometrial cancer, blood-clotting abnormalities, liver dysfunction and breast problems, possibly including breast
cancer. Moreover, it may not be of significant benefit in
established disease. Estrogen can slow but not prevent or
reverse osteoporosis.

Since the mid-1970's when the estrogen/endometrial cancer link was noted, hormone replacement has included both
estrogens and progestins. However, which hormone is
doing what has still not been addressed. Dr. John Lee, who
has studied the effects of natural progesterone in his clinical
practice since 1982, presents evidence that natural progesterone in a program of whole foods diet, vitamin/mineral
supplementation and modest exercise can prevent and reverse osteoporosis.[53]

Dr. Lee suggests a few reasons why research has not

pursued this line of inquiry, but the bottom line is that natural progesterone cannot be patented and offers much less commercial profit. There is quite a lot of confusion regarding progesterone vs. synthetic progestins.

Progesterone vs. Synthetic Progestins

There is a vast difference between progesterone and synthetic progestins. Progesterone is a single hormone made by the ovarian *corpus luteum,* which emerges after ovulation and which is responsible for the maintenance of the thickened endometrium necessary if a pregnancy ensues. Thus, progesterone allows for implantation of the egg and, if a pregnancy is achieved, the *corpus luteum* will support the pregnancy until the seventh to twelfth weeks of the pregnancy, at which time, after a period of shared production, the placenta emerges as the supplier of progesterone. Progesterone, essential for the survival and development of the fetus, is an important precursor for other sex hormones and adrenal steroids and functions to balance many of estrogen's effects in the body.

Synthetic progestins pale next to natural progesterone. Progestins are simply laboratory-derived chemicals that can sustain the thickened (secretory) endometrium. Pharmaceutical progestins are not found in nature and may be more suitably called xenoprogestins. Natural progesterone itself has no side effects. A very partial list of side effects from Provera the most popular synthetic progesterone, as listed in the *Physician's Desk Reference* (1993) follows:

Warning:
    Increased risk of birth defects.
    Beagle dogs given this drug developed malignant mammary nodules.
    Discontinue this drug if there is sudden or partial loss of vision.
    This drug passes into breast milk, consequences unknown.

May contribute to thrombophlebitis, pulmonary embolism, and cerebral thrombosis.

Precaution:

May cause fluid retention, epilepsy, migraine, asthma, cardiac or renal dysfunction.

May cause breakthrough bleeding or menstrual irregularities.

May cause or contribute to depression.

May decrease glucose tolerance; diabetic patients must be carefully monitored.

Adverse reaction:

May cause breast tenderness.

May cause acne, alopecia and hirsutism.

Edema, weight changes (increase or decrease).

Cervical erosions and changes in cervical secretions.

When taken with estrogens, the following have been observed:

Rise in blood pressure, headache, dizziness, nervousness, fatigue.

Changes in libido, hirsutism and loss of scalp hair.

Premenstrual-like syndrome, changes in appetite.

Cystitis-like syndrome.

Healthy Ways to Prevent Osteoporosis

Osteoporosis is a multifactorial disease. Bone is a living tissue that is constantly undergoing remodeling. By failing to provide the substrates for this process our nutritionally depleted diets are promoting the development of osteoporosis. The hormonal aspects cannot be oversimplified; osteoporosis is not simply caused by estrogen deficiency.

Osteoporosis needs to be seriously addressed with an individualized approach that includes:

- A whole foods, plant-based diet that is high in all the minerals necessary for bone metabolism.
- Vitamins, minerals and soy isoflavone supplementation.

- Regular weight bearing exercise
- The judicious use of dual photon densiometry to assess results.
- Progesterone preparations instead of synthetic progestins.

The safest hormone regimens must be our goal—consideration should be given to the incorporation of estrogens that have been shown to be the safest (estriol) and, if necessary, combined with the smallest doses of estradiol and estrone to achieve the desired relief and results.

A Suggested Osteoporosis Prevention/Treatment Program

I offer some general guidelines and points to be aware of. As always, individualizing a regime with respect for your particular condition is most beneficial:

Diet. Include leafy greens, whole grains, legumes, seeds and nuts in your diet to assure adequate calcium and magnesium. Tofu, sardines, and canned salmon are also good calcium-rich choices. Avoid soda, coffee, sugar, alcohol and heavily processed foods. Limit meat as the high phosphate content works against calcium balance.

Soy Isoflavones. Functioning both as antiestrogens and weak estrogens, soy isoflavones can perform two roles, depending on a woman's particular biochemistry. As antiestrogens they can block unopposed endogenous estrogens and/or potent xenoestrogens, thereby ameliorating potential carcinogens. As weak estrogens they can provide mild estrogenic activity for women who are in deficiency states and at risk for osteoporosis. I take Harmonizer, a vitamin, mineral and herbal blend prepared in a base of isoflavones.

Vitamin/Mineral Supplements

- Calcium, 600 mg per day; calcium citrate is a well-absorbed form. Also include magnesium at 300 mg/day. The calcium/magnesium ratio in a supplement should be approximately 2:1. In the winter add a vitamin D supplement of 400 IU.
- Many postmenopausal women are thought to be deficient in gastric acid secretions, which hinders the absorption of calcium and other important minerals. The aging process, diets that have been excessively high in animal protein and overconsumption of antacids can all contribute to this problem. Gastric acid supplements may be helpful to assure the absorption of calcium.
- Vitamin C, 3-5 gm per day. If you are currently being treated for breast cancer, 5-10mg/day.
- Betacarotene or mixed carotenoid supplement, 25,000-50,000 IU per day.
- Multivitamin and multimineral combination to assure intake of vitamin B6 (50 mg), folic acid (800 mcg), zinc (30 mg), copper (1 mg) and manganese (10 mg). The roles of boron, silicon and strontium in the prevention of osteoporosis have not been fully elucidated. Dr. Alan Gaby's book *Preventing and Reversing Osteoporosis* is excellent (see Resources).

Progesterone. An over-the-counter 3-to 5-percent progesterone cream is available by mail order or through local health food stores (see Resources) and may be used once or twice daily, one quarter to half a teaspoon, three weeks per month. This would be best discussed initially with a knowledgeable health care provider. Your gynecologist can advise how to use natural progesterone in conjunction with any estrogen replacement that you may be taking and how to go about switching from synthetic progestins to natural progesterone.

Exercise Aim for one hour four times a week of weight-bearing exercise. Brisk walking is an excellent choice. Daily sunshine is necessary for the production of vitamin D, another component of the calcium equation.

Avoid smoking.

Stress reduction. Decreasing stress levels is an important part of osteoporosis prevention and management.

Take the time to educate yourself and to find physicians who are open to these holistic approaches (see Resources).

Cardiovascular Disease and Estrogen

Research on the effect of estrogen on heart disease is conflicting. Some studies have shown reductions in the risk of heart disease for women on hormone replacement therapy, yet other studies have shown estrogen raises blood pressure, increases the level of triglycerides and increases blood clotting (leading to strokes). Dr. Graham Colditz writes that "women over 55 should carefully consider the risks and benefits of estrogen therapy . . . It is not clear that benefits outweigh risks for all women, particularly women with few risk factors for heart disease."[54]

Advocates of HRT maintain that it saves more lives from heart disease than it takes with cancer but if this is true it is only true if women are uninformed, unwilling or otherwise unable to take care of themselves. Eating a nutrient-dense heart-healthy diet, exercising, eliminating smoking and opening to our emotional needs will all result in normalizing blood pressure, weight and stress levels leading to healthy hearts, healthy bones, healthy breasts and healthy women.

Alternatives for Menopausal Symptoms

There are many ways to approach the issues that arise in menopause without resorting to conventional HRT. A more natural symptom-free menopause can be achieved by eating a whole foods diet, with balanced supplementation, herbs, homeopathy and even aromatherapy as valuable adjuncts. Combined with exercise, meditation or yoga one can approach menopause as a natural process rather than as a medical condition.

Hot Flashes. Emphasizing raw foods such as salads and fresh vegetable juice for their cooling effects will help alleviate hot flashes. Soy foods, high in phytoestrogens, will also diminish vasomotor symptoms. Bioflavonoids, found in lemon and orange skins, will ease hot flashes so use these skins in lemonade, teas or dessert recipes. Bioflavonoids are often found in supplement form combined with vitamin C. For some women 800 IU of vitamin E at bedtime relieves hot flashes and night sweats, in addition to its other health benefits.

Progesterone alleviates vasomotor complaints in addition to preventing and reversing osteoporosis. If hormones prove necessary, progesterone is the most sensible first choice. Natural progesterone, derived from the soybean plant or the wild yam, is available in various forms and dosages. It can be applied as a topical cream, ointment, gel or suppository or taken as an oral tablet, capsule, sublingual or suspension, as well as by injection. Progesterone can be obtained in over-the-counter preparations or compounded in stronger dosages as USP progesterone by prescription. I personally use progesterone products, which have been effective in eliminating my hot flashes. I believe that progesterone is restorative in today's high-stress world and in fact protective against breast cancer.

Vitex, black cohosh, sage and alfalfa are all menopausal herbal remedies. Homeopathic remedies, specifically pulsatilla or lachesis, can be effective adjuncts for menopausal symptoms. In Europe, where homeopathy has been used for generations, utilizing naturally occurring substances from plants, minerals and animals in minute doses for the purpose of stimulating one's own innate healing response is not even considered alternative medicine. French pharmacies are required to carry homeopathic remedies along with conventional drugs. In the practice of homeopathy the remedies are matched to the individual rather than the symptom, so one woman's hot flash remedy may be different from another's.

Aromatherapy makes use of essential oils; these oils are applied as massage oils or as compresses; they can be used in your bath or as inhalants; they can also be used internally but only under the proper medical guidance. Each oil contains, on average, 100 different chemicals which work on many different levels. Aromatherapy is effective because of the medicinal properties of the oils, which modify the immune response and harmonize moods and emotions. Aromatic molecules enter the olfactory system and travel to the limbic system of the brain which organizes our emotional experiences; aromas have powerful psychological effects. Essential oils are also effective because they are absorbed through the skin; no less important is the therapeutic value of receiving these oils through our sense of touch, either through soft-tissue or pressure-point massage. Clary sage, among other essential oils, can benefit hot flashes.

Insomnia. Many times the amelioration of hot flashes and night sweats will help menopausal women resume healthy sleep patterns. For some women other remedies are useful such as the combination homeopathic remedies for insomnia available in health food stores. If sleeplessness is associated with anxiety and grief, ignatia is a good homeopathic remedy. The essential oil of lavender can also improve sleep disturbances, as can the herb valerian taken as a tincture, tea or in capsules.

Melatonin, secreted by the pineal gland, regulates day/night cycles and can be used as a natural sleeping aid by menopausal women with sleep disturbances. Melatonin, in its role as a regulator of other hormones, may also help prevent hormone dependent cancers such as breast cancer.

The connection between pineal function, melatonin levels and breast cancer has been and continues to be an area of research. Melatonin has been shown to inhibit the growth of human breast cancer cells in tissue culture[55] and has also been shown to block the growth of breast tumors in laboratory animals. Dr. Paoli Lissoni has used melatonin alone as a cancer treatment and in combination with chemotherapy with encouraging results.[56] I think it is reasonable to use supplements that have multiple indications and to use what we know about the mechanisms of action in the most practical ways.

In their book, *The Melatonin Miracle,* authors Walter Pierpaoli, M.D. and William Regelson, M.D. write,

> Our findings are consistent with those of other researchers who have shown that chemotherapy is often more effective and less toxic when given at night, presumably because melatonin levels are at their peak. In fact, many chemotherapy patients are now given intravenous pumps with timers that automatically pulse anticancer drugs into their bodies while they sleep.[57]

Vaginal Dryness. The typical American diet, loaded with bread at every meal, contributes to dry mucus membranes. Select whole grains like whole oats, millet, barley and brown rice instead of processed grains. Kelp is beneficial to vaginal health. Essential fatty acids will relieve symptoms of dryness including sexual discomfort from the lack of vaginal secretions. Incorporate flaxseed oil and Udo's Choice into your diet. Vitamin E in the diet and by supplementation is useful for vaginal health. Vitamin E oil can be massaged directly into the vagina or can be used in suppository form to relieve dryness. Vitamin C supplementation will also help with vaginal lubrication.

Creme de la Femme (see Resources) is a useful nonhormonal product developed by Marilynn Pratt, M.D. that can be used for vaginal lubrication, and has been reported by reliable sources to enhance the sexual experience when treatment-induced or natural menopause has caused excessive dryness. Saw palmetto improves vaginal atrophy and slippery elm can aid in moisturizing the vagina. The homeopathic remedies lycopodium and bryonia are also used for promoting lubrication.

Fatigue. High quality protein combats fatigue. When women are tired they crave sugar to maintain their energy levels; sugar consumption then depletes mineral levels, further stressing the adrenals and contributing to a vicious cycle of sugar intake and fatigue. Eating more protein-rich legumes, nuts, seeds, tofu, tempeh, organic eggs and fish helps combat fatigue. The elimination of sugar and coffee and a good stress reduction program can improve adrenal function. Adrenal vitality increases energy, particularly sexual energy. Vitamin C supplementation also supports adrenal function. A good multi-vitamin and essential fatty acids are energizing. Siberian ginseng is a menopausal herbal remedy that has energizing effects. The essential oils of grapefruit, rosemary and ginger also help energy levels.

6

The Culture That Loves and Hates Breasts

"We cannot hope to reclaim our bodily wisdom and inherent ability to create health without first understanding the influence of our society on how we think about and care for our bodies."[1]

—CHRISTIANE NORTHRUP M.D.

WOMEN IN THE 90'S

SUPERWOMEN

In our culture, women are expected to meet everyone's needs. Women are given mixed messages: in some instances we are pushed to choose between motherhood and careers and in other cases forced to pursue both. As we attempt to do it all, we are devalued in both arenas. Women often take on both the role of a full-time mother and full-time worker because of financial pressures. We earn less money in the job market and then come home to household chores after a full day's work: cleaning, cooking, arranging daycare, overseeing household help and all the responsibilities of child-rearing from school lunches and clothing to playdates and vacation activities.

In the workplace the "mommy track" is the buzzword used to rationalize the sexist practice of unequal pay for equal jobs, a practice that exists in both high- and low-paying professions. As I went through medical school in the 1980's it was rare to find a female professor; a female department chair was unheard of. Aggressive men are considered powerful and successful while an aggressive career woman is devalued as "unfeminine" or "hard."

Sometimes it seems no socially acceptable role exists for women today. Even though motherhood is still a key part of the cultural stereotype of the perfect woman, full-time mothers aren't valued in our society. And neither are the women who work and choose not to have children. Both are looked upon as "unfulfilled." I have seen so many tormented professional women in their late 30s and early 40s in my practice who are conflicted about motherhood. These women have full lives with satisfying careers and relationships but, without children, they are judged and judge themselves "incomplete." All their extraordinary achievements are dimmed in their eyes if they fail to conceive.

On the other hand, those of us who combine motherhood with career often receive little appreciation for the tireless physical and emotional work of juggling 24-hour-a-day childcare and household responsibilities with 8-hour-a-day (at best) professional responsibilities. Although both my husband and I were full-time physicians, all organizational activities related to the house and the children were my domain. This is common practice for working women; it is the rare man who truly shares the burden and all the responsibilities of parenthood.

When I was working as a full-time obstetrician-gynecologist I was always taken aback when other women remarked how involved my husband was simply because he frequently dropped the children off at school. When men participate in bringing up their children they are applauded; women, on the other hand, are expected to do this job in its entirety, regardless of and in addition to any professional commitments. Anything less is unacceptable by our society's unwritten standards. I clearly remember the fury with which the news of my third pregnancy was met by my male medical partners, the very professionals who ought to be most sensitive to the special needs of women.

There are very few role models of women who successfully and creatively integrate their roles at home and at work. We are torn between our roles as mothers, wives, workers, and women; there is never enough of us to go around. Our nurturing capacities have been stretched to the limit. Is it any wonder that breast cancer has become such an epidemic? In *Women's Bodies, Women's Wisdom,* Christiane Northrup, M.D. writes:

> Our culture has skewed the nurturing metaphor in order that women will give themselves away to others, without nurturing themselves. Women give and give and give until the well runs dry. If men and women generally went around without shirts, people would see that the major wound for women is the mastectomy scar. In contrast the major scar for men would be the coronary artery bypass scar down the center of their chests—because men need to learn how to open their hearts."[2]

We need to empower ourselves by making choices that reflect our goals *via à vis* our own internal standards and then creatively integrate our lives on this basis. We must acknowledge and honor our own needs.

THE BATTERED WOMAN

Every 15 seconds a woman is battered in the United States.[3] This year three out of five women in the U.S. will be battered. Violence will occur at least once in two-thirds of all marriages. Domestic violence is the single largest cause of injury to women in the United States, more common than injuries sustained from car accidents, muggings and rapes combined. The FBI notes that 2,000 women are killed by their partners in the U.S. each year. Physical violence is a factor in 52 percent of middle-class divorces. Ninety-five percent of all domestic violence is male against female.

There are many kinds of domestic violence: physical, emotional, sexual as well as violence involving property. Physical violence occurs when one person attempts to establish and maintain control through the use of or threat of physical violence. More pervasive is psychological abuse: the constant use of intimidation, harassment, criticism and humiliation to control another's thinking and behavior. Sexual abuse occurs with the use or threat of force to coerce sexual activity. When a person breaks, destroys or takes away meaningful objects this is another form of domestic violence.

We need to get in touch with how this accumulated violence to women in our culture feels in our bodies and where we hold it. We need to know how and where it touches us in our own lives. We cannot simply understand violence intellectually; we need to feel it inside. This endemic violence affects us profoundly. We need to stop being "good" to everyone but ourselves and begin to pay attention to what we are allowing to take place in our lives. Dr. Northrup writes: "Once an experience is consciously named and internalized, physically and emotionally, it can no longer influence us unconsciously. Naming something that has affected us adversely is part of freeing ourselves from its continued influence." Abuse, in any form, needs to be named. "Many times healing cannot begin until we allow ourselves to *feel how bad things are* (or were in the past). Doing this frees the emotional and physical energy that has been stuffed, stuck, denied, or ignored for many years."[4]

Women, the perpetual nurturers, are wounded in our culture in many ways, putting us at risk for illness. We need to empower ourselves by recognizing and refusing to be abused in any form.

THE CULTURAL MAKEOVER OF OUR BREASTS

Our breasts have assumed proportions that are greater than life. Men are attracted to these "objects of desire." Depending on this season's fashion silhouette, we are told by the media that our breasts are either too small or too big. Flat-chested models on magazine covers look prepubescent and contrast with voluptuous, big-breasted Playboy bunnies. We have become conspicuously self-conscious. Whatever the size and shape of our breasts, they are not good enough.

In our culture women's breasts are commercialized. We are taught to measure our value by how we look, and specifically how we look to men. Our identity as women is connected to our feelings about our womanly bodies, and our breasts are very much part of that identity. From a young age girls get mixed messages about breasts. They are eager for their first bras, but often ashamed as their breast buds emerge. As women, our culture encourages us to reveal ourselves in scant bikinis or sexy lingerie, yet at the same time, such attire is considered too provocative. Too much, not enough. On a deep level we are confused by the conflicting messages about the acceptability of our breasts.

We are embarrassed by our breasts when they emerge, we are aghast as they age, and we measure our breasts by standards that are physically unachievable. Enter plastic surgery—cosmetic plastic surgery on the breasts has become commonplace. Our breasts are augmented; our breasts are reduced. In the past 20 years plastic breast procedures have increased dramatically. Approximately two million American women have had breasts implants,[5] about 80 percent for purely cosmetic reasons. According to statistics from the American Society of Plastic and Reconstructive Surgeons, there were 39,247 cosmetic breast augmentations and 36,074 reductions in 1994.

Plastic surgery of the breast is neither right nor wrong; the changes it effects can be very positive. However, as

Naomi Wolf so aptly points out in *The Beauty Myth,* plastic surgery is not a panacea. It will not heal a woman's life or her relationship with her body. The most important factor in a successful outcome, aside from a skilled surgeon, is the context in which the procedure is done and the expectations that a woman has of it. Our breasts cannot make up for what is missing in our lives. They can nurture but they cannot sustain us. They are beautiful but they cannot create the beauty in our lives. They are sensual but are not the source of our sensuality. Our breasts are expressions of the divine but they cannot be imbued with divinity.

So here we are in this culture of male obsession with breasts where women never feel quite right about their bodies. We need to commit ourselves to respecting and accepting our breasts, respecting their function in the nourishment of our children and lovingly accepting the sensual pleasure they bring to us.

Bras and Breast Cancer

Around the world certain attitudes and behaviors are passed along within various cultures. The way we dress, specifically the custom of wearing a bra, is a behavior that is affected by societal attitudes. Bra wearing is supported by a 20th century industry that mass produces these garments. Bras help create the image of the aesthetically perfect Playboy breast. Fashion in modern America demands bra wearing. In *Dressed To Kill* authors Sydney Ross Singer and Soma Grismaijer compare bra wearing and the fashion they support to a modern day religion. "All religions have devoted followers who willingly sacrifice comfort and health as a sign of devotion to their god."[5]

These authors document interviews with over 4,500 women, about half of whom had breast cancer and found that bra wearing is associated with a remarkable and dramatic increase in breast cancer incidence. Statistics revealed that "going braless is associated with a 21-fold reduction in breast cancer incidence compared with a general standard population. Further, wearing a bra for fewer than 12 hours daily is associated with a 10 percent greater incidence of breast cancer than is not wearing a bra at all, while wearing a bra all the time is associated with a 125-fold greater incidence of breast cancer then is wearing no bra at all."[6]

The theory behind these statistical observations is that the bra hampers the immune system of the breast. By causing chronic constriction of the lymphatic circulation, bra wearing impairs the ability of the breast to filter out toxins and repair damage. As part of everyday life we are exposed to increasing amounts of toxins; the breasts experience longer term toxin exposure because of this reduced lymphatic drainage. The breasts are particularly susceptible to the accumulation of fat-soluble toxins because they contain fatty tissue. Breast feeding and pregnancy may exert their protective effects by stimulating the development of more extensive lymphatic drainage. The authors of *Dressed To Kill* make sense out of many seemingly disparate facts about breast cancer with their theory.

Never sleep in a bra and consider going braless, at least part of the day.

> To every woman who is my daughter
> To every woman who is my sister:
>
> I will you my bras, my bra with underwires
> that pushed me up,
> my cross-my-heart bra that pushed me out,
> my padded bras that made me fuller,
> my natural bras that made me natural,
> a garbage can full of bras—
> a dresser full of bras—
> and the everlasting indecision about whether to or not
>   to . . .[7]
>
> —CLAIRE BRAZ-VALENTINE

Honoring the Feminine

Breast cancer means different things to different women; we each must look for our own personal messages, yet we live in a culture where our basic female nature is seen as problematic. Menstruation is regarded as "the curse" rather than a healthy manifestation of female cyclicity. Menopause is considered a deficiency state, not the transformational rite of passage of a woman into her more potent elder power. As long as women live in this negative cultural context we will remain out of touch with what breast health is. Breast health is part of female health, and the breast cancer epidemic is in part a rift with our own female nature. We have been separated from our own basic instincts on how to nurture ourselves, to feed ourselves and our families, to touch ourselves, to express ourselves, to create order, beauty and poetry in our lives.

Breast cancer is in the news. Breast cancer is talked about endlessly, but just who is doing the talking? We keep hearing about the importance of mammograms and breast self-exams, how early detection is the key. We hear about the tamoxifen trial. Conventional medicine's answer to prevention is not surprising—yet another drug for healthy women to ingest on a daily basis despite the known risks. Breast cancer is in the news, but what is being said is often not news, it's the same old story: If I submit to frequent early detection procedures, breast cancer might not happen to me. But if it does and I follow all the doctor's orders and keep my feelings to myself, it may go away.

On the contrary, breast cancer will *not* go away unless we start paying attention to ourselves *before* the dreaded diagnosis.

OUR CULTURE'S MISGUIDED APPROACHES TO THE BREAST CANCER CRISIS

THE TRUTH ABOUT BREAST SELF-EXAM

Women are told over and over again that breast self-exam and mammograms are the only way for us to survive the epidemic of breast cancer. We are taught how to touch our breasts in order to find cancer. This monthly procedure is fraught with fear for many women; many avoid the experience altogether, afraid of finding a lump that wasn't there before.

Is there any scientific evidence that self-exams actually increase a woman's chances of surviving cancer? Breast cancer experts are divided. In a 1991 study at the University of Wisconsin Comprehensive Cancer Center involving over 200 women with advanced stage breast cancer and over 400 controls, researchers found that those who practiced BSE were as likely to have developed late-stage cancer as those who did not. John Gohagan of the National Cancer Institute says, "We have very little science, or evidence anywhere, on the benefit of breast self-examination."[8] In contrast, researchers in Finland found more optimistic results after following 29,000 women who were taught BSE and regularly performed it over two years. These women had death rates that were 25 percent lower than in Finland as a whole. Each woman in the Finnish study had a designated breast specialist to consult for follow-up if she found an abnormality.

There are a number of important details to take into account when we try to understand the efficacy of a procedure like BSE. First, do women really understand how to examine their breasts, and second, are they comfortable doing so? Just as comfort and sexuality issues are pertinent to the development of breast cancer, they also affect a woman's ability to do BSE. Dr. Judy Dean of the Women's Mammography Medical Group in Santa Monica, California says, "I think the success of BSE is strongly related to one's cultural milieu. If you look at a country like Sweden, where women are much more comfortable touching their bodies, the average size of a self-discovered tumor is two-and-a-half centimeters. But in the United Kingdom, where there's still this Victorian hangover, the average size is four-and-a-half centimeters. Maybe, if women were more accustomed to touching their breasts, they'd be better at BSE."[9]

There can be no doubt that a woman who is comfortable with her body can be the best examiner of her own breasts. There is no reason to think that a clinical exam by a physician who examines countless women could be any better than the invested exam of a woman who communes with her own breasts daily, lathering them, massaging them, touching them.

No medical authority can say why a breast lump will manifest at a particular time, that all breast cancers are detectable when they are one to two cm or that the tissue reaction that is necessary to make the cancer palpable always occurs at a particular size or progresses in a linear fashion. Once breast cancer is discovered, we can always second-guess ourselves, but this is never helpful.

∾

I was a trained gynecologist, I had examined so many breasts including my own. But on this particular morning, after breast-feeding Oliver, there was no doubt that there was a hard mass, the size of a tennis ball. Where had it been hiding?

One of my consultant physicians commented afterwards, "You might have assumed that we would be judging you harshly for being a physician with such a large tumor . . . I hope you have learned and can believe that a large breast cancer is usually due to the cruelty of biology and not to any sort of negligence on the part of the woman afflicted with it."

❧

Dr. Suzanne Fletcher, professor in the department of ambulatory care and prevention at Harvard Medical School was quoted in *Ms.* magazine, "It's not that we know self-exams don't work, it's that we don't know they do."[10] The success of self-exams depends on what our goal is in examining ourselves. I believe the value of BSE is in becoming intimate with our own bodies and breasts when they are healthy. If at some point, something feels different, this is the time to consult with your doctor. Breast self exam should not be undertaken as a search-for-cancer mission. In sending out this kind of energy and expectation we are at odds with our own purpose, which is to treat our bodies with loving kindness and not to instill fear. When done with the express intent of finding a lump, BSE promotes a seek-and-destroy attitude that is not conducive to breast health.

Susun Weed, herbalist, feminist and author of *Breast Cancer? Breast Health! The Wise Woman Way* talks about breast self-massage. The purpose of breast massage is to put a woman in touch with her breasts, focusing on intimate self-knowledge as well as promoting lymphatic flow by deep pressure. The value of massaging the breasts and promoting lymphatic drainage as a means of prevention makes intuitive sense. Susun writes, "Breast self-massage is a piece of women's wisdom. . .Regular, loving touching of our breasts allows us to recognize normal breast changes without fear, and gives us time to respond thoughtfully to abnormal changes. Breast self-massage is also a quiet, focused time that allows the Wise Healer Within to alert us to any changes that require our attention."[11]

The kind of breast exam I suggest is qualitatively different than the one described on American Cancer Society shower cards, the express purpose of which is to find cancer. Fear-driven exams send the wrong message. Knowing your body well will have a positive impact on your health and well-being and will make it easier to know when something is wrong.

Fear and False Reassurances

In one BSE instruction pamphlet I read, "You may not feel a lump—the change may be more subtle." Fear, fear, how will I know? . . .Better go to the doctor. . .She/He will know, I'll be safe then. . . .The safety net is out there. Sorry, but there is no safety net. How many stories do we have to read about false reassurances by the so-called experts. In *First, You Cry,* Betty Rollin talks about her experience detecting a lump and the false reassurances of her internist and radiologist who based their conclusions solely on her mammogram.

> I had a lump for a year . . . It was a hard little thing—about the size of a yellow grape—and it resided, imperceptible except to the touch, on the far side of my left breast, due west of the nipple. I knew it was there, my (ex-) internist knew it was there, my (ex-) husband knew it was there and my (ex-)mammographer knew it was there. Of the four, only [my husband] was worried about it.

Less than a year later Betty went back to her doctor . . .

> "That's my lump," I said when he got to it. He looked at me. "I had it a year ago. You said it was nothing and that I should come back in a year." I was annoyed at having to explain. He nodded and drew a black circle around the lump with a pen. "That'll wash off," he said and walked out.

Rollin called Dr. Smith to get the results.

> . . . He did not speak immediately, and when he spoke he pronounced each word as if he had had a rehearsal. The

words I remember were "...nothing to worry about, but it really should come out."[12]

"What more could I do?" you wonder. "The doctors said it was okay, the mammogram said it was okay. But what is this lump? Our bodies speak to us in whispers and screams. We need to pay attention to both. Don't just bury the uncertainty. Do not live with the anxiety of a lump that you feel may be cancerous; be proactive. Go inside—explore the lump from the inside.

Even benign lumps have a message and may be calling for us to change to a plant-based diet, to eliminate caffeine, to take Vitamin E supplements or to assure adequate daily intake of essential fatty acids. Perhaps we need to explore unfinished emotional business, deal with buried childhood traumas or simply spend more time and energy nurturing ourselves. Benign fibrocystic breast disease is diagnosed in upwards of 70 percent of women. If a so-called breast disease is afflicting the majority of women in our culture then we must look closer. We need to address the underlying issues. Until we take charge of our lives we will live in fear of this disease. Make a point of getting to know your breasts from the inside and the outside: look at them, feel them, love them, be at ease with them and hear their messages. Get another opinion; have your own opinion. Consider making some of the changes we have talked about.

We all breathe a sigh of relief when a doctor says "it looks benign." So many times, as a gynecologist, I have seen the great relief in the faces of my patients, as I reassure them all is well. And then it is business as usual until the next exam, when once again the fear of discovery comes alive. Let us come to a more mature relationship with our bodies—one of mutual respect. Our bodies will not betray us if we pay attention to them. Relax and accept your body as your friend.

The Politics of Mammography

"Trust in mammography goes to the core of breast cancer's most sacred truth: early detection is your best protection."[13] In her inspiring book *Patient No More,* Sharon Batt challenges the conventional assumptions about breast cancer: "Our love affair with mammography fits critic Ivan Illich's description of industrial hubris, the dream that we can find technical answers to irrational fantasies. We imagine that we can escape sickness, pain and the threat of death through the medicalization of health. . . ."[14] We desperately need to get in touch with our health as a process, with the cycle of life, death and rebirth, and to affirm our respect for nature, apart from technology, apart from the so-called experts. We need to get in touch with our bodies to understand on a gut level what we need to be nourished; then the technology can serve us rather than the other way around. Right now we are slaves to our high-tech health care. Health care spending has no bounds because our priorities are misplaced. We need to get back to basics.

The energy invested in our culture's obsession with disease screening may be more wisely invested in actively creating health. A more balanced view on mammography can help us to refocus on better ways to actively create health in our lives. Regardless of the media blitz, early detection is not prevention.

National Breast Cancer Awareness Month, with its narrow and weighted focus on mammography for early detection, is a campaign sponsored by industry. We need to keep in mind an awareness of all the issues surrounding the breast cancer epidemic and be alert to one-sided presentations of complex issues. Zeneca, formerly owned by the pharmaceutical giant, Imperial Chemical Industries (I.C.I.) co-sponsors National Breast Cancer Awareness Month. Zeneca manufactures mammography equipment and the breast cancer drug, tamoxifen. "Don't be an easy target—get a mammogram *now,*" women are warned. It would be especially lucrative for Zeneca if tamoxifen were approved for prophylaxis in healthy women. Science, public interest and capital profits may not always mix well. In an interview with Dr. Sandra Steingraber, published in *Safe Food News,* the interviewer remarked, "It seems ironic that chemical corporations are taking breast cancer on as a cause."[15] Dr. Steingraber's reply was apropos: "I worry anytime biology is explained by someone who wants to sell a product."

There are certainly self-serving aspects to the campaign that we need to be aware of: the more women screened and diagnosed with breast cancer, the more money is made. We also need to look at what is conspicuously absent in the awareness campaign literature (the role of meat and dairy and environmental carcinogens in the genesis of breast cancer) and why (who would such a discussion offend?). Zeneca Pharmaceuticals make chlorine and petroleum-based products. Referring to an exposé of Breast Cancer Awareness Month, Sharon Batt noted that, "In Quebec, an I.C.I. paint subsidiary single-handedly dumps one-third of the toxic chemicals into the St. Lawrence River. These are precisely the kind of estrogen-mimicing toxins now suspected of promoting breast cancer."[16]

What then is the role of mammography and for whom do the benefits outweigh the rarely discussed risks? Fear is so rampant that we blindly consent to annual mammography screening without considering the very real limitations of the test and the fact that it is not appropriate for women of all ages. I well remember how many 30-year-old women in my practice would nervously ask, "Do you think I should get a mammogram? My company is offering them at work." or "My mother was just diagnosed with breast cancer; I'd like to go for a mammogram." The combined analysis of the best international studies indicate that routine screening mammography has no benefit in women under 50,[17] although a few studies do suggest the opposite.[18] The experts in this country are divided, and much controversy surrounds mammography guidelines. Although the American Cancer

Society still recommends screening mammography for women in their 40s, both the National Cancer Institute and the U.S. Preventive Health Services Task Force advise against it on the grounds that it hasn't convincingly been shown to reduce breast cancer mortality for women in their 40s. The eight-nation European Group for Breast Cancer Screening opposes it on the basis that there is no demonstrated benefit.

The problem with screening in younger women is that premenopausal women have denser and more fibrous breast tissue which can both resemble and obscure cancer. For premenopausal women substantial false negative rates have been reported, that is, cancer is present but goes undetected. A study from Australia found more than half of the breast cancers in younger women were not detectable on mammograms.[19] Statistics indicate that premenopausal breast cancer may be a more aggressive disease and therefore can easily become detectable in the interval between exams. Screening tests are better suited to slow-growing tumors. The upshot may be that although mammography may extend some younger women's lives, when the studies are analyzed this effect is so diluted by the greater number of missed and delayed diagnoses in younger women that the combined results of clinical trials show that mammography has essentially no benefit for women under 50.

False-positive tests, which indicate cancer is present when actually it is not, are also a problem leading to anxiety, unnecessary biopsy procedures, scarring and distortions of the breast which further strain the future accuracy of testing. According to researchers at the University of California School of Medicine and the Centers for Disease Control and Prevention, mammography reports often have serious shortcomings including omission of important information and absence of recommendations. The recent study which was presented at the Radiological Society of North America found that nearly all of the reports reviewed failed to address one or more of the key elements regarded as essential components of a complete mammography.[20] Another consideration is that a screening procedure only makes sense in the context of efficacious treatment.

Baseline mammograms are political hype; a woman's first mammogram will serve as her baseline to which all future studies can be compared. Postmenopausal women, the group that has shown a consistent survival benefit, may choose to get a mammogram every one to two years.

What are the hazards of mammography? Dr. John C. Bailar III calculated that if young women in their 20s started having mammograms every six months, we'd cause more cancer than we'd cure.[21] What is safe? Although the radiation doses from mammography units have been significantly reduced, radiation risks are cumulative and there is no proven safe minimum dose. The Mammography Quality Standards Act which took effect in October of 1994 was past due in addressing wide variations in quality among mammography centers. According to the National Council on Radiation Protection and Measurements, an American woman is exposed to 84-360 millirads per year from environmental sources over her entire body. So by age 65 a woman could be exposed to 30 rads or more from various sources.

Mammograms present one of the higher levels of diagnostic radiation. One mammogram exposes a woman to 25 to 30 times the dose of radiation of an average chest x-ray. One study suggests a safe exposure is below 300 millirads (1 rad = 1000 millirads). The ACS recommends no more than one rad of exposure per breast. Absorbed doses range from 200 millirads to one rad per breast for each x-ray exposure.[22] Before age 50 a woman's breast tissue density requires higher levels of rads to get a clear image. A standard mammogram takes two shots of each breast, four exposures to radiation per exam. The American College of Radiation does not put a limit on the number of views taken during any one visit.

Mammography can be a grueling experience. Women are often kept waiting, imagining the worst, wanting only to be reassured by a negative exam. As our breasts are compressed to get accurate pictures we say to ourselves the benefits are well worth the discomforts. Still we wonder if the invisible x-rays are indeed innocuous. Terror mounts after the mammogram is completed and we are asked to get undressed again for some additional views. Returning home, the doctor calls the following day explaining that another mammogram in six months will clarify the current reading. The reassurances we wanted were not there this time.

No one is keeping track of individual exposures. And no one really knows whether mammograms are contributing to the breast cancer epidemic. Some physicians believe that breast cancer risk is increased through exposure to mammograms. "The risk of developing cancer is directly related to the amount of exposure and the damage is cumulative with repeated exposure," says John McDougall, M.D. Furthermore, there's no safe threshold below which an increased risk of developing cancer does not occur. Cancers of the thyroid, female breast, bones, liver, lung and leukemia are the forms most likely found following excessive exposure to radiation. The potential risk of inducing cancer of the breast after years of exposure will not be distinguishable from non-radiation induced cancers. There is no sure method of determining the cause of breast cancer after it occurs.

Technology leads to more technology

Check and recheck. I remember the apprehensive way conclusions were often phrased and the all too frequent suggestions for repeating studies, in three-, four- and six-month intervals. Twenty-seven million films per year (of all types) are done as retakes of faulty films, and a significant percentage of the 271 million x-ray examinations per year are done as a consequence of the practice of defensive medicine in our malpractice era.[23]

Regular small doses of radiation may pose a danger that is not fully appreciated. As the investigation of toxic pesticides has revealed, the whole of a woman's exposure is surely greater than the sum of the parts, i.e., synergism between radiation exposure, xenoestrogens and other chemical carcinogens is quite likely. Dr. Michael Swift, formerly of the University of North Carolina in Chapel Hill, researched a particular gene that may confer a unique susceptibility to the effects of radiation in as many as 1.4 percent of the population in this country.[24]

Screening has been in use for more than 20 years while mortality has remained the same, which calls into question what effect all our efforts are really accomplishing; that is, are our diagnostic and therapeutic efforts making a difference?

There's big money in diagnosing breast cancer. The question of profiteering is always an issue. I cringe when I see designer-decorated mammo vans advertising discount rates. Whether conscious or unconscious, the fact that physicians invest in the mammography units that they recommend feels like a conflict of interest to me. I remember reading the advertisements in the obstetrical-gynecologic journals and newsletters hawking in-office mammo units, the implication being, both subtle and overt, don't let profits get away. The ultimate result for those who buy the units may be overuse.

∾   *Remember...*

Mammograms subject the most sensitive organ in the human body to direct radiation. In the 1970s exposure of 2 to 15 rads was considered safe; in 1991, 300 millirads was considered safe; and in 1994 the ACS recommended exposures up to 1 rad. Mammography does not prevent breast cancer. Screening mammography is beneficial for women between the ages 50 and 70; still, the optimal screening interval has not been established. For women under 50 and over 70 the data is inconclusive and must be considered as such.

Reframing Mammography, Making It Safer

Begin to actively create breast health rather than screening for and waiting for disease to strike. Take care of your breasts by eating in a health-supportive style, by developing a personally satisfying balance of rest and exercise in your life and by cultivating and honoring your identity as a creative woman.

If you choose to get a mammogram, make sure the facility is certified by the ACR and that the technician is accredited by the American Registry of Radiological Technologists. Check on the date of the last inspection. Find out the level of exposure that you will be exposed to and compare it to the 300 millirads mentioned here.

In the week before going for a mammogram be sure to take antioxidant supplements, especially vitamins E and C, the carotenes and selenium for the best protection against radiation. Eat lots of miso soup and seaweed in the weeks following the mammogram to enhance the removal of radioactive isotopes.

There really is no simple way to reduce the problem of breast cancer to a screening test. Breast Cancer Awareness Month in the best of all possible worlds would be renamed Breast Health Action Month and would impel women to get in touch with the day-in, day-out process of health—not to just get on line for a mammography screening.

PROPHYLACTIC MASTECTOMIES: FEAR OF KEEPING OUR BREASTS, FEAR OF LOSING OUR BREASTS

In some instances women are advised that the best strategy is to surgically remove their breasts before they develop cancer. This procedure is known as a prophylactic mastectomy. However, removing the breast tissue with this procedure does not eliminate the risk of breast cancer. Mastectomies do not remove all breast tissue. Many surgeons think if they remove 95 percent of the breast tissue they will remove 95 percent of the risk of breast cancer, but this is not so. As Susan Love says regarding this issue, "The question isn't how much breast tissue you have, it's how much whatever tissue you have is acted on by the carcinogens and the other factors that cause breast cancer."[25] This procedure probably removes some of the risk, but we have no idea how much. There are no good studies looking at this issue.

In considering this drastic operation women need to be clear about the potential risk and benefits. If they are at "high risk" for breast cancer the risk must be clearly and practically defined. Cancer phobia is another indication used to justify this procedure; it would certainly be wiser to address the phobia through psychotherapy rather than through mutilating surgery. It is rare indeed that we as doctors suggest removing a normal organ to prevent a disease from occurring. "If a surgeon tells you that you are at very high risk for getting breast cancer and your breasts are so lumpy that they'll conceal a cancerous tumor until it's too late, you will very sensibly react with fear," writes Dr. Love. "Whether this fear is warranted and whether it justifies removing a normal breast is another matter. To put these recommendations into perspective, I suggested (on ABC's "Nightline") that we take out men's testicles and replace them with Ping-Pong balls to prevent testicular cancer. Somehow the men in the audience didn't take to the idea."[26]

In too many instances our breasts have become strangers, not friends. How can one be intimate with a stranger? The answer is not to remove our breasts. The answer lies in reconnecting with the experience of knowing our bodies. And what is proposed after a prophylactic mastectomy—that we become flat-chested goddesses? No, that won't do. We are offered the perfect breasts—silicone or saline implants, perhaps the size your husband told you he always admired, perhaps the size you think every man would worship, the size that will make your life everything it isn't. No, the answer is not to replace our breasts. A prophylactic mastectomy is clearly the most horrifying example of technology and fear overcoming our inborn intuition and common sense.

CHEMOTHERAPEUTIC PROPHYLAXIS

Tamoxifen was synthesized in the 1960s when the FDA was developing contraceptives. In the early 70s it was tested for its effect on breast cancer. The drug was found to decrease recurrence rates and to also decrease the rate of cancer in the opposite breast. What's wrong with tamoxifen?

- The majority of women on tamoxifen do not live longer, and recurrences do occur on the drug.
- Resistance to tamoxifen eventually develops.
- There are cases of life-threatening complications in patients using tamoxifen.
- Long-term toxicity of this drug has not been explored.

The uncontrolled use of tamoxifen in all subgroups of breast cancer patients and in healthy high-risk populations may prove very dangerous. Its use in otherwise healthy women is reminiscent of the diethylstilbestrol (DES) disaster. DES was a synthetic estrogen given to millions of women to prevent miscarriages and which instead caused an increase in a previously rare vaginal cancer. Daughters and sons of the women who took DES also developed a variety of reproductive abnormalities. One study of 3,029 women who took DES, published in 1993, showed that the mothers themselves have a 35 percent increased risk of breast cancer.[28]

There are gentler and more effective ways to proactively prevent breast cancer, but there is no profit to be made from encouraging a healthy diet and lifestyle.

POLITICS AND PROFITS

WHO PROFITS FROM BREAST CANCER

There is a great deal of money to be made in the cancer industry. There are billions of dollars available for research, diagnosis and treatment. Breast cancer is a highly profitable disease for those who screen for, diagnose, and treat it. Look at these statistics:

- There are more biopsies performed to diagnose breast cancer than for any other cancer.
- Breast cancer is the cancer for which the most x-rays are taken.
- In 1992 an estimated 23.5 million mammograms were performed in the United States at a cost of $2.5 billion.
- Breast cancer is the cancer for which the most radiation therapy is given.
- No other cancer is treated with so much chemotherapy.
- No other cancer is treated with as much hormonal therapy.
- There are more drugs in development for the treatment of breast cancer than for any other cancer.

Researching and selling magic-bullet cures such as the ever more toxic chemotherapy protocols can be a financial bonanza, while teaching lifestyle changes, nutritional counseling and environmental activism for the prevention and treatment of breast cancer yield no profits at all. Often, in our society, when there's no money to be made there's little incentive to invest research money. Although emotional factors are incredibly important in the genesis of breast cancer there is no "mind-body lobby" vying for funds in Congress, nor is there a "low-fat lobby."

Ralph Moss was hired in 1974 as Assistant Director of Public Affairs at Memorial Sloan-Kettering Cancer Center

(MSKCC) in New York City; he was fired in 1977 after a press conference on laetrile during which he tried to give an accurate account of the controversial cancer treatment. In his 1980 expose, *The Cancer Industry,* Moss lists the various members of key policy committees at MSKCC, the world's largest private cancer center, and their affiliations. The entire structure is built upon pharmaceutical, petro-chemical, automobile industry, corporate investment and cigarette industry affiliations, all with obvious vested inter-ests. Some of the country's largest polluters were repre-sented on the Cancer Center's board.

The fact that directors of pharmaceutical companies sit on the board at MSKCC does not mean they are doing something illegal or immoral, says Moss, but "on the other hand it must be said that their drug company positions cer-tainly predispose them to direct research in a manner con-sistent with the interests of the profit-making sector."[28] Since the 1950s, all the major pharmaceutical companies have par-ticipated in the production of anticancer drugs. Worldwide chemotherapy sales are $5 billion annually, and drug sales are projected to be $13 billion by the year 2000. In compari-son, the budget for the Office of Alternative Medicine (OAM) is just $4 million out of a $10-billion-dollar allotment to the National Institute of Health. It is a sobering fact that the budget for the OAM is less than one-tenth of a percent of worldwide chemotherapy sales.

Although chemotherapy has a role in the treatment of breast cancer it is unlikely that it will take us any further. Despite the research and development of new and more effective chemotherapeutic agents for breast cancer, ac-cording to Richard Margolese, an oncologist at the Sir Morti-mer B. Davis Jewish General Hospital in Montreal, "We've exposed cancer cells to something like 50 agents in the past 30 years. It's not likely that one more agent is going to make a difference. The cancer cell is too adaptable and it has a programme for survival and it's going to adapt again and again to these kinds of things."

Chemotherapy succeeds because it is a systemic poison which is also the reason it does harm. The chemotherapy era began during World War II when researchers involved in chemical weaponry realized that mustard gas was a cellular poison that might be effective against cancer. The National Cancer Institute estimates that 200,000 patients each year receive chemotherapy but most are not cured by these treatments. A number of uncommon tumors respond very well to chemotherapy: choriocarcinoma, Burkitt's lymphoma, acute lymphoblastic leukemia, acute lymphocytic leukemia and a few others. However, John Cairns, professor of microbiology at the School of Public Health at Harvard University commented in an article for *Scientific American,*[29] "Whether any of the common cancers can be cured by chemotherapy has yet to be established."

Ralph Moss reviews the history of the development of radiation treatment and notes "A realistic appraisal of radiation might have resulted if it hadn't been for the events of August 1945—the bombing of Hiroshima and Nagasaki, which ushered in the atomic age."[30] Atomic energy, its use and safety became a political question. Atomic medicine became a good public relations guise for the Atomic Energy Commission agenda which included the pile-up of nuclear weaponry, open-air atomic testing and the scandalous nuclear waste problem. The citizens of this country have been exposed and continue to be exposed to radioactive wastes in our environment. Major leaks have been documented in Ohio, South Carolina, Colorado and the State of Washington—and cancer rates continue to climb.

Unfortunately the radiation research community is intimately connected with the atomic energy and defense establishments, calling into question accurate information about the hazards of radiation from both an environmental and therapeutic standpoint. There are 17 comprehensive reviews of tumors associated with diagnostic and therapeutic radiation between 1957 and 1975.[31] Dr. Bross, a prominent U.S. scientist, is outspoken about what he feels is a cover-up of the hazards of radiation by the medical establishment. It is no surprise that his grant application to the National Cancer Institute to answer the question What are the long-term hazards of radiation therapy? was approved for only a fraction of the money necessary to answer this important question. Although many doctors believe that radiation is a harmless procedure, others believe it can be positively harmful. There are very small numbers of cancers that are cured by radiation and no one knows how many cancers are caused or promoted by its long-term effects.

Radiation is a large source of revenue for doctors and hospitals in both the diagnostic and therapeutic arenas. We need to be sure those who are in a position to profit are not in control of treatment recommendations.

The Supplement Industry vs. the FDA

Ironically, while drugs like DES and tamoxifen find their way into the marketplace and are offered to healthy women without adequate assessment of long-term risks, while cigarettes and alcohol are condoned by our society and its regulatory agencies, the FDA has been busy "protecting" consumers from the false claims of the supplement industry.

The FDA has prevented the food and supplement industry from claiming that antioxidants protect against cancer. In reality, the inverse link between antioxidants and cancer risk has become so accepted by the scientific community that 16 leading nutrition researchers from all over the United States have publicly condemned the FDA's position, "An incorrect decision has been reached to disallow a claim that antioxidant nutrients may decrease the risk of cancer . . . [We] believe the data clearly support approval of a health claim."[32] The FDA has been and continues to be involved in trying to classify vitamins as drugs and thereby limit over-the-counter access to vitamins and other nutritional supplements.

CONFLICTS OF INTEREST: WHO IS PROTECTING WOMEN'S BEST INTERESTS?

The Falsification of Data

In 1994 it was reported that the National Cancer Institute (NCI) and researchers from the National Surgical Adjuvant Breast and Bowel Project (NSABP) knew for several years about the falsification of data used in the critical breast cancer studies that have set the standard for treatments around the world, including the role and the efficacy of tamoxifen. This information was not made public in a responsible or timely way.

The public outcry that followed this news prompted a top official at the NCI to say if he had "intuited" women's concerns regarding the NCI/NSABP behavior, the agencies would have acted differently. The National Breast Cancer Coalition got to the heart of the matter when it replied, "There is a fundamental deficiency in a system where a public servant believes he must intuit how the public may react to decisions made by his agency. Had a consumer advocate—a woman with breast cancer—been part of the process, the public's peace of mind and women's lives would not have been left to the uncertainties of an individual's intuitive abilities. This self-imposed separation between the public agencies and the citizenry they serve is unacceptable."[33] One of the coalition's basic premises is that the biomedical research system needs a restructuring—one that encourages consumer activism and that does not consolidate power in the hands of the few.

Inappropriate Conclusions

In 1992, an article in the *Journal of the American Medical Association* about the Harvard Nurses' Health Study caused quite a stir. Authored by Dr. Walter C. Willet, M.D. and based at the Harvard Department of Nutrition, the study concluded that there was no connection between dietary fat and breast cancer. This study received enormous media attention and deeply impressed the American public.

However, there were many methodological flaws in the Nurses' Study, not the least of which was the fact that it was a giant mail survey which relied on the recall of how often and in what amounts the nurses consumed various foods over the preceding two years. Resembling a poll more than a scientific study, the Nurses' Study was conducted by researchers who never had any contact personally or by telephone with the participants. Dr. Kradjian critiques the study thoroughly in his book, *Save Yourself From Breast Cancer*. He writes:

> Consider this comparative example. If you wish to learn the effect of speed on automobile safety, you might measure motor vehicular deaths in a group of motorists driving 90 to 120 miles per hour. If you did this, you would find little difference in death rates among the 90- or 95-mile-per-hour drivers compared with the 110- or 115-mile-per-hour motorists. A "logical" conclusion could then be made that "speed has nothing whatever to do with motor-vehicular fatalities," which is, of course an erroneous statement. That is essentially what the Harvard study has done! By following a group of women ingesting from 27 to over 50 percent of calories as fat (average 39 percent in their 1980 group and 33 percent in their 1984 group), they were looking at a group all of whom were at risk to develop breast cancer."[34]

Dr. Kradjian discusses his attempts to call the NIH about the complete list of the sources of funding for the Nurses' Study, specifically food industry monies. After nearly a year of persistent probing, access to this information was denied. Dr. Kradjian was subsequently informed by one of the authors of the study that the dairy industry was involved in funding "some part of the study."

We need to be aware of potential and real conflicts of interest between industry funding and impartial scientific research, and strive to keep the boundaries intact.

THE CULTURE THAT LOVES AND HATES BREASTS

A New Role for Women: Social Activist

Breast cancer is a woman's issue. Upwards of 10 percent of women in this country will be faced with breast cancer at some point in their lives. The other 90 percent will see the suffering of their mothers, sisters, daughters and friends. The 90 percent who are spared may choose to deny or may fear this collective breast cancer experience. But the experience profoundly affects all women. It is a woman's crisis, and we are deeply connected in the commonality of the struggle.

Yet we are afraid to own our female experience. Once we embrace this disease in all its physical, mental, emotional and social contexts, we will be able to heal on all these levels. We can transform this disease and heal our lives. We can harness the power of this crisis to nurture ourselves through our food choices, conditioning programs and the work of emotional processing. We can organize around this issue and call for social and political action. We can bare our breasts and learn how to really care for ourselves. We can turn our lives around and recreate the meaning of our lives. We can create a more meaningful life. We can create.

As poet Audre Lorde writes:

What would happen if an army of one-breasted women descended upon Congress and demanded that the use of carcinogenic, fat-stored hormones in beef feed be outlawed? . . . women with breast cancer are warriors . . . I have been to war and still am. . . . I refuse to have my scars hidden or trivialized behind lambswool or silicone gel. I refuse to be reduced in my own eyes or in the eyes of others from warrior to mere victim, simply because it might render me a fraction more acceptable or less dangerous to the still complacent, those who believe if you cover up a problem it ceases to exist.[35]

Bare-chested Amazons marching, not to be ignored, stark reality—what an incredible display of power!

Get involved politically; the National Breast Cancer Coalition is a grassroots advocacy effort that is made up of over 290 organizations and thousands of individuals. It is a national action network that is outspoken on many issues including:

- Advocating the collection of data from randomized clinical trials to determine optimal screening guidelines for mammography.

- Epidemiologically assessing breast cancer risk at different dose levels for all types of radiation exposure.

- Addressing environmental breast cancer issues aggressively.

- Bringing women with breast cancer into decision-making positions with respect to the direction and pace of funding and research.

- Access to screening, diagnosis, treatment and care.

- Investigation of dietary factors in the development and prevention of breast cancer.

- Investigation of the different endogenous and exogenous hormones.

- Increasing the involvement and influence of women with breast cancer in legislation, clinical trial designs and access to clinical trials.

- Initiation of research programs directed at lifestyle exposures.

ᐁ *Remember...*

Breast cancer is woven into our culture. To decrease breast cancer incidence we must stop being superwomen and refuse to be abused physically or emotionally. We might consider removing our bras, coming into a freer, more comfortable and more respectful relationship with our breasts. Let us stop searching for and fearing breast cancer and instead begin to actively create breast health. Actively creating breast health involves making choices in both the personal and the political arenas—personal habits as well as public policy issues. Breast cancer is not a disease of the breasts but a disease of women within a cultural context.

PART FOUR

❧

Putting It All Together

7

Your Own Breast Cancer
Healing/Prevention Program

At a conference on Women and Cancer in 1991 Dr. Susan Love, speaking for the medical establishment, said, "We don't know who will get breast cancer. We don't know why it develops. And we don't know why some are cured."[1] Keep that in mind when you look *outside* yourself for the answers.

INTUITION AND DECISIONS—YOU CAN TRUST YOURSELF

After the great news about the pathology of my lumpectomy specimen in October 1991—no residual cancer—I'd begun talking a lot to Tullia about ending my chemotherapy. The size of the original mass and the DNA studies showed a very aggressive tumor, so Dr. Zelkowitz suggested continuing my treatments to complete a full year. But I wondered, is more really better in this case? According to Dr. Love there really weren't any convincing data to support my doing anything more. No one really knew what to do; it was scary. I had read the scientific literature and I was torn. I felt kind of protected by the ongoing treatments. Yet at the same time I felt I had had enough and that what I needed was to re-build rather than continue to be bombarded with toxic chemicals. I wasn't sure, in the wake of all the treatments I'd been through, if by itself my immune system could stand up to the cancer. Thus, I couldn't say no to the chemotherapy just yet. . .I didn't trust myself enough.

After two more cycles of chemo I ended up with herpes zoster, otherwise known as shingles, an infection known to affect immunosuppressed patients, a category I was certainly not happy to be in. I knew immediately what was going on—my body was saying a definitive NO to any further chemotherapy. Meanwhile I began to run a 105° temperature. I'd never been so hot and cold at the same time. A local infectious disease specialist met me in the Emergency Room and strongly suggested I be admitted to the hospital. When I balked, he told me I could die; after all I'd been through I couldn't imagine dying of this ridiculous complication, so I agreed to his recommendation.

I was pumped up with various antibiotics, my already low white blood count went even lower and it was clear no one was sure if my problem was a reaction to the simultaneous bombardment with chemotherapy and radiation, to herpes zoster or to the various antibiotics I was now receiving. Thanks to Mother Nature my fever and chills subsided, but not before I was black and blue from endless blood tests and innumerable intravenous lines. I couldn't even get a good night's sleep with all the vital signs checks ordered round the clock. After a few days, the IVs were discontinued and I went home. It was a horrible experience, but I learned the great lesson of trusting my own intuition. The treatments were coming to an end. It was December 31, 1991. Happy New Year!

∾

Developing Compassion for Yourself

I grew in innumerable ways through my experience with breast cancer—from the very personal realm and relationships, past and present, to my place in the larger global community. Transformation was happening in so many ways. Of course, there is no guarantee that such transformation will result in a cure of physical disease. Nor did I feel responsible for the illness. Rather I felt responsible *to* the illness. As Treya Wilbur wrote:

> I try to focus on what I can do now. . . .I am also very aware of the many other factors that are largely beyond my conscious or unconscious control. We are all, thankfully, part of a much larger whole. I like being aware of this, even though it means I have less control. We are all too interconnected, both with each other and with our environment—life is too wonderfully complex—for a simply statement like "you create your own reality" to be simply true. A belief that I control or create my own reality actually attempts to rip me out of the rich, complex, mysterious, and supportive context of my life. It attempts, in the name of control, to deny the web of relationships that nurtures me and each of us daily.[2]

Treya talks about the exquisite balance between effort and surrender, success and failure in a most inspiring way. Her life and her death, chronicled in *Grace and Grit,* thoroughly opened my heart to the common experience of these challenges.

Responsibility *to* our illness often gets mixed up with responsibility *for* our illness and the whole issue of blame/guilt. Women, alas, are particularly susceptible to accepting blame for the psychological factors leading to breast cancer. If a woman believes that she brought breast cancer on herself, the guilt she feels can further intensify her illness. We need so badly to develop self-compassion and to help one another along this path instead of casting blame. Treya writes,

> I need you to try to understand what [cancer] must feel like, just a little, to put yourself in my place and hopefully treat me more kindly than I sometimes treat myself.[3]

THE POWER OF YOUR INTENTION

Intention is very powerful. Remember, our thoughts help shape our reality, and the work of creating physical realities begins with our intention. We need to be clear about our intention to heal. Just how much energy are we really willing to put toward our healing? The obstacles we see are those we, for various reasons, choose to put ahead of our own health. Healing is a full-time commitment; there is really no room for hidden agendas, procrastination or laziness. We are not aiming for perfection, but rather clear commitment. Author Gary Zukov says, "An intention is not only a desire. It is the use of your will."[4] The more we understand and believe in the immense power of our will, the greater our healing capacity.

How can we heal? We must use the power of our intention and at the same time allow ourselves to surrender to a force that is greater than ourselves. Out of this blend healing comes. This is our task:

- Willing ourselves to make the necessary changes yet completely accepting ourselves as we are in the present moment.
- Seeing the difficulties in our lives with clarity and, when possible, making the commitment to work through them.
- Letting go of the situations that are no longer workable and no longer serve us.

COMMITMENT ON ALL LEVELS

Make a Commitment to Nourish Your Body

Food

Using the principles outlined in the nutrition and supplements chapter, begin to make healthy changes. Remembering that breast cancer is a process that develops over years, it is important to proceed whether you are currently under-going treatment, are in recovery from breast cancer or are simply wise enough to pursue a preventive dietary ap-proach. *The dietary goal is a whole foods, organically grown plant-based diet with a wide variety of fresh land and sea vegetables, whole grains and legumes.*

FIRST STEPS

1. Locate sources of organic food within your community and begin to purchase organic grains, legumes and produce. Replace the foods in your pantry with or-ganic products.
2. Throw out products with hydrogenated oils and margarine.
3. Minimize all processed foods.
4. Use unheated flaxseed oil or Udo's Choice (see Re-sources) on salads, pasta, cereal or lightly steamed vegetables daily. Small quantities of fresh organic but-ter are fine for those in good health. Minimize the use of heated oils; use sesame oil or extra virgin olive oil on occasion.
5. Minimize saturated fats from red meat, poultry and dairy food. It is essential that the consumption of even small quantities of these products be from free-range animals that have been organically fed without the ad-ministration of antibiotics and hormones.
6. Fish once or twice a week is a good choice for non-vegetarians.
7. Purchase a few cookbooks from the ones listed on page 375 to help you with new healthier recipes.
8. See a knowledgeable nutritionist, natural foods coun-selor or other health professional for guidance. Women with breast cancer either undergoing treat-ment or in recovery should consult with appropriate health care professionals regarding the use of supple-ments and herbs as well.

Reducing Toxic Exposures

1. Eliminate from your kitchenware any potentially toxic products. For cooking use stainless steel, porcelain enamel, cast iron or Corningware. Avoid aluminum pots and pans and Teflon coatings. For storage and general purpose use Pyrex, glassware, ceramic bowls or wooden bowls.
2. Avoid plastics for storage and never use plastic in the microwave. Use wax paper bags for lunch boxes.

Be thankful

1. It is crucial that your food choices be health-supportive; they can make the difference between health and disease. Cultivate your deepest feelings of wonder and gratitude that the very foods we eat are brimming with healing medicines.
2. Affirm at meals and throughout the day that the food you are eating is healing nourishment.
3. Begin to develop your own ritual for saying grace and blessing your food with each meal.
4. Treat yourself with respect at mealtime. Allow yourself to sit, relax and enjoy the meal. Create a sacred eating time for at least one meal each day. Don't eat scraps or leftovers from your children's plates. Make a plate for yourself. As Dr. Christiane Northrup says, "Treat yourself as you would treat an honored guest."[5]
5. Take enough time to eat in a relaxed atmosphere and to chew properly. Digestion starts in your mouth, and chewing properly gives a message of respect to your body.
6. Allow the food you choose to be an expression of self-love. As you begin to cultivate respect for your body you will make food choices that support your health and improve your physical well-being.

Exercise

Exercise is also essential nourishment for the body. A balance of exercise with adequate rest is the goal. Our bodies need to stretch out, allowing energy to release and realign. When we exercise, we remember and honor our physical aspect, which empowers our emotional, mental and spiritual dimensions.

Dozens of research studies have shown that regular vigorous exercise enhances the immune system and decreases the risk of cancer. Women who are physically active have lower cancer rates, better immune system function and enjoy many other overall health benefits. One of the largest studies looking at this relationship was done at the Harvard School of Public Health in 1985. Fifty four hundred women who had graduated from college between 1925 and 1981 were asked about their diet, their health and their reproductive and exercise histories. Half the subjects were athletes and half nonathletes. Dr. Rose Frisch, Associate Professor of Population Sciences Emerita, who headed the research said, "We found that the former athletes had a significantly lower rate of breast cancer and cancers of the reproductive system."[6] More recently researchers at the University of Southern California studying more than 1,000 women have found that one to three hours of exercise per week during the reproductive years cuts the risk of breast cancer by 30 percent; four or more hours by 60 percent.[7]

It is postulated that exercise can speed the transit of wastes through the intestines, moving food-borne carcinogens along, giving them less contact time with the intestinal wall and ultimately less time for absorption. It has also been firmly established that body fat contributes to estrogen production; leaner fitter women make less estrogen and are therefore exposed to less estrogen, which we know plays a role in breast cancer. Exercise is also a great tissue-draining activity. During exercise, muscles move lymph fluid 10 to

15 times faster than the usual rate. Effective lymphatic drainage may be a significant mechanism in the protective effect of exercise with respect to breast cancer.

Young women should be encouraged to take up sports including basketball, field hockey, softball, tennis, soccer, volleyball, martial arts and dance. Many women feel inadequate about their skills at sports because they were never taught. We need to address this deficit at the earliest possible time for our daughters as we overcome our own self-limiting beliefs in this regard. Younger girls should be encouraged to participate in ballet, gymnastics, swimming, running and other age-appropriate activities. The earlier in life these routines start the better both in terms of establishing healthy lifestyles and in achieving the greatest benefits with respect to hormone balance. The 10 years following puberty are very important years for young women to get into regular exercise routines.

As Dr. Love has said, "More emphasis should be put on female athletics and less on chemotherapy." Studies indicate that fewer than 20 percent of high school junior and senior girls exercise at least three times a week.

FIRST STEPS

Whether you are healing from breast cancer or are trying to prevent breast cancer by establishing a health supportive lifestyle, your exercise program needs to be tailored to your individual needs and preferences. A general guideline would be to aim for one half to one hour of an enjoyable activity three to five times per week. Walking, aerobics, weight training, jogging, biking and dancing are all possibilities. Yoga has the added benefit of providing relaxation, stretching, stimulation and alignment of the body. I'm convinced that setting aside time to nurture yourself in this way is as important emotionally as physically, as your body gains strength, endurance and flexibility.

As in all endeavors, balance is the key. Avoid excess. With some women exercise can become the arena in which to strive for the perfect body. Don't fall into this trap. Begin with love and respect for your body as it is and then begin a sensible program that is right for you. Listen to your body's need for exercise—and for rest.

Touch

On the most basic physical level we need to be touched. It is well-known that newborns who are deprived of touch fail to thrive.[8, 9] Dr. John Larson, a psychiatrist and Chief of Stress Medicine at Norwalk Hospital in Connecticut has said, "The two most important components in a recovery program for women with breast cancer are touch and the development of assertiveness."

Women who have breast cancer need to be nurtured and the skin can take in this message through our sense of touch. Massage on a regular basis can be an important part of recovery. If you are in a loving relationship, allow yourself the pleasure of receiving. The skin is our most pervasive sense organ and touch is the language of sensuality. Allow your body to be soothed by loving touch.

Breast Self-Massage

Touch can be both therapeutic and preventive. Manual lymph drainage, a form of massage therapy that has been successful in treating lymphedema, can accelerate the rate at which our body processes lymph fluid. The lymphatics are key in removing bacteria, viruses, dead cells and toxins from our system. A massage technique that improves lymphatic circulation and helps the body to more effectively remove contaminants like estrogenic pesticides certainly has the potential to help prevent breast cancer.

If you wear a bra, massage your breasts daily when you remove it. Susun Weed describes her version of breast self-massage in detail in her new book *Breast Cancer? Breast Health! The Wise Woman Way*. When performing deep massage consider the direction of lymphatic flow and move outward from the nipple toward the armpit. This massage will have the side benefit of completely familiarizing you with your breasts and obviate the need for your monthly breast exam. Do not wear a bra to sleep. Consider going braless, at least occasionally, to improve lymphatic circulation in the breasts. After reading *Dressed to Kill,* by Sydney Ross Singer and Soma Grismaijer, which describes in detail the association between bras and breast cancer, I replaced my bras with cotton undershirts. I feel much freer.

Make a Commitment to Nourish Your Mind, Emotions, Spirit

Rest

Acknowledging, expressing and releasing emotions that have been stored for a lifetime requires energy, time and space. Rest is nourishment for both the body and the soul. In order to have the energy to do the work, rest is a prerequisite.

If you are undergoing active treatment (chemotherapy, radiation) or are recovering from surgery, you need to honestly assess how much rest you need. This includes adequate sleep at night, plus a midday nap perhaps, or short rest periods at intervals throughout the day. This is in addition to the time that must be set aside for personal inner work. In fact, only adequate rest makes the other work possible; if you are too tired you will not be effective. Nurturing oneself means allowing time for rest and time for emotional work. Breast cancer patients are often women who have not been able to nurture themselves. We need to learn how to do this. Women who are developing strategies to prevent breast cancer need to make adequate rest a priority within their lives. Rest is a gift that only we can give to ourselves.

Inner Work

The preliminary requirements to explore your emotions are time and space. Set aside time and create a space. You can start with at least one half hour each morning or evening. If you can arise before the rest of your household, before the gears of the world get going, the morning can be a quiet and private time. The evening can also work provided you set privacy limits. If you work too late, you will be too tired for anything but sleep. If you can find private time both morning and evening, even better, but be sure that one of those time spans is at least one half hour. You can't do the work of a lifetime in a hurry! Remember, you are the priority, whether you are sick or not. If you can only give to yourself when you are sick, you are setting up a very unhealthy situation. Initially, set aside about 15 minutes for breathing and relaxation and the rest of the time to do one of the various exercises that follow.

To begin, you need a "sacred space," a special and comfortable place where you will not be disturbed. A candle, a flower, perhaps a few pillows in a comfortable corner, some treasured objects on a small silver tray—make your space as simple or elaborate as you like. As this space becomes your spiritual home you can go there whenever you need a respite, if only through visualization. I chose a space in my bedroom: a chair facing a window overlooking my backyard. My walkman, the tapes I used, and important books I was working with were easily accessible.

Inform everyone who needs to know not to disturb you for any reason. Shut off the phone in the room. Each night after my little ones were put to bed I went upstairs and did my personal work, throughout my treatment and beyond. One night, while sitting in my chair, in walked one of my little angels, Zachary, only three at the time. He came silently into the room, put his arms around me, gave me a tender hug and with remarkable wisdom quietly left.

When we honestly and respectfully take the time and

space that we need for ourselves that time and space becomes available. If we expect others to resent us for taking this time and are tentative about meeting our own needs then we participate in the creation of an ambiguous situation. Remember, as we honor and respect ourselves we honor and respect others, but self-respect comes first.

Take Time Out for Yourself

Taking regular time out for yourself could save your life. Set aside time each day for something slow like reflection, a walk in nature, an activity that has no immediate goal.

- Watch out for the pattern of being there for everyone all the time. Give yourself a day without a schedule, without obligations.
- Be aware that endless giving can turn into unhealthy resentment.
- Experience nurturance from the inside. Check in with yourself throughout the day, take short healing moments to settle any uncomfortable feelings.
- Take a long, hot bath infused with lavender oil. Light a candle and play some soft music.
- Buy yourself a present. When I got sick I bought myself a gold ankle bracelet that I had always wanted. It remains one of my special treasures and reminds me that I can give to myself.
- Take a vacation that allows you to experience life without rushing, without producing, without doing.

Exercises for Body-Mind-Spirit

Breathing and Relaxing

Allow your breath to expand the belly, then fill the chest. Notice how you do not have to think about breathing—how the body just knows. You can use the breath to affirm your body's wisdom. Take a deep breath and then blow it out completely through your mouth like a sigh: push out every last bit of air. Then consciously soften your belly and allow the breath to fill the belly again, then the middle and upper chest up to the collarbone. As you shift to abdominal breathing remember to exhale completely and to keep the belly soft as you inhale. Your body will feel immediately relaxed. Focus on abdominal breathing for about ten minutes.

Releasing Muscle Tension

We store tension in the body and need to release it. Take a mental journey from your toes to your head, releasing tension where you find it. Tighten the muscles in each area as you come to it, then release the tension, let go and relax. Start with your toes, then feet, ankles, calves, knees, thighs, genitals, buttocks, lower back, abdomen, upper back, chest, breasts, shoulders, arms, hands, fingers, neck, face, eyes, ears, nose, mouth, scalp. After deep breathing and muscle release you are more relaxed and ready to choose an emotional exercise or meditation. Plan to spend at least 15 minutes on the exercise you choose and increase the time as you feel the benefits and are more comfortable spending time alone.

Imagery, Tapes, Music

What I did with my personal time and space changed over time and continues to evolve. The important matter is to claim it. Early on I used some guided imagery exercises suggested by the Simontons in their groundbreaking work *Getting Well Again*. After attending Bernie Siegel's workshop I began to use his tape, *Healing Meditations*, which evoked some very important images and emotions from my past which I found very useful. Feelings came up over and over again that had been pushed down for years. After the tears, the incredible value of my life came back to me; I began to feel renewed.

Feelings and emotions are different than thoughts. We can learn new facts quickly but blocked emotions must be processed. They must be dealt with over time, again and again, and released when you are ready. We can't rush through emotional learning. Stephan Rechtschaffen, M.D., co-founder and director of the Omega Institute for Holistic Studies talks about "mind time" and "emotional time."[10] He claims the way we are living our lives in the modern world has created a chasm so that our minds are functioning at a speed that our emotions cannot keep pace with. Thus, if we don't take the time to deal with these emotions as they come up, they are repressed and resurface when we slow down. So be prepared for uncomfortable feelings to come up as you slow down and start to relax. All the unresolved encounters and unfinished business will call for resolution.

Emotional healing is a journey out of the silence and into the silence. Australian author Grace Gawler writes, ". . . Real healing can only take place when there is a conscious transition from the state of 'bottled up,' emotionally distressed silence, to the state of open communication and expression, the state of inner nourishing silence and its product, peace of mind."[11] Sit in a room lit only by natural light or outside in nature to do this work.

Imagery can be used in many ways. For example, you can visualize the cancer in your body in a way that seems right to you. In my cancer support group we did an imagery exercise under the loving guidance of my therapist Tullia Kidde who suggested that we picture our disease. I saw my cancer as a small gray rock which, in the course of the guided imagery, simply dissolved into sand and disappeared. At the time the visualization confirmed what I knew: my tumor was responding to the chemotherapy treatments. My spirit was strong and the image assured me that I was healing.

Work with your images. If your images are frightening,

then fears need to be confronted. Dr. Bernie Siegel writes in *Peace, Love and Healing,* "Intuitively and instinctively, the unconscious knows what is needed. Our job as individuals confronting disease is to set it free. . . ."[12] See what comes up for you when you visualize your cancer; explore the images and interact with them. You can transform your images with your positive energy, enhancing the communication between your subconscious and your body. Transforming the rock into sand, my soul gave permission to my body to eradicate the cancer; confirming what was happening on a physical level and bringing it to consciousness, my mind and emotions could more fully partake of my healing experience.

Early in my treatment, using the Simontons' book, I worked with the image of cancer cells in my bloodstream being surrounded and then destroyed by my own white blood cells. These images came straight out of my medical background: cell biology 101 materialized. The imagery that arises can be an important way to access deeper levels of your consciousness and can also communicate your support of your body's ability to effectively deal with this cancer. You are not a passive player but an active participant.

The Simontons[13] list the following features of effective images which provide a good starting point for this exercise.

1. The cancer cells are weak and confused.
2. The treatment is strong and powerful.
3. The healthy cells have no difficulty repairing any slight damage the treatment might do.
4. The army of white blood cells is vast and overwhelms the cancer cells.
5. The white blood cells are aggressive, eager for battle, quick to seek out the cancer cells and destroy them.
6. The dead cancer cells are flushed from the body normally and naturally.
7. By the end of the imagery, you are healthy and free of cancer.

8. You see yourself reaching your goals in life, fulfilling your life's purpose.

The Simontons's list is only a suggestion for one type of visualization. There are infinite approaches. Creating your own images is part of your healing; accessing creative energy can assist you in your healing, which itself is a creative process.

Visualization and Affirmation of Wholeness

See yourself as whole. Picture yourself in perfect health, radiating well-being. Even though you have breast cancer, you are still whole—your spirit is still intact. Feel your healthy spirit. Know you can heal. Repeat to yourself a phrase that is meaningful to you over and over. Try to keep your mind clear except for this phrase; if your mind wanders, bring it gently back.

- I am healthy.
- My deepest spirit is always in perfect health.
- My disease allows me to rise above challenging circumstances and reach new levels of health.
- Healing energy is always available to me.
- Fear blocks my access to healing. I can let go of fear.

Repeat the phrase; stay with it for the duration of the meditation. When your mind wanders, bring it back to the phrase. Create a meaningful affirmation for yourself. You can use these or your own affirmations throughout the day. Keep them in your consciousness instead of incessantly replaying past injuries or worrying about the future.

Sometimes, instead of guided imagery, I would just listen to music and open myself to what came up. Daniel Kobialka's *Timeless Motion* is wonderful meditative music. Everytime I hear this music it brings me immediately back to a state of exquisite introspection that I had never experienced before my illness. Later on, I worked in silence.

℘ *Remember...*

We must pay attention to the images that come up but we do have the power to transform these images and to consciously create new ones with our intention. Images and dreams are the connection between our highly intuitive subconscious and our body. By accessing the information in our images and dreams we release healing energy. It takes a lot of energy to keep uncomfortable feelings buried in our subconscious. Use your intention. Work with images of the cancer dissolving. Work with images of your body and spirit as healthy.

Meditation on Feeling the Fear and Freeing the Fear

Sit quietly and allow your emotions to rise; let the fear come up. For me, as the fear came up it initially showed itself as the fear of impending death. The fear of death then became the fear that I wasn't living my life as I really wanted to, now, in this moment. How could I begin to approach the mistake that my life had become; how could I arrive at a different place; how far back did I need to go in order to heal, in order to live without this dread? I began to let the fear of death come in and relaxed into an awareness of my own, our shared mortality. We are all going to die. Let this feeling open you to the most authentic living possible in the present moment. Fill yourself with the feeling of how you want to live today.

༄   *Remember..*

Very often, people who get busy living forget to die of their diseases. Use what comes up for you in this meditation in a very practical way in your daily life. Even if you believe you are going to die soon, what do you want to do with your last day, week, month? Do it!

Fear of Recurrence

Sometimes I feel like I can not let go of it
If I do
when it comes flooding back—I will drown.
If I stay with it
I know its dimensions
If I let go of it
anything can happen

I no longer have the luxury of living
as if I might live forever
as if I hadn't been warned

A recurrence
might be more terrifying than the initial diagnosis
Cancer may be incurable
but a recurrence . . .
and after all my hard work.

—B.J.

Directly dealing with fear can effectively help process the denial that we have regarding extremely painful issues. If you can face the possibility of your own death, speak to it and let it speak to you, you can stop hiding. Many times family, friends and doctors minimize the possibility of death. If people avoid this issue it is because they are uncomfortable and are not in touch with their own fears regarding their mortality. Despite the media coverage of the rights of dying patients, despite the hospice movement and the AIDS crisis, despite the epidemic of breast cancer, there is still an unnatural fear of death in our culture. Death is not viewed as part of the natural life process.

How many of us have been with a person in the final stages of his or her life with whom we could talk openly about this inevitable event? Our culture is fascinated with death—open the newspaper, turn on the TV—but it's all happening to someone we don't know. We need to encounter our personal feelings about death. It really does not matter what stage you have been assigned to or what your physician has said regarding your eventual prognosis. The point is, no matter what the statistics show, the very real emotional issue of breast cancer eventuating in death must be dealt with.

The word cancer is equated with death in our culture. I know many woman whose fear is quite profound even though they have Stage I cancer with good "five-year survival statistics." Five years? I don't want to die in six years either. What happened to one day at a time? That's okay for other people, but I can't live knowing I'm going to die, you say. What about the statistic that 80 percent of women with breast cancer will die of their disease within 20 years of the diagnosis?[14] Breast cancer brings us face to face with our mortality, so it is not surprising that there are many women who live in mortal fear of breast cancer.

The meditation, sitting with our fear of death, frees us to live effectively now. The fact that we are mortal gives our lives meaning. Putting a frame around our lives allow us to set priorities and accomplish goals. If we had forever, we would never get the job done. Live the days as if you are going to die and see what happens. Accept your mortality, not in a giving-up sense, but in the spirit of a frame, a context for your Life's Story.

This exercise also helps you to see the things that really have meaning. My children began to look so precious at every moment. My awareness of my mortality allows an ever-deepening sensitivity to life. At any moment I can break into tears of joy just looking at my children and then I know—now I am really living. Everybody dies. Bernie Siegel reminds us that "life is terminal." Let the fear open your heart to living in this moment. As many times as necessary, open to the fear, breathe deeply, relax and allow space around the fear. Only by allowing the fear can it begin to dissolve.

Even if you do not believe in life after death, allow for the possibility that we live on when our bodies die. This can be very comforting.

> I hope children downt get kanser.
> And gronups downt get kanser
> and I hope all people are well
> and I know its very sad when people
> die in a family and I'm sorry that hapins
> When my mom was sick I felt
> very sad and felt bad for her
> when she got kanser and I hope it
> never hapins agen and I hope I downt get kanser
>
> by Hannah, age 7

Meditation on Self-Esteem

This meditation is to help you work on the feeling that you're not good enough. Part of this feeling usually has to do with low self-esteem—feelings of unworthiness that we have carried with us from childhood. "Can't you ever do it right?" gets internalized. Some people grow up getting a "don't be" message. Because their parents were incapable of loving them as they were, they grew up believing that something was wrong with them. They were too alive, too enthusiastic and the way to please their parents was to diminish their life force, their will. Part of "not good enough" has to do with our inability to love ourselves or accept ourselves. Our life energy is diminished because of these old messages.

Let the feelings arise in the context of not feeling good enough. Where did your body hide this message? Perhaps the message is hidden in your breast. Repeated feelings of anger, resentment and pain that were never expressed may contribute to the development of breast cancer. Some of these feelings may be stored in your breasts. The negative messages that our parents, teachers and peers drummed in to us need to be aired. The negative messages became our beliefs and then became encoded in our cellular memory banks. We need to step back and reprocess these messages so that we can be free of their crippling influence.

Go back to a time when you were told you did not do it right, when you were criticized for not being perfect. From infancy, were you unwanted, were you the wrong sex? From childhood, were you never neat enough, not smart enough, too loud, too shy? From adolescence, was your emerging sexuality shamed? Were you told you would never amount to anything? Close your eyes and go back to the time of a hurtful negative message. Trust that the memory will come. Feel how you felt at the time and let it come in; sit with the feelings. Allow all of what you felt then, the anger, the resentment, the bitterness and pain to come up. Feel how vulnerable, how defenseless you were. With great compassion, appreciate your predicament at that time. Unable to express your feelings, check where you stored these emotions. The feelings may be stored throughout your body and some may be in your breasts. Explore where they are now and soften wherever you stored these unexpressed emotions. With great self-love, release them.

Meditation for Releasing Self-Blame

Is the diagnosis of breast cancer giving you that "not good enough" message again? Is there a part of you that blames yourself for getting this disease? Close your eyes and allow for the thoughts that you didn't eat right, that you didn't exercise enough, that you held too much anger in, on and on: wait and watch as the endless self-blaming thoughts come in. Let them go; do not hold on to them. And, when you are ready, take a deep breath and allow yourself to feel infinite compassion for your present circumstances. Be with yourself not in pity, but in love. Allow room for the belief that to everything there is a purpose, that in everything there is a lesson and that with deep respect for ourselves we can go beyond "not good enough" and cross into our own acceptance.

There is no room for bitterness and self-blame. This old Sufi saying tells us to embrace the circumstances of our lives and that in the embrace comes the healing.

> Overcome any bitterness that may have come to you because you were not up to the magnitude of the pain that was entrusted to you.
>
> Like the mother of the world who carries the pain of the world in her heart, each one of us is part of her heart and therefore endowed with a certain measure of cosmic pain. You are sharing in the totality of that pain.
>
> You are called upon to meet it in joy instead of self-pity. The secret is to offer your heart as a vehicle to transform cosmic suffering into joy.

Meditation for Releasing Anger and Resentment

Unexpressed anger becomes resentment, a chronic ill will that persists long after the anger-provoking situation, and it undermines our health. The word *resentment* comes from the French, *ressentir*—to feel strongly and to feel again. When we feel resentful, we feel strongly the pain of the past again and again. Robin Casarjian likens resentment to holding a burning ember with the intention of throwing it at another, all the while burning yourself.

Begin with a reflection on a time, past or present, when you felt angry. Take a deep breath and go deeper. Underneath anger is the pain of a more primary emotion; allow yourself to feel it. Were you really feeling sad, scared, hurt, abandoned, disappointed? Go even deeper to the longing underneath the pain. Were you really longing for acknowledgment, appreciation and love? Anger needs to be processed moment to moment; optimally it arises and passes through us as we immediately allow access to the more primary feelings. In order for this to happen, we need to be clear and trust that we are safe. To get through anger and resentment we need to go back with clarity to old hurts and feel and release them in safety. Put yourself in a safe place and linger there. Work on visualizing a safe and comfortable place to release old hurts. Sitting with the anger, slowly, gently allow yourself to become vulnerable to the feeling underneath. Be patient; it will come. Slowly and gently go deeper to the longing and feel it in the safety that you have created. Know that the universe is safe.

Meditation on Forgiveness

In her book, *Forgiveness, A Bold Choice for a Peaceful Heart,* Robin Casarjian writes: "There are many ways to define forgiveness, because forgiveness is many things. It is a decision, an attitude, a process and a way of life. It is something we offer others and something we accept for ourselves."[15] Forgiveness implies an understanding that insensitive behavior is a call for love, help and respect. Forgiveness is an attitude that seeks to shift our perceptions and the emotional reactions that follow so that they reflect this understanding. Forgiveness is the process of shifting our perceptions so that we see others and ourselves with ever more compassion. Forgiveness as a way of life transforms us from being ruled by the past to reacting cleanly and clearly to whatever life presents, moment by moment.

Go to a safe and comfortable place. Breathe and relax.

Think of someone whom you would like to forgive and picture them in your mind. Look at this person and communicate all the feelings that have been left unsaid. Allow yourself to hear their truth. Let go of all your judgements, the resentments you hold for that person and your feelings of self-righteousness. Let go of the way you have conditioned yourself to see this person. Look at this person through the eyes of compassion. Open your heart to yourself and your power to see and feel in this new way. Honor and respect the power of forgiveness.

Meditation on the Light

Begin with abdominal breathing, and as you feel relaxed visualize a healing light entering your body at the crown of your head and illuminating your entire body. Allow every cell in your body to be bathed in this primordial light. Remember that every cell is a microcosm of the entire body, and within each cell's DNA and deeper still into its submolecular structure is the wisdom of the universe. The light you are meditating upon goes to the core of the cell, at its deepest level, allowing it to resonate with its own true nature. Let every cell open to light and love. Spend an entire meditation on the light or begin or end any of the other exercises with this meditation.

ASKING FOR HELP

By asking for help we open, the pain is diminished and in its place there is room for love and for healing. Yale surgeon Bernie Siegel told his patients. "Share your needs. Reach out for help. Express yourself. If you love yourself, you will give your body all the help it needs, but that can only happen if you accept yourself and your needs. . . . Let out the pain and love will fill the space."[16]

Accept love and support when offered honestly by your

family and friends. This is not the time for us to be attending to others but rather we must allow ourselves to be cared for. Although we can benefit from the love and support of close family members, this is not always possible. Sometimes those closest to us are at a loss; they may be so overwhelmed with the pain our illness has evoked in their lives, they are unable to give to us. Author Ken Wilbur, whose wife had breast cancer writes, "For the many men who do stay with their mates during cancer and its treatment, the feeling that comes up most is fear."[17]

We need to explore and give voice to our unmet needs in meditation, counseling, discussion and support groups. The important work of recognizing and forgiving old hurts can be done in various ways, sometimes directly, sometimes not. We need not ask for help from those with whom we have emotional difficulties or from those who are unable to give at this time, though we would wish otherwise. Yet we do need to feel comfortable in opening and asking the universe for help in creative ways; sometimes we need to take a chance, a leap of faith. Help will come from unexpected directions but only if we open to it.

A counselor can offer vital help. Your counselor could be a psychologist, psychiatrist, social worker, minister, art therapist, a dear friend . . . the degree is not important, skill and devotion to the healing arts is vital.

SUPPORT GROUPS

We came together each week. Tullia, myself and the others. I looked forward to that once-a-week meeting, that time was mine. My time. My time to listen and to speak without judgments. It was a holy experience. We supported one another at such a vulnerable time. Bill died of pancreatic cancer after far exceeding his expected prognosis. He lived well up until the end. His emotions became much clearer and his expression easier. We all thought his wife should have been easier on him; Bill was such a gentle soul. I learned how gentle a man could be. Ellen lives. Heavyset, gentle, a lover of animals. She had breast cancer and was in remission. She was beginning to take the first steps in creating a profession for herself. She was learning word processing. We encouraged her. Ellen often spoke about her family of origin, it dominated her to such an extent that it was months before I had any notion of her current situation. Nora died. We heard so much about her children, her miserable ex-husband and her demanding mother. It was so hard to let go of all the hurts. Nora couldn't let go but she worked so hard at it. She outlived her doctor's prediction. I honor her spirit, her thick flesh, her headscarf and her wonderful sense of humor. Jayne died this year. She did not exceed the five-year survival, as statistics had predicted. She reminded me of my mother, not because she had ovarian cancer but because I knew deep down she believed it would kill her, just like my mother. And she couldn't let go of that belief no matter what she did. She kicked and screamed and went to all sorts of political meetings, representing beleaguered cancer patients in pleas for more governmental funding. She submitted to innumerable invasive procedures, experimental procedures. She was explored and re-explored following the progression of her illness, cell by multiplying cell. And she always ran back to her oncologist who was closely following her serum CA 125 levels for yet another indication. The tumor finally encased her heart. Gisela lives. Gisela had recurrent breast cancer, she did not let that get her down. Gisela is German and very methodical. She took on the challenge to clear her emotional life, she worked through her conflicts with her aged wheelchair-bound mother whom she regularly visited in Germany and she opened more to the love she and her husband shared. Gisela and Steve moved to Santa Fe, and we get together once a year now. I live; I did a lot of work. I approached my healing like it was an assignment, the outcome of which was life or death. I studied hard. I brought in all I had. I held nothing back. The group still lives in my heart.

∾

GROUP

May I sit with wisdom and compassion
  at the ancient fires
  of dashed hopes
  and lost dreams.

May the pain which brings us together
  become the cave we enter
  in reverent descent
  and surrender
  to what Is.

May we have the courage
  to bear this rebirth together.[18]

—CAROL HOWARD, M.F.C.C.
Therapist, Support Group Leader

ACTIVELY CHOOSING AND COMMUNICATING WITH YOUR PHYSICIANS

. . . April 25th, 1991, the day I first learned I had breast cancer at Yale . . . I got the news in the waiting room—I had cancer . . . the waiting room had no formal boundaries, just bunches of modular furniture clustered around nursing stations. It reminded me of an airline terminal, with the same stale air. I thought for sure if the news was bad the doctor would have a nurse call us into a consultation room, so I was slightly off balance as he sat down next to us and the words came out of his mouth . . . you have cancer . . . there were no walls for the words to bounce off, they just kept going and floated through that huge room . . . you have cancer; he quickly went on to say it wasn't life-threatening, it looks like an in situ *on the frozen section but you know how unreliable frozen sections are. Don't*

worry, we'll take care of it, I'll be in touch with the final pathology, and he was gone ... I walked out in a daze; now I knew I had cancer. He did say cancer, I heard him, but he hedged—in situ—*was that something I should cling to until the final pathology report was in? I knew it was going to be invasive, there was no security in the hope it might be otherwise. ... The people around me were going about their business, the crowd had really thinned out since we'd arrived for the biopsy hours ago, it was the end of the day. ... Was it the end of my life? A private room may have allowed me to sit with the reverberating shock but we were in the middle of the Yale Comprehensive Cancer Center's waiting room. We walked outside and got into the car; the world looked no different but all feeling was gone; I was numb; my private world had just collapsed. I vaguely remembered my husband's promise of a dinner to celebrate the good results. I sensed that I had failed and I was annoyed with him—he had, after all, assured me all would be fine. It was a quiet ride home ...*

∾

My first doctor-patient interaction at Yale strongly contrasts with the style of communication that went on with the surgeon I eventually chose.

Dr. Susan Love believes in the importance of frankness, privacy and individualization within the context of a team approach. Her's is the model I consider to be essential in a proactive doctor-patient relationship:

When a patient comes to me with what I think may be a malignancy, I start talking with her right away about the possibilities, from the most hopeful to the most grim, and ask her to consider what it would be like for her in the worst possible scenario. We discuss the general range of treatments we'd be likely to want to choose from. Then we talk about when I'm going to call her with the results of her biopsy, so she can decide where she'll be and who will be with her. I

was taught in medical school that you should never tell a
patient anything over the phone, but I've found that it works
better if I do. If the patient doesn't have cancer, why keep
her in suspense any longer? And if she does, I prefer that
she find out in her own home, or in whatever environment
she's chosen beforehand. Then if it's bad news, she doesn't
have to worry about being polite because she's in my office
and there are all these other people around. She can cry,
scream, throw things, get drunk, deal with the blow in whatever way she needs to. And she won't have to lie awake all
night hoping I'm not going to tell her something awful the
next day but knowing the worst already. So I'll tell her on
the phone, and then make an appointment to see her within
24 hours. By that time, the shock will have worn off a little
bit, and she can absorb information about her options a little
better. . . . In the long run, I'm convinced that you're better
off when you've consciously chosen your treatment than
when it's imposed on you as a matter of course. But in the
short run, it's more difficult. . . . Of course, different patients
have different needs. Some women still want an "omni-
scient" doctor to tell them what to do. . . . They did better
with old-fashioned paternalistic surgeons who told the
women what was best for them, giving them minimal information. Others liked to feel in control of their lives, and to
know all they could about their illness and its ramifications.
They did better with surgeons like me, who wanted to discuss everything with them.[19]

Out of Bernie Siegel's pain as a surgeon he was able to
articulate many of the ways medical training and medical
practice serve to foster avoidance of true relationship with
patients and prevent a healing partnership.

. . . I didn't have a class on healing and love, how to talk
with patients, or the reasons for becoming a doctor. I was
not healed during my training, and yet I was expected to
heal others . . . I was finding my job very painful . . . my
typical physician's response—to hide my pain when something went wrong—helped no one. . . . The pressure never

let up. . . . Too often the pressure squeezes out our native compassion. The so-called detached concern we're taught is an absurdity. Instead, we need to be taught a rational concern, which allows the expression of feelings without impairing the ability to make decisions . . . it is not hard to understand why today's young doctors, many of whom have never had to confront death or serious illness in their own lives, have no idea how to help their patients. Overwhelmed by the magnitude of what they must tell patients and families facing serious disease, they withdraw. The patient, however, sees only the detachment, not the concern. Too often, the result of maintaining our "professional distance" is that we build a wall around ourselves. When we do this, our patients are not the only one who suffer. We hurt ourselves as well . . .[20]

Bernie speaks the truth about the medical profession. It is my experience that most physicians are not in touch with themselves, their reasons for entering the profession, their need to be in control of the interactions with their patients (controlling the range of choices that are open to their patients, controlling the limits of what is acceptable to talk about within the medical model, controlling how much time they will talk) and are only comfortable holding the power. Bernie offers many suggestions and has many ideas about the way humanity can be brought back into the healing profession. Many doctors have lost touch with their humanity, and their irrational obsession to cure at any cost, leads to the dispersal of facts without feeling, "more is better" recommendations regarding treatments, and the destruction of those whom they cannot assure of cure. So many die on schedule when they are told how long they have to live. By holding out to women the grim probabilities of dismal statistics rather than the real possibilities of deep healing, women are denied honest confrontation with breast cancer.

When I see seminars being offered on "how to talk to your physician," I am distressed that we have gone so far astray as a culture that we need a course to learn how to talk to one another. I get more invitations to seminars on the topics of insurance coding, strategies for reimbursement, preferred providers and malpractice issues than for preventive medicine in women's health care.

Physicians need to come to terms with the limitations of the conventional methods in breast cancer treatment and begin to integrate complementary modalities and healing partnership into patient care. Physicians are frightened; failure to diagnose breast cancer is one of the most common grounds of malpractice litigation and awards in the profession. As physicians, we need to educate ourselves and our patients regarding the role of lifestyle in disease prevention, long- and short-term risks and benefits of diagnostic and treatment interventions and the necessity for responsibility on both sides of the physician-patient equation. Women need to rely on themselves, to read, to network and to involve open-minded physicians and other health professionals in their health care.

As a culture, we need to foster the birth of a new paradigm in health care—one in which physicians do not feel protected by overprescribing and overtreating—in which simple, inexpensive and effective measures such as nutritional counseling, vitamins, minerals and herbs, yoga and meditation classes and group therapy are considered essential in supporting health. We need to educate our government and insurance carriers that this approach is not only health promoting but cost-effective.

I saved my own life by stepping out of the medical model to take part in the integration of my own medical care. You can do it too. I am not suggesting that doctors should abandon the best that high-tech medicine has to offer. But as physicians we do need to open a dialogue and consider other options. We need to acknowledge that what conventional medicine has to offer is not enough for true healing, that conventional methods cannot stand alone, that they are not enough. We need to support each individual's quest to find healing and empowerment. It is also important to broaden our awareness of the larger political and environmental issues that are so obviously part and parcel of the breast cancer epidemic.

Do your best to find physicians and other health professionals who you can talk to, who listen and who make it clear that they have the time to listen and, most importantly, who honor your ability to make choices.

∾   Remember...

You have a right to private and thorough communications with your doctors. Reflect on the quality of your interactions with your health care team and make changes, if necessary.

∾

I was scheduled to go up to Boston, I had completed four cycles of chemotherapy and I was to meet with Dr. Love so that she could evaluate my response to the chemo and plan the strategy over the next few months. I was in an ongoing relationship with Richie Zelkowitz, who was my medical oncologist, and he and I both knew I was responding well. Nevertheless, seeing is believing and, since Susan was going to do my surgery when the time came, it was important that she know how I was doing.

Marie, the funny Marie, as my children called her, arrived early to babysit for the day. My husband and I were ready to go. It was windy and raining heavily and I had heard on the radio about hurricane warnings, but I didn't pay too much attention. The storm I was weathering inside was enough for me. Just to be sensible I dialed the Faulkner Breast Clinic just before leaving and I was assured that as long as I came they were sure to be open; I wasn't about to let a little rain—or even a lot—get in the way of this important visit.

As we headed north on I-95, the all-too-familiar route to

the Boston area hospitals, the rain picked up. It was so heavy that despite the wipers going at full speed we could barely see the road ahead. We slowed down and the rains continued; we listened to music. I always brought things to read with me, so I read until I was carsick. As we got closer to Boston the winds picked up and the radio continued to issue hurricane warnings. Finally the radio alerted us to the fact that we were now in the midst of a hurricane. We were advised to get off the roads; it had all the markings of an adventure. Suddenly, the roads seemed deserted, obviously everyone else was taking this quite seriously.

We arrived at Faulkner and, despite what the office had said in the morning, the parking lot was suspiciously empty. We walked over to the Breast Clinic with the wind and rain upon us; the door was locked. I pulled harder and shook the door. I refused to take no for an answer. They told me they would stay open, and I meant to get in. We wandered around the building like two thieves, my husband, following, knowing I was not to be dissuaded. We found a side entrance unlocked and wandered through the building until we found our way to the offices of Dr. Love and her associates. And there pasted on the door of the office was a note:

Barbara Joseph
We tried to reach you
this morning. We're sorry
but due to the weather
we had to close. We
will call you to reschedule.

Thanks

By this time an officer from Faulkner security had been sent over to investigate the intruders—us! I explained the circumstances to the security guard and he stayed around while I telephoned Dr. Love's answering service. In a short time I got a call back from the doctor. She couldn't have been more gracious, and what we finally decided was to meet. She gave me directions to a doctor's office which was accessible to her, and we followed the Boston street map from Jamaica Plains to an office in Watertown. The roads were deserted. Some trees were down, but eventually we found our way. There was no sign of Dr. Love, so we waited. Finally, a red Jeep approached. It was Dr. Love. We joined her and followed her upstairs. She examined me and agreed that the tumor had been remarkably responsive to the chemotherapy (and whatever else I was doing). We talked for a while, laughed about the circumstances and our determination not to let the hurricane change our plans! She understood, without explaining, the difficulties of undergoing the aggressive chemotherapy treatments, traveling three hours each way to and from Boston, making provisions for watching three little children . . . here was a doctor with HEART. I'll never forget that I had a doctor who came out in the middle of Hurricane Bob to see me, as long as I live . . . and the real adventure that life sometimes is.

ॐ

ॐ **Remember...**

Your doctor can limit you, your doctor can inform you. Your doctor can bully you, your doctor can be your ally. Your doctor can harm you, your doctor can help you. Find a doctor you like. Find a doctor who empowers you. Find a doctor who has an open heart.

The effect of sensitivity is inestimable. In the collection, *Cancer As a Women's Issue,* Dian Marino writes, "One incident that stands out in my mind as a turning point was when I shifted from Princess Margaret Hospital to the Sunnybrook Cancer Clinic. A woman doctor introduced herself as the head of my team (of seven doctors of different specialties). She then gave me a physical exam (number 347) and instead of admiring the many incisions and scars that I had on my body and inquiring who had given me this beauty or that wonderful piece of work, she said 'I can see you have been through a lot.' She was the first doctor to use those scars as symbols of painful experiences . . . I told her that I appreciated her open and non-distractive way of communicating and asked if she could teach her peers to come to people this way."[21] Dian's story moved me deeply. As a woman and a physician I connected to both the enormity and the simplicity of being a physician and the awareness necessary for real communication.

TAKING CHARGE

Remember—you are in charge, it's an awesome responsibility, not unlike mothering a child. In *My Breast,* Joyce Wadler discusses the problems of dealing with so many "specialists."

It's a relief on Monday to get back to research. The only thing is, I am finding a new problem: I am dealing with a growing group of specialists—a breast surgeon, plastic surgeon, oncologist, radiologist. Each specialist puts his field first and is somewhat ignorant—at times even disdainful—of the others. The cancer surgeons, when they discuss reduction surgery—an idea I haven't dismissed—seem to regard it as a hideous, even frivolous, procedure. Dr. Luke, when I talk things over with him after seeing Dr. Veteran, suggests doing a reduction *after* I'm done with lumpectomy and radiation; he isn't aware plastic surgeons have difficulty working with irradiated tissue. Even if I give up my idea of reduction, there will be three or four people involved.

"I understand that I don't see the oncologist until after the lymph node surgery, and the radiation doctor comes in after that," I tell a nursing assistant at Sloan-Kettering, when I make an appointment. "But who's in charge?"

"There will be a group of doctors, who will all be monitoring you along the way," she says cheerfully, "but as far as who's in charge—in a sense, you are."

In a sense, that's good—I should be the one to have the final say about what happens to my body. In another, it's terrifying. I know nothing about science; I'm one of those people who's still not sure what makes planes stay up. What this disease needs, I decide, is a contractor—or at least a place where we could get all the specialists in one room.[22]

My friends—you are the contractor! And there's no one in a better position to pull it all together. In all the personal accounts I've read I have noticed a common thread as breast cancer patients go through the conventional medical system. A major complaint is the lack of leadership. We have all heard from experts with conflicting opinions. Some of us have been recipients of a paternalistic censoring of information or have been given misleading information that conveyed a false sense of emergency which in turn frightened us into scheduling surgery before thoughtful consideration of all the options.

We have also been subject to careless mistakes and policies of questionable benefit:

- In my own case one surgeon forgot to examine my lymph nodes, omitted a metastatic work-up, and immediately booked me for a partial mastectomy. Had I been an obedient patient, his oversights might have cost me my life.
- In Joyce Wadler's book she tells about being invited back for chemotherapy a year after completing her treatment. The doctors at Memorial Sloan-Kettering Cancer Center did not have all her slides when they made their initial recommendations, and when the slides were received a year later the pathologists at Sloan disagreed with the original diagnosis:

It all seems crazy to me, but there's nothing I can do. I have two doctors who have looked at the same slides and made different diagnoses. I have been thinking about medicine, I realize, as a science of absolutes. I assumed a doctor would look at a cancer cell and tell you with certainty what it was, just as one looks at the liquid in a measuring cup and gives you a precise count. But breast cancer is apparently not like that; its more like two coaches disputing a play at a basketball game . . .[23]

- For Virginia Soffa, it was a discovery early in her journey. After thoroughly researching all her options she could not find a surgeon to agree with and support her treatment plan—lumpectomy along with many complementary techniques to improve her immune status. Her innovative thinking and determination to create her own best treatment program went up against the orthodoxy of conventional medicine, where a Stage I tumor without clear margins gets either a mastectomy or a lumpectomy with radiation and or chemotherapy.

Since then, I have heard so many other women describe having had this same experience that I think many doctors don't want to be challenged. They are tired of explaining the grim probabilities, and they hope for blind compliance. When I verbalized my understanding of the significance of my disease—that my life was in danger—and my desire for my illness to be treated with the seriousness it warranted, I found it more difficult to find supportive physicians.[24]

INNER LISTENING—HOW TO MAKE UP YOUR MIND ABOUT TREATMENT OPTIONS

Having gone to many physicians and received second opinions from many specialists, the time comes for us to make a decision. Our mind goes round and round weighing alternatives; the indecision can be exhausting. Jessie Crum describes a helpful technique in her book, *The Art of Inner Listening*.[25]

- Think the problem through from every angle, writing down every option and any questions that still remain.
- After this ask your intuitive self for help.
- Close your eyes, quiet your restless outer mind and let the answer come. Write any thoughts down that come.
- If the answer is not forthcoming, ask your inner guidance to give you insight during the night.
- Before going to sleep write down any remaining questions, being specific about the choices and potential actions.
- Have a pad and pencil by your bed so you will be able to write any answer down immediately if it comes during the night. Never wait until morning to write any dreams or insights down.
- In the morning, if you have not had an answer during the night, sit down and relax; ask the question again and once again ask your intuitive self for the answer. Listen expectantly and write down whatever comes to you.

The most important ingredients for inner listening are discipline (taking the time to ask the question and thinking it through), effort (quieting the mind in the service of listening) and trust (knowing that the answer will come).

DEALING WITH YOUR EVERYDAY WORLD

Obviously, it is appropriate to consider how to talk to your children and prudent to reflect on a suitable time and setting in which to tell the news of a recent diagnosis to concerned family and close friends. The way in which you inform and involve your children very much depends on their ages and the specific circumstances of your illness. For children of all ages, it is crucial to keep in mind their need

for love and their fear of abandonment. After I was diagnosed with cancer I stopped working; I was able to spend
considerable time with my children expressing my love for
them. The details of my illness, for the most part, were not
shared because my children were newborn, two and three
years old at the time of my diagnosis. However, the fact
that I had breast cancer was not hidden, and the older
children, now seven and eight, know I recovered from
breast cancer, use the word cancer freely and have even
contributed some of their thoughts about my illness to the
book. *The Fall of Freddie the Leaf* by Dr. Leo Buscaglia is
an inspiring story that I read to my children about the delicate balance between life and death. It is appropriate for
children of all ages.

Selma Miriam, in *A Witch Recipe for Grievers,* says, "Consider your friends. Withdraw from the ones who are frightened by your pain ... When you're hurting, you need
especially considerate tenderness ... A griever's friend is
one who is there, who spends more time than seems reasonable with a griever ..."[26]

This is not a time to obsess about being polite, who to
tell that you have breast cancer, who not to tell, how to tell
people, or to be overly concerned about how those not
close to you will take it. We all are surrounded by a bevy
of peripheral people in our lives and it is not in our best
interest to spend long hours on the phone answering everyone's questions and curiosities. Conserve your energy.

Tell those you are close to, those you want to tell, those
who will support you. Our time is precious. When your
diagnosis is fresh and your feelings are raw you cannot
afford the resentment that comes with allowing anyone to
interrogate you. Get comfortable with your own boundaries
and insist that others respect them. Talking to people you
don't want to talk with is an energy leak. You need all your
energy, so pay attention.

To everything there is a season. There is no shame in

taking what you need and learning to say no. Take what those who love you offer. Receive with an open heart. Open to the love that is there for you. Allow yourself to be loved.

CREATIVITY CAN HEAL

Healing Legacies is a collection of visual, literary and performing artworks by women with breast cancer in which the experience of breast cancer is explored. Virginia Soffa, who first put out the call for the Healing Legacy Arts Registry, noted that all 33 women who entered their own work in 1993 are alive today. She says, "This fascinates me, since no other breast cancer group I have been part of has had similar efficacy . . . This does not mean that people engaged in creative work don't die . . . I hope to better understand how regular creative activity can enhance our quality of life and improve survival . . . This to me is the medicine of art . . ."[27]

In *Cancer As A Turning Point,* author Larry LeShan discusses the hopelessness of the cancer patients he worked with. Many were people who, despite their successes, were suffering from a lack of expression in their lives. ". . . Over and over again I found that the person I was working with reminded me of the poet W.H. Auden's definition of cancer. He called it a 'foiled creative fire.' "[28]

The deep place where we can confront and process the emotions that breast cancer engenders is a place from which creativity springs. If through this dis-ease, we can access this creative place then not only can we work through the experience, but we can experience healing, the joy of knowing ourselves and the power that comes from communicating our creative force. It takes courage when one is diagnosed with a life-threatening illness to look for this place—some women find it on canvas, with sculpture, by quilting, writing poetry or prose, journaling, playing music, gardening, drawing. Creating artwork is a mirror that helps us see who we are, where we've been and who we are becoming. Go into your creative self; find the way that suits you best and you can connect with your true path in life and recreate your life. Creativity can be the ultimate healing.

MAKING CHANGES

There is an old Chinese definition of insanity: doing the same thing over and over again and expecting it to turn out differently.

If we surgically remove cancer or treat it with chemotherapy or radiation and do not change or optimize the other areas of our lives, that is, our internal and external environments, we will be faced with the same biochemical pathways, leading to perhaps the same illness, a greater likelihood of recurrences or to the development of other chronic debilitating degenerative illnesses in the future.

We need to strengthen all aspects of our lives if we want to individualize our acute care, have a true cancer prevention program, prevent disease recurrence or prevent other illness.

ᔛ   *Remember...*

Breast cancer arises in an environment in which we play an interactive role. We can change our internal and external environment.

The following tips may help:

1. Accept the fact that life will never be the same.
2. Release all notions of what women with breast cancer are like.
3. Be yourself. Don't worry about what other people expect.
4. Be your own best advocate.

5. Forgive yourself for all the things you might have done differently and honor yourself for arriving at this point.
6. Find a doctor who has heart, someone you like— someone who would come out in a storm for you.
7. Find therapists/support groups/mates/friends that are empowering—you can't have a therapeutic alliance without equality, camaraderie and cooperation.
8. Read, read, read. Discover the truth for yourself and don't doubt that it may be in the fine print! See the bibliography for suggested reading.
9. Nurture your sense of gratitude.
10. Remember the healing power of creativity. Find work you love and in which you believe; this can be a valuable healing tool.
11. Continuously create who you are. As Plato said, "Be what you wish to appear."
12. Don't forget to have fun along the way.

11/14/91 Things to do:

Be gentle with myself.
Love myself.
Be kind to myself.
Take care of myself.
Understand myself.
Ask for what I need.
Say no to what I don't want.

—B.J.

THE ESSENTIALS OF A HEALING PROGRAM

- Healing is a full-time commitment. If your intent is to transform your life in the process of recovering from breast cancer you must be willing to put forth the effort. Your energy output needs to be organized and prioritized around this crisis.

- Strength of body and mind will assist you in your journey. Rest will conserve your strength for the healing. Clean food and water will allow your body to do the work. Meditation, visualization, affirmation will enlist your mind in the service of your greater purpose.
- Let love into your life: love yourself and where you are in your recovery, love the adversity that awakens you to your fighting spirit, love your Creative Power and align with it, love those in your life who are there to help you learn the lessons of your life.

Alchemy

Breast cancer
a woman's rite of passage
Through the crab
emerges
a sense of purpose, respect for nature, our creative fire,
gratitude for life
the light within the blackness.

—B.J.

Appendix

A **diagnostic procedure** is a procedure that is done to identify a disease. In the case of breast cancer an incisional biopsy removes a section of suspicious tissue in order to scrutinize the tissue under the microscope and make a diagnosis. A pathologist has been trained to make diagnoses based on certain criteria viewed under the microscope. In some cases there can be disagreement as to whether a particular tissue specimen meets the criteria of a cancer diagnosis. Cancerous type changes often form a continuum between normal, atypical, contained but cancerous and frankly invasive. Second and third opinions can be obtained from pathologists if there is controversy.

A **staging procedure** is a procedure that is done in order to help determine which stage a cancer is in at the time of diagnosis. Ostensibly these procedures are done to make therapeutic decisions but this may not always be so. In the case of lymph node dissections, microscopic disease in the lymph nodes may or may not impact on treatment decisions and unnecessary procedures may themselves prove harmful.

A **therapeutic procedure** is a procedure that is done to treat a disease. In the case of breast cancer an excisional biopsy done on a suspicious lump can be both diagnostic and therapeutic.

* * *

Currently the TNM (tumor, nodes and metastases) system of classification is used to stage breast cancer. It is based on combining the size of the tumor in the breast with the

THE STAGING OF BREAST CANCER

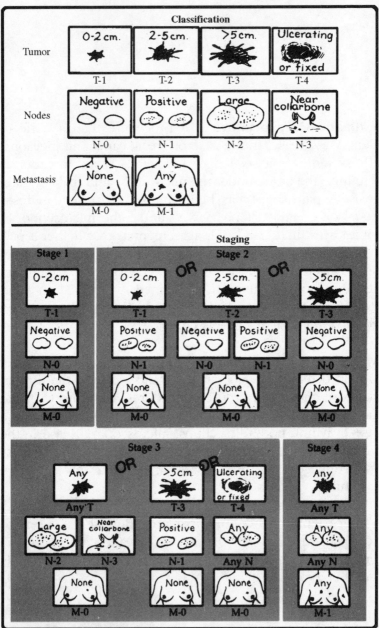

Reprinted with permission from Dr. Susan Love's Breast Book
(Addison-Wesley, 1995)

presence or absence of lymph node involvement as well as spread to other organs. The following chart shows how the Stages I-IV are arrived at. This system does not take into account the aggressiveness of the tumor cells or the fact that lymph nodes are not the only route of spread. The TNM system is helpful to statisticians so that the efficacy of different treatments can be compared but doing the procedures necessary to accurately determine the stage may or may not offer benefits to an individual.

Resources

Barbara Joseph, M.D.
Joel M. Evans, M.D.
The Center For Women's Health
Stamford, CT
203-323-9666

FOOD AND WATER

Food and Water, Inc.
RR1, Box 114
Marshfield, VT 05658
800-EAT-SAFE
A non-profit consumer advocacy organization working for safe
   food and a clean environment. Publishers of *Safe Food News*.

Kushi Institute: Macrobiotics
P.O. Box 7
Becket, MA 01223
413-623-5742

Annemarie Colbin: The Natural Gourmet Cookery School
48 West 21rst St.
New York, NY 10010
212-645-5170

Multi-Pure Water Filters
Available through distributor 203-847-4690

NUTRITIONAL SUPPLEMENTS

Flora Products for essential fatty acids:
flax seed oil, Udo's Choice, The Missing Link

Check your health food store or order directly from:
Flora 800-446-2110

ECOLOGICALLY-SOUND HOUSEHOLD PRODUCTS

Seventh Generation 800-456-1177

PERSONAL CARE

Bajamar Women's Health Care Pharmacy. Individualized compounding of hormonal products including progesterone and estriol by prescription or natural progesterone cream without prescription, 800-255-8025.

Creme de la Femme Non-hormonal Vaginal Lubricant
Hickey Chemist 800-724-5566
Wilner Chemist 800-633-1106

Natural Menstrual Products
WomanKind
P.O.Box 1775
Sebastopol, CA 95473
707-522-8662

ORGANIZATIONS

National Breast Cancer Coalition
P.O. Box 66373
Washington, DC 20035
202-296-7477

National Alliance of Breast Cancer Organizations
(NABCO)
9 East 37th Street
New York, NY 10016
212-719-4154

Y-Me
National Breast Cancer Organization
212 W. Van Buren
Chicago, Il 60607
800-221-2141

American Academy of Environmental Medicine
4510 West 89th Street
Prarie Village, Kansas 66207
913-642-6062
Will help you locate a physician who specializes in environmental medicine

American Holistic Medical Association
4101 Lake Boone Trail
Raleigh, NC 27607
919-787-5181
Will help you locate a physician with a holistic orientation.

Physician's Committee for Responsible Medicine
P.O. Box 6322
Washington, DC 20015
202-686-2210

Menstrual Health Foundation
P.O. Box 1775
Sebastopol, CA 95473
707-522-8662
Educational resource, Coming of Age workshops

American Menopause Foundation, Inc.
Madison Square Station
P.O. Box 2013
New York, NY 10010
212-475-3107

PRIME PLUS/Red Hot Mamas
203-431-3902
Menopause education programs

Greenpeace
1611 Connecticut Ave., NW
Washington, DC 20009
Environmental concerns

EarthSave Foundation
P.O. Box 949
Felton, CA 95018-0949
Environmental concerns

ECaP (Exceptional Cancer Patients)
300 Plaza Middlesex
Middletown, CT 06457
203-343-5950

The Wellness Community
2716 Ocean Park Blvd.
Santa Monica, CA 90405
310-314-2555

The National Lymphedema Network, Inc.
221 I Post Street, Suite 404
San Francisco, CA 94115
800-541-3259
Information on prevention and management

SPECIAL SERVICES

Dr. Ralph Moss, author of *The Cancer Industry, Cancer Therapy: The Independent Consumer's Guide to Non-Toxic Treatment and Prevention and Questioning Chemotherapy* will provide an individualized report for cancer patients who want to know their treatment options, including nontoxic therapies. You can contact him at:

Healing Choices
144 St. John's Place
Brooklyn, NY 11217
718-636-4433

Commonweal Cancer Help Program
P.O. Box 316
Bolinas, CA 94924
415-868-0970
Non-medical education programs to reduce the stress associated with a cancer diagnosis.

References

INTRODUCTION

1. Epstein, Samuel, M.D. Correspondence to Dr. David Kessler, Commissioner of the FDA, February 14, 1994.
2. Cancer and Steroid Hormone Study of the Center for Disease Control and the National Institute of Child Health and Human Development. 1986. Oral Contraceptive Use and the Risk of Breast Cancer. *New England Journal of Medicine* 315: 405-411.
3. Malone, K. et al. 1993. Oral Contraceptives in Relation to Breast Cancer. *Epidemiologic Reviews* 15 (1): 80-97.

CHAPTER 1: CONVENTIONAL AND COMPLEMENTARY APPROACHES TO HEALING

1. Klijn, J.G. et al. 1992. Clinical Breast Cancer, New Developments in Selection and Endocrine Treatment of Patients. *Journal of Steroid Biochemistry and Molecular Biology* 43 (1-3): 21-22.
2. Plotkin, D. and Blankenberg, F. 1991. Breast Cancer—Biology and Malpractice. *American Journal of Clinical Oncology* 14 (3): 254-266.
3. Rutqvist, L.E. et al. 1984. Is Breast Cancer a Curable Disease? A study of 14,731 Women with Breast Cancer from the Registry of Norway. *Cancer* 53: 1793-1800.
4. Alleger, I. July 1995. BookCorner, *Townsend Letter for Doctors:* 104.
5. Meares, Ainslie. *Cancer Another Way?* (Melbourne, Australia: Hill of Content, 1977).
6. Chopra, Deepak. *Quantum Healing* (New York: Bantam, 1989).

7. Moss, Ralph W. *The Cancer Industry* (New York: Paragon House, 1980), pp. 48-49.
8. Kradjian, Robert M. *Save Yourself from Breast Cancer* (New York: Berkley Publishing Group, 1994).
9. Fisher, B. et. 1985. Ten-Year Results of a Randomized Clinical Trial Comparing Radical Mastectomy and Total Mastectomy with or without Radiation. *New England Journal of Medicine* 312: 674-681.
10. Kern, K. August 1994. Connecticut Board Surgeons Survey of Surgical Approach to Breast Cancer, 1993. *Connecticut Medicine* 58 (8): 468-469.
11. Meares, *Cancer Another Way?*
12. Fisher, B. et al. 1985. Five-Year Results of a Randomized Clinical Trial Comparing Total Mastectomy and Segmental Mastectomy with or without Radiation in the Treatment of Breast Cancer. *New England Journal of Medicine* 312: 665.
13. Fisher, B., Redmond, C., Poisson, R., et al. 1989. Eight-Year Results of a Randomized Clinical Trial Comparing Total Mastectomy and Lumpectomy with or without Irradiation in the Treatment of Breast Cancer. *New England Journal of Medicine* 320: 822-828.
14. Fisher, B. et al. 1985. *NEJM* 312: 665.
15. Fessenden, F. July 1995. The Mastectomy Question *Ladies Home Journal:* 77.
16. Margolis, G.J. et al. 1989 Psychological factors in the Choice of Treatment for Breast Cancer. *Psychosomatics* 30 (2): 192-197.
17. Soffa, Virginia. *The Journey Beyond Breast Cancer* (Rochester, Vermont: Healing Arts Press, 1994), pp. 47, 106
18. Boscher, S. Dec. 1, 1994. Without Mortality Benefit, Axillary Dissection Up to Doctor's Discretion. *ObGyn News:* 10.
19. Singer, Sydney Ross and Grismaijer, Soma. *Dressed To Kill* (Garden City Park, New York: Avery Publishing Group, 1995), p. 85.
20. Baum, Michael. *Breast Cancer: The Facts* (New York: Oxford University Press, 1988), p. 65.
21. Center For Medical Consumers. December 1994. Latest Breast Cancer Information from Three Experts (Susan Love, Larry Norton, Dennis Slamon). *HealthFacts* 19:1.
22. Courtesy of the American Society of Plastic and Recon-

structive Surgeons 1994 statistics which represents 97 percent of all physicians certified by the American Board of Plastic Surgery.

23. Lorde, Audre. *The Cancer Journals* (San Francisco: spinsters/ aunt lute, 1980), p. 61.

24. Markisz, Susan B. Spring/Summer 1995. *Breast Cancer Action News* 3 (1): 7.

25. Metzger, Deena *Tree* (Topanga, California: Wingbow Press, 1978), p. 91.

26. Lorde, *The Cancer Journals,* pp. 42-44.

27. Soffa, *The Journey Beyond Breast Cancer,* p. 127.

28. Rollins, Betty. *First, You Cry* (New York, Warner: 1976), pp. 157-158.

29. Levy, S. et al. 1991. Mastectomy Versus Excisional Biopsy: Mental Health Effects on Long-Term Follow-Up. Unpublished manuscript. Pittsburgh Center Institute p. 10.

30. Lorde, *The Cancer Journals,* p. 60.

31. Edelson, S. Clinician of the Month, December 1994. *Preventive Medicine Update Summary Cards* 14 (12): 295.

32. Stephenson, J. December 15, 1994. Silicone Implants and Illness: Research Doesn't Support Link. *ObGyn News:* p. 3.

33. January 21, 1994. Study of Children Breastfed by Women with Breast Implants. *FDA's Talk Paper.*

34. August 2, 1994. Test To Study Breast Implant Made with Soybean-Oil Fat. *L.A. Times*

35. Meares, *Cancer Another Way?*

36. Tokunaga, M. et al. "Breast Cancer Among Atomic Bomb Survivors." *Radiation Carcinogenesis Epidemiology and Biological Significance.* eds., Boice, J.D., Jr. and Fraumeni, J.F., Jr. (New York: Raven Press, 1984), p. 45.

37. Hildreth, N.G. et al. 1989. The Risk of Breast Cancer after Irradiation of the Thymus in Infancy. *New England Journal of Medicine* 321: 1281.

38. Hoffman, D.A. et al. 1989. Breast Cancer in Women with Scoliosis Exposed to Multiple Diagnostic X-rays. *Journal of the National Cancer Institute* 81:1307.

39. Mettler, F.A. et al. 1969. Breast Neoplasma in Women treated with X-rays for Acute Pospartum Mastitis: A pilot study. *Journal of the National Cancer Institute* 43: 803-811.

40. Miller, A.B. et al. 1989. Mortality from Breast Cancer after

Irradiation During Fluoroscopic Examinations in Patients Being Treated for Tuberculosis. *New England Journal of Medicine* 321: 1285.

41. Laszlo, John. *Understanding Cancer* (New York: Harper and Row, 1987).
42. Bishop, J. May 14, 1993. Study Links Breast Cancer Treatment to a Higher Risk of the Disease in the Lungs. *Wall Street Journal.*
43. Austin, Steve and Hitchcock, Cathy. *Breast Cancer What You Should Know (But May Not Be Told) About Prevention, Diagnosis, and Treatment* (Rocklin, California: Prima, 1994), p. 57.
44. Israel, Lucien. *Conquering Cancer* (New York, Random House, 1978).
45. Haybittle, J.L., et al. 1989. Postoperative Radiotherapy and Late Mortality: Evidence from the Cancer Research Campaign Trial for Early Breast Cancer. *British Medical Journal* 298: 1611-13.
46. Early Breast Cancer Trialist's Collaborative Group. 1995. *New England Journal of Medicine* 333: 1444-55.
47. Ibid., pp. 1496-98.
48. Neugut, A. et al. 1993. New Warning for Breast Cancer Patients Who Smoke. *Oncology Times* 15 (6):1.
49. Jancin, B. Feb 16, 1996. Breast Cancer Therapies up Leukemia Risk. *ObGyn News:* 19.
50. Jack, Alex, ed. *Let Food Be Your Medicine.* (Beckett, Mass.: One Peaceful World Press, 1991), p. 92.
51. Batt, Sharon. *Patient No More* (Charlottetown, P.E.I., Canada: Gynergy Books, 1994) p. 87.
52. Meares, *Cancer Another Way?*
53. Love, Susan. afterword to *My Breast* by Joyce Wadler (New York: Simon and Schuster, 1992), p. 173.
54. Love, Susan. *Dr. Susan Love's Breast Book* (Reading, Mass.: Addison-Wesley, 1990) p. 210.
55. Early Breast Cancer Trialists' Collaborative Group. 1992. Systemic Treatment of Early Breast Cancer by Hormonal, Cytotoxic, or Immune Therapy. *Lancet* 339:1-15, 71-85.
56. Batt, *Patient No More,* p. 96.
57. Fisher, B. et al. 1985. Leukemia in Breast Cancer Patients Following Adjuvant Chemotherapy or Postoperative Radiation: The NSABP Experience. *Journal of Clinical Oncology* 3: 1640.

58. Cairns, J. November 1985. The Treatment of Diseases and the War Against Cancer. *Scientific American* 253: 51-59.
59. Grant, J.P. July-August 1990. Proper Use and Recognized Role of TPN in the Cancer Patient. *Nutrition* 6 (4 suppl): 6S-7S, 10S
60. Wood, L. 1985. Vitamin E in Chemotherapy Induced Alopecia. *New England Journal of Medicine* 312 (16): 1060.
61. Stahelin, H.B. et al. 1989. Preventive Potential of Antioxidative Vitamins and Carotenoids on Cancer. *International Journal of Vitamin and Nutritional Research Supplement* 30: 232-241.
62. Rogers, Sherry A. *Wellness Against All Odds* (Syracuse, New York: Prestige Publishing, 1994), p. 187.
63. Simone, Charles B. *Breast Health* (Garden City Park, New York: Avery Publishing Group, 1995), p. 83.
64. Spiegel, David. *Living Beyond Limits* (New York: Ballantine Books, 1993), p. viii.
65. Wilbur, Ken. *Grace and Grit Spirituality and Healing in the Life and Death of Treya Killam Wilbur* (Boston, Mass.: Shambhala, 1991), p. 38-44.
66. Bates, B. September 1, 1995. False Hope for Breast Cancer Patients? Costly Bone Marrow Transplant Sparks Debate. *ObGyn News:* 10.
67. Sakai, F. et al. 1978. Increases in Steroid-Binding Globulins Induced by Tamoxifen in Patients with Carcinoma of the Breast. *Journal of Endocrinology* 76: 219-226.
68. Pollack, M. et al. 1990. Effect of Tamoxifen on Serum Insulinlike Growth Factor I Levels in Stage I Breast Cancer Patients. *Journal of the National Cancer Institute* 82:1693-1697.
69. Noguchi, S. et al. 1993. Down-Regulation of Transforming Growth Factor—Alpha by Tamoxifen in Human Breast Cancer. *Cancer* 72: 131-136.
70. Butta, A. et al. 1992. Induction of Transforming Growth Factor Beta-1 in Human Breast Cancer *in vivo* Following Tamoxifen Treatment. *Cancer Research* 52: 4261-4264.
71. Rose, C. et al. 1985. Beneficial Effect of Adjuvant Tamoxifen Therapy in Primary Breast Cancer Patients with High Oestrogen Receptor Values. *Lancet:* il6-19
72. Fisher, B. et al. 1989. A Randomized Clinical Trial Evaluating Tamoxifen in the Treatment of Patients with Node-Negative Breast Cancer Who Have Estrogen-Receptor-Positive Tumors. *New England Journal of Medicine* 320: 479-484.

73. Seoud, M. et al. 1993. Gynecologic Tumors in Tamoxifen-Treated Women with Breast Cancer. *Obstetrics and Gynecology* 82:165-169.
74. Fisher, B. et al. 1994. Endometrial Cancer in Tamoxifen-Treated Breast Cancer Patients: Findings from the NSABP B-14. *Journal of the National Cancer Institute* 86: 527-537.
75. Committee on Gynecologic Practice. February 1996. Tamoxifen and Endometrial Cancer. *ACOG Committee Opinion* Number 169: 1
76. Margriples, U. et al. 1993. High-Grade Endometrial Carcinoma in Tamoxifen-Treated Breast-Cancer Patients. *Journal of Clinical Oncology* 11: 485-490.
77. Schwartz, P. September 1994. Gynecologic Surveillance of Women on Tamoxifen. *Connecticut Medicine* 58 (9): 515-520.
78. Pavlidis, N.A. et al. 1992. Clear Evidence that Long-Term, Low-Dose Tamoxifen Treatment Can Induce Ocular Toxicity. *Cancer* 69: 2961-2964.
79. Jancin, B. February 1, 1996. NCI Urges 5-Year Limit on Tamoxifen. *ObGyn News* : 3.
80. Brinkley, D. and Haybittle, J.L. 1984. Long-term Survival of Women with Breast Cancer. *Lancet:* i1118.
81. Messina, Mark and Virginia. *The Simple Soybean and Your Health* (New York: Dell, 1989).
82. Meares, *Cancer Another Way?*
83. Bach, Richard. *Illusion—The Adventures of a Reluctant Messiah* (New York: Dell, 1989).

CHAPTER 2: GENES AND HORMONES

1. Chopra, D. interviewed by Mauro, J. November/December 1993. From Here and Now to Eternity. *Psychology Today:* 37.
2. Love, Susan. *Dr. Susan Love's Breast Book* (Reading, Mass.: Addison-Wesley, 1990).
3. Chopra, Deepak *Ageless Body, Timeless Mind* (New York: Crown Publishing, 1993), pp. 113-117.
4. Kradjian, Robert M. *Save Yourself From Breast Cancer* (New York: Berkley Publishing Group, 1994), p. 27.
5. Love, *Dr. Susan Love's Breast Book.*

6. Swift, M., et al. December 26, 1991. Incidence of Cancer in 161 Families Affected by Ataxia-Telangiectasia. *New England Journal of Medicine* 325 (26): 1831-1836.
7. Northrup, Christiane. *Women's Bodies, Women's Wisdom* (New York: Bantam, 1994), p. 130.
8. Rosenberg, C.R. et al. 1994. Premenopausal Estradiol Levels and the Risk of Breast Cancer: A New Method of Controlling for Day of the Menstrual Cycle. *American Journal of Epidemiology* 140: 518-525.
9. Toniolo, P. et al. 1993. Prospective Study of Endogenous Oestrogens and Breast Cancer. *American Journal of Epidemiology* 138: 601.
10. Lemon, H.M. et al. 1996. Reduced Estriol Excretion in Patients with Breast Cancer Prior to Endocrine Therapy. *Journal of the American Medical Association* 196: 1128-1134
11. Follingstad, A.H. Jan 2, 1978. Estriol, the Forgotten Estrogen? *Journal of the American Medical Association* 239 (1): 29-30.
12. Michnovicz, J. et al. 1991. Altered Estrogen Metabolism and Excretion in Humans Following Consumption of Indole-3-Carbinol. *Nutrition and Cancer* 16: 59-66.
13. Schatzkin, A. et al. 1994. Alcohol and Breast Cancer: Where Do We Go From Here? *Cancer* 74: 1101-1110.
14. Cowan, L.D. et al. 1981. Breast Cancer Incidence in Women with a History of Progesterone Deficiency. *American Journal of Epidemiology* 114: 209-217.
15. Fentiman, I.S. et al. May 25, 1991. Timing of Surgery During Menstrual Cycle and Survival of Premenopausal Women with Operable Breast Cancer. *Lancet* 33: 1261-1264.
16. Associated Press. 1991. Cancer Study: Time Surgery.
17. Soffa, Virginia M. *The Journey Beyond Breast Cancer* (Rochester, Vermont: Healing Arts Press, 1994).
18. Love, *Dr. Susan Love's Breast Book*, p. 146.
19. Lee, John R. *Natural Progesterone The Multiple Roles of a Remarkable Hormone* (Sebastopol, California : BLL Publishing, 1993), pp. 71-74.
20. MacMahon, B. et al. 1970. Age at First Birth and Breast Cancer Risk. *Bulletin of the World Health Organization* 43: 209-221.
21. Gallagher, R.P., December 15, 1993. History of Lactation and Breast Cancer Risk. *American Journal of Epidemiology* 138 (12): 1050-1056.

22. United Kingdom National Case-Control Study Group. 1993. Breast Feeding and Risk of Breast Cancer in Young Women. *British Medical Journal* 307:17-20.

23. Newcomb, P.A. Jan. 13, 1993. Lactation and a Reduced Risk of Premenopausal Breast Cancer. *New England Journal of Medicine* 330: 81-87.

24. Ing, R. et al. July 16, 1977. Unilateral Breast Feeding and Breast Cancer. *Lancet* 2(8029): 124-127

25. Gammon, M.D. and John, E.M. 1993. Recent Etiologic Hypotheses Concerning Breast Cancer. *Epidemiologic Reviews* 15 (1): 163-168.

26. Ekbom, A. et al. October 24, 1992. Evidence of Prenatal Influences on Breast Cancer Risk. *Lancet* 340: 1015-1018.

27. Kelsey, J.L. et al. 1993. Reproductive Factors and Breast Cancer. *Epidemiologic Reviews* 15 (1): 36-47.

28. Apter, D. et al. 1989. Some Endocrine Characteristics of Early Menarche, a Risk Factor for Breast Cancer, are Preserved into Adulthood. *International Journal of Cancer* 44: 783-787.

29. Love, Susan,. June 20, 1991. Testimony to the United States Subcommittee on Aging, Committee on Labor and Human Resources. Response to committee topic: *Why Are We Losing the War on Breast Cancer?*

30. Cuzick, J. 1987. Women at High Risk of Breast Cancer. *Reviews on Endrocrine-Related Cancer* 25: 5.

31. Dunn, J.E. 1977. Breast Cancer Among American Japanese in the San Francisco Bay Area. *National Cancer Institute Monograph* 47: 157-160

32. Seidman, H., Stellman, S.D. and Mushinski, M.H. 1982. A Different Perspective on Breast Cancer Risk Factors: Some Implications of the Nonattributable Risk. *CA : A Cancer Journal for Clinicians* 32: 301.

33. Kvale, G. et al. 1988. Menstrual factors and breast cancer risk. *Cancer* 62: 1625-1631.

CHAPTER 3: NOURISHING BODY AND SOUL—FOOD, SUPPLEMENTS, HERBS

1. Reuben, Carolyn. *Antioxidants: Your Complete Guide* (Rockland, California: Prima, 1995), p.114.

2. Baker, S. 1991-92,. Magnesium in Primary Care and Preventive Medicine: Clinical Correlation of Magnesium Loading Studies: *Magnesium and Trace Elements* 10: 251-262.

3. Brody, Jane E. May 15, 1979. Research Yields Surprises About Early Human Diets. *New York Times* Science Section.

4. Select Committee on Nutrition and Human Needs, U.S. Senate. *Dietary Goals for the United States* (Washington, D.C.: U.S. Government Printing Office, 1997).

5. *Healthy People: The Surgeon General's Report on Health Promotion and Disease Prevention* (Washington, D.C.: Government Printing Office, 1979).

6. National Academy of Sciences. *Diet, Nutrition, and Cancer* (Washington D.C.: National Academy Press, 1982).

7. Cohen, L.A. et al. 1991. Modulation of N-Nitrosomethylurea-Induced Mammary Tumor Promotion by Dietary Fiber and Fat. *Journal of the National Cancer Institute* 83: 496-500.

8. Goldin, B.R. et al. 1982. Estrogen Excretion Patterns and Plasma Levels in Vegetarian and Omnivorous Women. *New England Journal of Medicine* 307 (25):1542-1547.

9. Rogers, S. Spring 1994. *Northeast Center for Environmental Medicine Health Letter:* 5.

10. Rogers, Sherry. *Wellness Against All Odds* (Syracuse, New York: Prestige Publishing, 1994), p. 99.

11. Courtesy of Robin Keuneke, natural foods counselor.

12. Milner, J.A. et. al. October 1992. Carcinogensis 13(10): 1847-1851.

13. Simone, Charles B. *Cancer and Nutrition* (Garden City Park, New York: Avery Publishing Group, 1992), p. 123.

14. Simone, Charles B. *Breast Health* (Garden City Park, New York: Avery Publishing Group, 1995), p. 75.

15. Ziegler, R. G., January 1989. A Review of Epidemiologic Evidence that Carotenoids Reduce the Risk of Cancer. *Journal of Nutrition* 119(1): 116-122.
Fontana, J.A. et al. February 1991. Retinoid Modulation of Insulin-like Growth Factor-Binding Proteins and Inhibition of Breast Carcinoma Proliferation. *Endocrinology* 128 (2): 1115-1122.

16. Michnovicz, J. and Bradlow, H. 1991. Altered Estrogen Metabolism and Excretion in Humans Following Consumption of Indole-3-Carbinol. *Nutrition and Cancer* 16: 59-66.

17. November 22, 1995, Do I Date Eat A Strawberry, *New York Times*.
18. National Research Council. *Recommended Daily Allowances*, 9th edition (Washington, D.C.: National Academy of Sciences, 1980), p. 46.
19. Messina, M. and Barnes, S. 1991. The Role of Soy Products in Reducing Risk of Cancer. *Journal of the National Cancer Institute* 83: 541-546.
20. Rao, A.V. and Sung M.-K. Saponins as Anti-carcinogens. 1995. *Journal of Nutrition* 125 : 717S-724.
21. Simone, *Cancer and Nutrition*, p. 124.
22. Fotsis, T. et al. 1993. Genistein, a Dietary-derived Inhibitor of *in vitro* Angiogenesis. *Proceedings of the National Academy of Science* 90: 2690-2694.
23. Peterson, G. and Barnes S. 1991. Genistein Inhibition of the Growth of Human Breast Cancer Cells: Independence from Estrogen Receptors and Multi-drug Resistance Chain. *Biochemical and Biophysical Research Communications* 179 (1): 661-667.
24. Wei, H. et al. 1993. Inhibition of Tumor Promotor-induced Hydrogen Peroxide Formation *in vitro* and *in vivo* by Genistein. *Nutrition and Cancer* 20: 1-12.
25. Messina, Mark and Virginia. *The Simple Soybean and Your Health* (New York: Dell, 1989).
26. Pritikin, N. quoted in *Vegetarian Times:* 43: 21.
27. Gray, G.E., Pike, M.C. and Henderson, B.E. 1979. Breast Cancer Incidence and Mortality Rates in Different Countries in Relation to Known Risk Factors and Dietary Practices. *British Journal of Cancer* 39: 1-7.
28. Lubin, J., Blot, W. and Burns, P. 1981. Breast Cancer Following High Dietary Fat and Protein Consumption. *American Journal of Epidemiology* 114: 422 Abstract.
29. Campbell, C. Summer 1994. The Latest from The China Diet and Health Study. *Good Medicine* 3 (3): 11-13.
30. Phillips, R.L. 1975. Role of Life-style and Dietary Habits in Risk of Cancer Among Seventh-Day Adventists. *Cancer Research* 35: 3513.
31. Barnard, N. Sept/Oct 1991. Women and Cancer. *PCRM Update*.
32. Kradjian, Robert M. *Save Yourself From Breast Cancer* (New York: Berkley Books, 1994), p. 45.
33. Hartmann, W.H., Sakamoto G. et al. 1979. Comparative Clinico-

pathological Study of Breast Cancer Among Japanese and American Females. *Japanese Journal of Cancer* 25 (3):161-170.

34. Wynder, E. et al. 1963. A Comparison of Survival Rates Between American and Japanese Patients with Breast Cancer. *Surgery Gynecology Obstetrics* 117: 196.

35. Gregorio, D.I. et al. 1985. Dietary Fat Consumption and Survival Among Women with Breast Cancer. *Journal of the National Cancer Institute* 75: 37.

36. Tannenbaum, A. 1942. The Genesis and Growth of Tumors III. Effects of a High Fat Diet. *Cancer Research* 2: 468.

37. Erasmus, Udo. *Fats That Heal Fats That Kill* (Burnaby BC, Canada: Alive Books, 1993), 2nd edition p. 111.

38. Baker, S. Winter 1984. Fat is Not Just to Hold Your Pants Up. *Gesell Institute of Human Development Update* 3 (2).

39. Speroff, Leon, Glass, Robert H., Kase, Nathan G. *Clinical Gynecologic Endocrinology and Infertility* (Baltimore, Maryland: Williams and Wilkins, 1989), 4th edition p. 301.

40. Brisson, G.J. *Lipids in Human Nutrition* (New Jersey: Burgess, 1981), p. 39.

41. October 1995. Spotlight Shifts to Enzymes: Indispensable Constituent of Physical and Mental Health. *Well Mind Association of Greater Washington, Inc. Newletter* 219: 4.

42. Steinmetz, K.A., Potter, J.D. 1991. Vegetables, Fruit and Cancer II. Mechanisms. *Cancer Causes and Control* 2 (6); 427-442.

43. Robbins, *Diet For A New America,* p. 150.

44. Lieberman, Shari and Bruning, Nancy. *The Real Vitamin and Mineral Book* (Garden City Park, New York: Avery Publishing Group, 1990), p. 21.

45. Weil, A. 1996. Is It Necessary to Take Supplements If You Eat a Healthy Diet? *Self Healing* 1 (1): 2-3.

46. De Felice, S. Summer 1993. *Regulatory Affairs* 5:169.

47. Simone, *Breast Health,* p. 71.

48. Israel, L. et al. 1985. Vitamin A Augmentation of the Effects of Chemotherapy in Metastic Breast Cancers after Menopause. Randomized Trial in 100 Patients. *Annales De Medecine Interne* 136 (7): 551-554.

49. Moss, Ralph W. *Questioning Chemotherapy* (Brooklyn, New York: Equinox Press, 1995).

50. Palan, P.R. 1989. Decreased Beta-Carotene Tissue Levels in Uterine Leiomyomas and Cancers of the Reproductive and Nonreproductive Organs. *American Journal of Obstetrics and Gynecology* 161: 1649-1652.

51. Potischman, N. et al. 1990. Breast Cancer and Dietary Plasma Concentrations of Carotenoids and Vitamin A. *American Journal of Clinical Nutrition* 52: 909-915.

52. Santamaria, L.A. et al. 1990. Cancer Chemoprevention by Supplemental Carotenoids and Synergism with Retinol in Mastodynia Treatment. *Medical Oncology Tumor Pharmacotherapy* 7: 153-67.

53. Garland, M. et al. 1993. Antioxidant Micronutrients and Breast Cancer. *Journal of the American College of Nutrition* 12: 400-411 [review].

54. Block, G. July 1992. The Data Support a Role for Antioxidants in Reducing Cancer Risk. *Nutrition Reviews* 50 (7): 207-213 [This statement was cosigned by fifteen leading American scientists].

55. Kritchevsky, D. Sept 15, 1990. Nutrition and Breast Cancer. *Cancer* 66 (6).

56. Calabrese, E.J. 1985. Does Exposure to Environmental Pollutants Increase the Need for Vitamin C? *Journal Environment Pathology Toxicology Oncology* 5: 81-90.

57. Shimpo, K. et al. 1991. Ascorbic Acid and Adriamycin Toxicity. *American Journal of Clinical Nutrition* 54:1298S-1301S.

58. Pauling, L. And Hoffer, A. 1990. Hardin Jones Biostatistical Analysis of Mortality Data for Cohorts of Cancer Patients with a Large Fraction Surviving at the Termination of the Study and a Comparison of Survival Times of Cancer Patients Receiving Large Regular Oral Doses of Vitamin C and Other Nutrients with Similar Patients Not Receiving Those Dosages. *Journal of Orthomolecular Medicine* 5:143-154.

59. Pauling, Linus. *How to Live Longer and Feel Better* (New York: WH Freeman and Co., 1986).

60. Block, G. 1991. Epidemiologic Evidence Regarding Vitamin C and Cancer. *American Journal of Clinical Nutrition* 54.

61. Howe, G. et al. 1991. Dietary Factors and Risk of Breast Cancer: Combined Analysis of 12 Case-Controlled Studies. *Journal of the National Cancer Institute* 54.

62. London, R.S. et al. 1981. Endocrine Parameters and Alpha-

tocopherol Therapy of Patients with Mammary Dysplasia. *Cancer Research* 41: 3811-3812.

63. Knekt, P. et al. 1988. Serum Vitamin E Level and Risk of Female Cancers. *International Journal of Epidemiology* 17: 281-286.
64. Shamberger, R.J. et al. 1971. Selenium Distribution and Cancer Mortality. *Clinical Laboratory Science* 2: 221.
65. Schrauzer, G. 1977. Cancer Mortality Correlation Studies III. Statistical Associations with Dietary Selenium Intakes. *Bioinorganic Chemistry* 7: 23-24, 35-56.
66. Ladas, H.S. 1989. The Potential of Selenium in the Treatment of Breast Cancer. *Holistic Medicine* 4: 145-156.
67. Ksrnjavi, H. et al. 1990. Selenium in Serum as a Possible Parameter for Assessment of Breast Disease. *Breast Cancer Research and Treatment* 16: 57-61.
68. Folkers, K. March 30, 1994. *Biochemical and Biophysical Research Communications* 199: 1504-1508.
69. The Burton Goldberg Group. *Alternative Medicine The Definitive Guide* (Puyallup, Washington: Future Medicine Publishing, Inc., 1994), p. 583.

CHAPTER 4: THE MENTAL AND EMOTIONAL ASPECTS OF BREAST CANCER

1. Le Shan, Larry. *Cancer as a Turning Point,* (New York: Penguin Books, 1990), p. 8.
2. Levy, S. personal communication, June 6, 1991.
3. Bernie Siegel discusses Exceptional Cancer Patients (ECaP) in his books (see Resources).
4. Temoshok, Lydia and Dreher, Henry. *The Type C Connection* (New York: Random House, 1992).
5. Greer, S. and Morris, T. 1975. Psychological Attributes of Women Who Develop Breast Cancer: A Controlled Study. *Journal of Psychosomatic Research* 19: 147-153.
6. Scherg, H. 1987. Psychosocial Factors and Disease Bias in Breast Cancer Patients. *Pychosomatic Medicine* 49: 302-312.
7. Wirsching, M. et al., 1982. Psychological Identification of

Breast Cancer Patients Before Biopsy. *Journal of Psychosomatic Medicine* 26: 1-10.

8. Greer, S. et al. 1990. Psychological Response to Breast Cancer and Fifteen Year Outcome. *Lancet* 1: 49-50.

9. Jensen, M.R. 1987. Psychobiological Factors Predicting the Course of Cancer. *Journal of Personality* 55 (2): 317-342.

10. Gawler, Grace. *Women of Silence* (Melbourne, Australia: Hill of Content Publishing, 1994).

11. Boyd, Peggy. *The Silent Wound* (Reading, Massachusetts: Addison-Wesley Publishing Company, 1984).

12. Edelman, Hope. *Motherless Daughters* (Reading, Massachusetts: Addison-Wesley Publishing Company, 1994), p. xxv.

13. Boyd, *The Silent Wound,* pp. 11-12.

14. Ibid., p. 63.

15. Chapman, Jnani, Remen, R.N. ed. *Woudned Healers* (Mill Valley, California: Wounded Healer Press, 1994), p. 34.

16. Siegel, Bernie. (see Resources).

17. Siegel, Bernie. *Love, Medicine and Miracles* (New York: Harper and Row Publishers, 1986), pp. 57-58.

18. Goldie, L. "The Interdisciplinary Treatment of Cancer: Cooperation or Competition?" *Psychosocial Oncology, Proceedings of the Second and Third Meetings of the British Psychosocial Oncology Group 1985 and 1986* (New York: Pergamon Press, 1988), p. 78.

19. Siegel, *Love, Medicine and Miracles,* p. 58.

20. Moyers, Bill. *Healing and The Mind* (New York: Doubleday, 1993), pp. 191-192.

21. Spiegel, D. et al. 1989. Effect on Psychosocial Treatment on Survival of Patients with Metastatic Breast Cancer. *Lancet* 2: 888-891.

22. Levy, S. et al. 1988. Survival Hazards Analysis in First-recurrence Breast Cancer Patients: Seven-year Follow-up. *Psychosomatic Medicine* 50: 520-528.

23. Gawler, *Women of Silence.*

24. Shealy, C. Norman, Myss, Caroline M. *The Creation of Health* (Walpole, New Hampshire: Stillpoint Publishing, 1988).

25. Remen, Rachel Naomi. *Wounded Healers* (Mill Valley, California :Wounded Healer Press, 1994), p. 90.

26. Kidde, Tullia Forlani, talk at Griffin Hospital, Derby, CT., 1994

27. Siegel, *Love, Medicine and Miracles.*

28. Williams, Wendy. *The Power Within* (New York: Harper and Row, 1990), p. 92.

29. Metzger, Deena. *Tree* (Oakland, California: Wingbow Press, 1978), p. 48.

30. Brandenberg, P. *Who Cares? Women With Breast Cancer and Social Support* (Syracuse, New York: Syracuse University, June 1991) Doctoral Dissertation.

31. Northrup, Christiane. *Women's Bodies, Women's Wisdom* (New York: Bantam, 1994), pp.4-5.

32. Gawler, *Women of Silence*, p. 50.

33. Levine, Stephen and Ondrea. *Embracing the Beloved* (New York: Doubleday, 1995).

34. Wilbur, Ken. *Grace and Grit Spirituality and Healing in the Life and Death of Treya Killam Wilber* (Boston: Shambhala Publications, 1991), p. 327.

35. Wexler, Merida. "From a Cancer Journal," *Cancer As A Woman's Issue,* Midge Stocker ed. Vol. 1 (Chicago: Third Side Press, 1991), p. 54.

36. Dossey, Larry. Spring 1995. *The Center Post* 7 (1).

CHAPTER 5: OUT THERE AND IN HERE: BREAST CANCER AND POLLUTION.

1. Carson, Rachel. *Silent Spring* (New York: Houghton Mifflin Company, 1962).

2. Davis, D.L. et al. 1993. Medical Hypothesis: Xeno-estrogens as Preventable Causes of Breast Cancer. *Environmental Health Perspectives* 101: 327.

3. Rogers, Sherry. *Tired or Toxic* (Syracuse, New York: Prestige Publishing, 1990).

4. Epstein, Samuel. *The Politics of Cancer* (New York: Anchor Books, 1979).

5. Environmental Working Group 1994. Washed, Peeled . . . Contaminated.

6. Wolff, M.S. et al. April 21, 1993. Blood Levels of Organochlorine Residues and Risk of Breast Cancer. *Journal of The National Cancer Institute* 85 (8): 648-652

7. Mussalo-Rauhamaa, H. et al. 1990. Occurrence of Beta-

hexachlorocyclohexane in Breast Cancer Patients. *Cancer* 66: 2124-2128.

8. Falck, F. et al. 1922. Pesticides and Polychlorinated Biphenyl Residues in Human Breast Lipids and Their Relation to Breast Cancer. *Archives of Environmental Health* 47:143-146.

9. Wolff, M. et al. 1993. *JNCI* 85 (8): 648-652.

10. Krieger, N.K. et al. 1994. Breast Cancer and Serum Organochlorines: A Prospective Study among White, Black and Asian Women. *Journal of the National Cancer Institute* 86: 589.

11. Dewailly, E. et al. 1994. High Organochlorine Body Burden in Women with Estrogen Receptor-positive Breast Cancer. *Journal of the National Cancer Institute* 86: 232-234.

12. October 24, 1993. EPA to Study an Insecticide for Links to Cancer. *New York Times:* 21

13. Soto, A. October 1994. *Delicious* :11

14. Westin, J. and Richter, E. 1990. The Israeli Breast-cancer Anomaly. *Annals of the New York Academy of Sciences* 609: 269-279.

15. September 1994. *Natural Health:* 18.

16. July 3, 1993. *Science News* 144:10-13.

17. Winter 1995. *ConnPRIG Reports The Newsletter of the Connecticut Public Interest Research Group Citizen Lobby* 9 (1).

18. February 14, 1994. Letter from Samuel Epstein, M.D. to David Kessler, M.D. the Commissioner of the FDA.

19. Environmental Research Foundation August 10, 1995. Milk Safety. *Rachel's Environment and Health Weekly* 454.

20. Testimony of Dr. Francis E. Ray, July 19, 1957. *"Food Additives" Hearings* 85th Congress, Subcommittee of Committee on Interstate and Foreign Commerce: 200.

21. Scheuplein, R.J. 1992. Perspectives on Toxicological Risk— An Example: Foodborne Carcinogenic Risk. *Critical Reviews in Food Science and Nutrition* 32 (2): 105-121.

22. American Lung Association. August 1994. *Healthy Attitudes* 4 (1).

23. Bennicke, K. 1995. *British Medical Journal* 310: 1431-1433.

24. Longnecker, M. et al. 1995. *Journal of the National Cancer Institute* 87: 923-929.

25. Kahn, J., July 13, 1995. Even Modest Alcohol Intake Raises Risk of Breast Tumors. *Medical Tribune:* 8.

26. Members of the Environmental Defense Fund, *Malignant Neglect* (New York: Alfred Knopf, 1979).

27. U.S. Environmental Protection Agency, 1991. Toxics in the Community: National and Local Perspectives, The 1989 Toxics Release Inventory National Report, Office of Toxic Substances, Washington, DC.

28. Mann, R. ed. *Hormone Replacement Therapy and Breast Cancer Risk* (London: Parthenon, 1992).

29. Kamen, Betty. *Hormone Replacement Therapoy Yes or No?* (Novato, California: Nutrition Encounter, 1993), p. 23.

30. Malone, K. 1993. Diethylstilbestrol (DES) and Breast Cancer. *Epidemiologic Reviews* 15 (1): 93.

31. Epstein, *The Politics of Cancer,* p. 222.

32. November 1988. Lower Dose Pills. *Population Reports* Series A, 7.

33. Epstein, *The Politics of Cancer,* p. 581.

34. Seaman, B. and Seaman, G., *Women and the Crisis in Sex Hormones* (New York: Rawson Associates Publishers, 1977), p. 66.

35. Soffa, Virginia, M. *The Journey Beyond Breast Cancer* (Rochester, Vermont: Healing Arts Press, 1994), p. 207.

36. Olsson, H. 1989. Oral Contraceptives and Breast Cancer. *Acta Oncologica* 28: 857

37. Soffa, *The Journey Beyond Breast Cancer,* p. 33.

38. Greenfield, Natalee S., *"First Do No Harm . . ." A Dying Woman's Battle Against the Physicians and Drug Companies Who Misled Her about the Hazards of The Pill.* (New York: Sun River Press, Two Continents Publishing Group, 1976).

39. Rinzler, Carol Ann. *Estrogen and Breast Cancer* (New York: Macmillan Publishing Company, 1993), p. 81.

40. Ibid., p. 83.

41. Brinton, L.A. et al. June 7, 1995. Oral Contraceptives and Breast Cancer Risk Among Younger Women. *Journal of the National Cancer Insstitute* 87 (11): 827-835

42. Source: American Cancer Society, Proportions of estimated new breast cancer cases in woman, by age, 1996.

43. Northrup, Christiane. *Women's Bodies, Women's Wisdom* (New York: Bantam, 1994), p. 430-431.

44. February 1, 1996. Opinion Column—From the Front Line, The Estrogen Sales Pitch, *Ob-Gyn News:* 24.

45. Love, Susan. *Dr. Susan Love's Breast Book* (Reading, Mass.: Addison-Wesley, 1990).

46. Gambrell, R.D. "Complications of Estrogen Replacement Therapy." *Hormone Replacement Therapy,* Swartz, D.P. ed. (Baltimore: Williams and Wilkins, 1992).

47. L. Bergkvist, et al. 1989. The Risk of Breast Cancer after Estrogen and Estrogen-progestin Replacement. *New England Journal of Medicine* 321: 293-297.

48. Colditz, G.A. et al. 1995. Use of Postmenopausal Estrogens and Progestins and Risk of Breast Cancer. *New England Journal of Medicine* 332: 1589-1593.

49. Capri, J. December 1, 1994. ERT Trial Called for in Postmenopausal Women with Breast Ca History. *ObGyn News:* 11.

50. The second annual evening of breast cancer information at the 92nd Street YMCA Center for Adult Life and Learning in Manhaattan, 1994.

51. Felson, D. T. et al. 1993. The Effect of Postmenopausal Estrogen Therapy on Bone Density in Elderly Women. *New England Journal of Medicine* 329:1141-1146.

52. Barzel, U.S. 1988. Estrogens in the Prevention and Treatment of Postmenopausal Osteoporosis: A Review. *American Journal of Medicine* 85: 847-850.

53. Lee, John. *Natural Progesterone, The Multiple Roles of a Remarkable Hormone* (Sebastopol, California: BLL Publishing, 1994), p. 53-71.

54. Colditz, G.A. et al. 1995. *NEJM* 32: 1589-1593.

55. Blask, D. et al. 1988. Effects of Pineal Hormone Melatonin on the Proliferation and Morphological Characteristics of Human Breast Cancer Cells (MCF-7) in Culture. *Cancer Research* 48: 6121-6126.

56. Lissoni, P. et al. 1994. Efficacy of the Concomitant Administration of the Pineal Hormone Melatonin in Cacner Immunotherapy with Low-dose IL-2 in Patients with Advanced Solid Tumors who had Progressed on IL-2 Alone. *Oncology* 51: 344-347.

57. Pierpaoli, Walter, Regelson, William with Colman, Carol. *The Melatonin Miracle* (New York: Simon and Schuster, 1995), p. 124.

CHAPTER 6: THE CULTURE THAT LOVES AND HATES BREASTS

1. Northrup, Christiane. *Women's Bodies, Women's Wisdom* (New York: Bantam, 1994), p. 3.
2. Ibid., pp. 287-288.
3. *"For Two Women Out Of Five, Love Doesn't Hurt,"* Women's Crisis Center, Inc. Norwalk, Connecticut.
4. Northrup, *Women's Bodies, Women's Wisdom,* p. 15
5. Singer, Sydney Ross and Grismaijer, Soma, *Dressed to Kill* (Garden City Park, New York: Avery Publishing Group, 1995), p. 154.
6. Ibid., p. 126.
7. Claire Braz-Valentine. "The Last Will and Testament of This Woman," in *On Women Turning 50,* Rountree, Cathlene, ed. (New York: Harper Collins, 1993), p. 21.
8. Gohagan, J. February 1996. Monitor. *OBG Management:* 23.
9. Wartik, N. and Felner, J. November/December 1994. Is Breast Self-Exam Out of Touch? *MS.:* 68.
10. Ibid., p. 67
11. Weed, Susun. *Breast Cancer? Breast Health! The Wise Woman Way* (Woodstock, New York: Ash Tree Publishing, 1996), p. 57.
12. Rollin, Betty. *First You Cry* (New York Warner: 1976).
13. Batt, Sharon. *Patient No More* (Charlottetown, P.E.I., Canada: Gynergy Books, 1994) p. 33.
14. Ibid., p. 53.
15. Steingraber, S. Winter 1995. *Safe Food News:* 12-15.
16. Batt, *Patient No More,* p. 245.
17. Elwood, J. et al. 1993. The Effectiveness of Breast Cancer Screening in Young Women. *Current Clinical Trials* 2: 227.
18. Nystrom, L. and Larsson, L. 1993. Breast Cancer Screening with Mammography. *Lancet* 341: 1531-1532.
19. Day, P.J. and O'Rourke, G.E. 1990. The Diagnosis of Breast Cancer: A Clinical and Mammographic Comparison. *Medical Journal of Australia* 152: 635-639.
20. Stephenson, J. February 1, 1995. Mammography Reports Show Information Gaps. *ObGyn News:* 1.

21. Bailar, J.C. 1976. Mammography: A Contrary View. *Annals of Internal Medicine* 84: 77.

22. Hung, Diana *The Doctor's Guide for Buying X-ray Equipment and Accessories* (Cottage Grove, Oregon: Springtime Interprises, 1987)

23. Shapiro, J. *Radiation Protection: A Guide for Scientists and Physicians* 1990, (Cambridge, Massachusetts: Harvard University Press, 1990), p. 94.

24. Swift, M. et al. December 26, 1991. Incidence of Cancer in 161 Families Affected by Ataxia-Telangiectasia. *New England Journal of Medicine* 325 (26): 1831-1836.

25. Love, Susan. *Dr. Susan Love's Breast Book* (Reading, Mass.: Addison-Wesley, 1995), 2nd edition p. 245.

26. Ibid., p. 247.

27. Summer 1993. DES and Breast Cancer Risk. *DES Action Canada Newsletter:* 1.

28. Moss, Ralph, W. *The Cancer Industry,* revised edition (New York: Paragon House, 1989), p. 93.

29. Cairns, J. November 1985. The Treatment of Diseases and the War Against Cancer. Scientific American 253: 51-59.

30. Moss, Ralph. *Questioning Chemotherapy* (Brooklyn, New York: Equinox Press, 1995) p. 9.

31. Schmahl, D. et al. *Iatrogenic Carcinogenesis* (Berlin: Springer-Verlag, 1977).

32. Block, G. July 1992. The Data Support a Role for Antioxidants in Reducing Cancer Risk. *Nutrition Review* 50 (7): 207-213 [This statement was so-signed by 15 leading American scientists including Bruce Ames, Elizabeth Barret-Connor and Richard Shekelle.]

33. National Breast Cancer Coalition Statement in Response to NSABP Data Falsification, Washington, D.C. 1994.

34. Kradjian, Robert M. *Save Yourself From Breast Cancer* (New York: Berkley Publishing Group 1994), p. 187.

35. Lorde, Audre. *The Cancer Journals* (San Francisco: spinsters/ aunt lute, 1980), p. 16.

CHAPTER 7: YOUR OWN BREAST CANCER HEALING/ PREVENTION PROGRAM

1. Susan Love, quote from lecture at Interface conference "Women and Cancer," Boston, Mass., 1991.
2. Wilbur, Ken. *Grace and Grit: Spirituality and Healing in the Life and Death of Treya Killam Wilbur* (Boston: Shambhala, 1991), pp. 253-254.
3. Ibid., p. 221.
4. Zukav, Gary. *The Seat of the Soul* (New York: Fireside, 1989).
5. Northrup, Christiane. "Creating Health tape series, Nutrition" (Boulder, Colorado: Sounds True Recordings, 1993).
6. Frisch, R. October 1993. *American Health:* 77.
7. Bernstein, L. et al. 1994. Physical Exercise and the Reduced Risk of Breast Cancer in Young Women. *Journal of the National Cancer Institute* 86: 1403-1408.
8. Field, S. et al., December 1993. "Brain/Mind Bulletin," *Science News* 127 (302).
9. Klaus, Marshall H. and Kennel, John H. *Parent/Infant Bonding,* 2nd ed. (St. Louis, Missouri: C.V. Mosby Co., 1982).
10. Rechtschaffen, S. December 1993. Time-Shifting. *Psychology Today:* 32-36.
11. Gawler, Grace. *Women of Silence* (Melbourne, Australia: Hill of Content Publishing, 1994), p. 8.
12. Siegel, Bernie. *Peace, Love and Healing* (New York: Harper and Row, 1990), p. 15.
13. Simonton, O. Carl, Matthews-Simonton, Stephanie and Creighton, James *Getting Well Again* (New York: Bantam, 1978), p. 155.
14. Ferguson, D.J. et al. 1982. Staging of Breast Cancer and Survival Rates. *Journal of the American Medical Association* 248: 1337-1341.
15. Casarjian, Robin. *Forgiveness* (New York: Bantam, 1992), p. 23.
16. Siegel, *Peace, Love and Healing,* p. 115.
17. Wilbur, *Grace and Grit,* p. 327.
18. Howard, Carol *Wounded Healers,* Remen, R.N., ed. (Bolinas, California: Wounded Healer Press, 1994), p. 91.

19. Love, Susan. *Dr. Susan Love's Breast Book* (Reading, Mass.: Addison-Wesley, 1990), p. 239-241.
20. Siegel, Bernie. *Love, Medicine and Miracles* (New York: Harper and Row, 1986).
21. Marino, Dian. "White Flowers and a Grizzly Bear: Finding New Metaphors." in *Cancer As A Women's Issue,* Stocker, Midge, ed. (Chicago, Illinois: Third Side Press: 1991) p. 191.
22. Wadler, Joyce. *My Breast* (New York: Simon and Schuster, 1992), pp. 81-82.
23. Ibid., pp. 157-158.
24. Soffa, Virginia M. *The Journey Beyond Breast Cancer* (Rochester, Vermont: Healing Arts Press, 1994).
25. Crum, Jessie K. *The Art of Inner Listening* (Wheaton, Illinois: Quest Books, 1989).
26. Miriam, Selma. "Thoughts on Cancer and Healing," in *Cancer As A Women's Issue,* Stocker, Midge ed. (Chicago, Illinois: Third Side Press: 1991), p. 50.
27. Soffa, Virginia. Spring/Summer 1995. "Executive Director News," *Breast Cancer Action News* 3 (1): 8.
28. LeShan, Larry. *Cancer As A Turning Point* (New York: Penguin Group, 1989), p. 14.

Suggested Reading List

BREAST CANCER—DIAGNOSIS, TREATMENT, PREVENTION, POLITICS

Breast Health by Charles B. Simone, M.D.
Breast Cancer: What You Should Know (But May Not Be Told) About Prevention, Diagnosis and Treatment by Steve Austin, N.D. and Cathy Hitchcock, M.S.W.
Dr. Susan Love's Breast Book by Susan Love, M.D.
Dressed To Kill by Sydney Ross Singer and Soma Grismaijer
Patient No More by Sharon Batt
Preventing Breast Cancer by Dr. Cathy Read
Questioning Chemotherapy by Ralph W. Moss., Ph.D.
The Journey Beyond Breast Cancer by Virginia Soffa

BREAST CANCER—THE EMOTIONAL JOURNEY

The Cancer Journals by Audre Lorde
Grace and Grit: Spirituality and Healing in the Life and Death of Treya Killam Wilbur by Ken Wilbur
Tree by Deena Metzger
Women of Silence: The Emotional Healing of Breast Cancer by Grace Gawler

FOOD AND YOUR HEALTH, COOKBOOKS

The Book of Whole Meals by Annemarie Colbin
Cooking With Sea Vegetables by Peter and Montse Bradford
Culinary Treasures of Japan by John and Jan Belleme
Diet For a New America by John Robbins
Don't Drink Your Milk by Frank Oski, M.D.

Fats That Heal, Fats That Kill by Udo Erasmus, Ph.D.
Macro Mellow by Shirley Gallinger and Sherry A. Rogers, M.D.
The Power of Your Plate by Neal Barnard, M.D.
The Self-Healing Cookbook by Kristina Turner
The Simple Soybean by Mark Messina, Ph.D. and Virginia Messina, R.D.
Super Nutrition For Menopause by Ann Louise Gittleman
When Food Is Love by Geneen Roth

INSPIRATIONAL

Cancer: Another Way? by Ainslee Meares, M.D.
Healing Into Life and Death by Stephen Levine
Love Is Letting Go Of Fear by Gerald G. Jampolsky, M.D.
A Path With Heart by Jack Kornfield
The Seat of the Soul by Gary Zukov
Silent Spring by Rachel Carson
Wherever You Go, There You Are by Jon Kabat-Zinn, Ph.D.
Wounded Healers: A Book of Poems by People Who Have Had Cancer and Those Who Love and Care for Them edited by Rachel Naomi Remen, M.D.

THE MIND-BODY CONNECTION

Cancer as a Turning Point by Larry LeShan, Ph.D.
The Creation of Health by C. Norman Shealy, M.D. and Caroline Myss
Forgiveness by Robin Casarjian
Getting Well Again by O. Carl Simonton, M.D., Stephanie Matthews-Simonton and James L. Creighton
Guilt is the Teacher, Love is the Lesson by Joan Borysenko, Ph.D.
Love, Medicine and Miracles by Bernie Siegel, M.D.
Minding The Body, Mending The Mind by Joan Borysenko, Ph.D.
Peace, Love and Healing by Bernie Siegel, M.D.

WOMEN'S ISSUES, MENOPAUSE AND HORMONES

Women's Bodies, Women's Wisdom by Christiane Northrup, M.D.
Cancer as a Women's Issue edited by Midge Stocker
Hormone Replacement Therapy, Yes or No? by Betty Kamen, Ph.D.
Natural Progesterone: The Multiple Roles of a Remarkable Hormone by John Lee, M.D.
Preventing and Reversing Osteoporosis by Alan Gaby, M.D.
Transformation Through Menopause by Marian Van Eyk McCain

Index

About the Author

Barbara Joseph, M.D. is a board certified Obstetrician and Gynecologist. She graduated from Downstate Medical College, State University of New York and completed her residency in Obstetrics and Gynecology at Rutgers Medical School of the University of Medicine and Dentistry of New Jersey in 1984.

She was in private practice in Norwalk, Connecticut from 1985 through 1991 when she was diagnosed with Stage III breast cancer. Her healing transformation and reorientation to the practice of medicine are documented herein.

After five years of self-reflection, self-healing, exploration of alternatives and integration of her own health care program Dr. Joseph now offers women's health care consultations by appointment at The Center for Women's Health 203-323-9666, where she practices with her associate Joel M. Evans, M.D. in Stamford, Connecticut. Her areas of special interest are breast cancer prevention and creative menopause; her focus is on nutrition and mindbody approaches. Dr. Joseph resides in Weston, Connecticut with her three children Zachary, Hannah and Oliver.